Leadership
FOR Literacy

Leadership
FOR Literacy

RESEARCH-BASED PRACTICE, PreK–3

Joseph Murphy

LEADERSHIP
for LEARNING

CORWIN PRESS
A Sage Publications Company
Thousand Oaks, California

For information:

Corwin Press
A Sage Publications Company
2455 Teller Road
Thousand Oaks, California 91320
www.corwinpress.com

Sage Publications Ltd.
6 Bonhill Street
London EC2A 4PU
United Kingdom

Sage Publications India Pvt. Ltd.
B-42, Panchsheel Enclave
Post Box 4109
New Delhi 110 017 India

Printed in the United States of America

Library of Congress Cataloging-in-Publication Data

Murphy, Joseph, 1949-
Leadership for literacy : research-based practice, preK-3 / by Joseph Murphy.
  p. cm. — (Leadership for learning)
Includes bibliographical references and index.
ISBN 0-7619-4579-2 (Cloth)—ISBN 0-7619-4580-6 (Paper)
  1. Reading (Early childhood) 2. Curriculum planning—United States.
3. School improvement programs—United States. I. Title. II. Series.
LB1139.5.R43M87 2004
372.4—dc22

                          2003015359

This book is printed on acid-free paper.

04   05   06   07   10   9   8   7   6   5   4   3

Acquisitions Editor:	Rachel Livsey
Editorial Assistant:	Phyllis Cappello
Production Editor:	Julia Parnell
Copy Editor:	Diana Breti
Proofreader:	Sally Scott
Typesetter:	C&M Digitals (P) Ltd.
Indexer:	Teri Greenberg
Cover Designer:	Tracy Miller
Production Artist:	Lisa Miller

Contents

Series Introduction

The American Association of School Administrators (AASA) is the largest association in the world representing school system leaders and, in particular, school district superintendents. These educational leaders know that the quality of America's schools depends heavily on the ability of school principals. AASA recognizes a pressing need exists to improve the skills and knowledge of current and prospective school leaders. To help address this need, AASA has put in place the Leadership for Learning initiative. This series of books plays a central role in this initiative.

The Leadership for Learning books address a broad range of knowledge and skills school superintendents, exceptional principals, and researchers believe are essential to ensure effective leadership at the school level. The content of this series of books reflects the "leaders' standards" developed for state licensure by the Interstate School Leaders Licensure Consortium (ISLLC), which was composed of representatives from several professional organizations representing educators, policymakers, and scholars. These standards have been adopted by more than two thirds of the states as the criteria by which the qualifications of school principals should be judged. Although the books in the series can be thought of as parts of a coherent curriculum, individual books stand on their own as syntheses of relevant research and expert consensus about best practice. The series as a whole reflects these commitments:

- All students should have the opportunity to maximize their potential for intellectual and social development.
- Enhancing the quality of teaching is the most important way to influence students' opportunities to learn.
- The actions of administrators, teachers, and school staff should be based on collaborative problem solving focused on the

systematic analysis of student performance and evidence of effective practice.

- School leaders need to foster the active engagement of parents and community organizations in the direct facilitation of student learning.

Leadership for Literacy examines the foundations of highly effective literacy programs in the primary grades. The focus is on the ways research on effective classrooms and productive schools can be used to ratchet up literacy achievement for all youngsters, especially children who have not fared well in school. The book helps leaders learn how to promote quality instruction, deepen the curriculum, and coordinate regular and special programs. The book also helps principals to promote higher reading achievement by fostering learning communities within schools and by nurturing collaboration between home and school.

—Willis D. Hawley
—Joe Schneider
Series Editors

Preface

A quarter century ago, the knowledge needed to power literacy programs that ensured that all youngsters learned to read well was in short supply. Theories and hunches were abundant. Research-based evidence was limited. As a consequence, teachers often pursued a course of action based on what they hoped might work, on local traditions, or on the most current initiatives afoot in the profession. Comprehensive school-based attacks on the literacy challenge were few and far between. The results were not surprising. Many youngsters did not learn to read well. We did not possess much confidence that we could address the problem. In addition, once children fell behind, we were unable on a consistent basis to help them right themselves on the path toward literacy success.

Over the last twenty years, we have progressed a long way in our ability to address the literacy challenge. Many hunches and philosophies of reading have proven to have fairly shallow roots. A significant body of empirical evidence has accumulated. And we are learning more and more about how to help youngsters that either come to school with language and reading deficits or fall behind once formal instruction begins.

Twenty years ago, there was also a firewall between school administration and teaching and learning. Leaders tended to know a good deal about the complex task of managing organizations, but they were poorly informed about the core technology of schooling. Surprisingly, they were also not well attuned to the task of leading school improvement, of ensuring that the systems at the school level (or district level) directed activities to promote the success of all students.

Over the last two decades, we have witnessed considerable progress in breaking down this barrier and in re-centering the field of school administration on our best understandings of learning, teaching, and school improvement. Beginning with the research on effective schools and instructional leadership, we have accumulated considerable knowledge about the role of school leadership in powering educational excellence for all students.

This book fuses knowledge from both of these areas, hence the title *Leadership for Literacy*. In so doing, I compile and integrate a considerable amount of research from four broad domains of scholarship: studies on school effectiveness, research on instructional leadership, investigations of teacher effects, and explorations of effective reading programs. It is this comprehensive strategy that permits me to capture and link findings that have rarely traveled together in the past. The end result is the crafting of a research-based platform that helps readers inform themselves about what is important and act to make literacy mastery a reality in schools and school districts throughout the United States.

The spotlight in this volume is directed toward literacy in the early years of schooling. I focus here because a consensus has emerged over the last twenty years about the critical nature of the primary grades (preK–3) in terms of literacy development. Much of this consensus emanates from data revealing that many youngsters arrive in kindergarten with literacy backgrounds that place them at significant risk of school failure. This knowledge, coupled with our inability until now to develop successful post-primary interventions for students with low literacy achievement and the growing recognition that students who remain behind after the second or third grade face very long odds in the race for school success, forcefully directs our attention to the literacy of young children.

While I cover the spectrum of students defined by ability and family background, I also provide space to investigating ways to ensure high levels of literacy for youngsters who historically have not fared well in our schools, that is, those children on the wrong side of the achievement gap. Given the moral imperative of addressing the underachievement of these children, as well as the shifting economic and political landscape that both heightens the problem and the demand for its resolution, it seems especially appropriate to target strategies that promise to strengthen literacy outcomes for students at risk. In understanding this endeavor, the featured mechanism is prevention of problems rather than their remediation, as recommended by a host of reading analysts. Throughout, however, the focus is on reading and writing for purpose, not as ends in themselves. In addition, I am concerned with explaining success as well as describing it.

It is my aim to influence political actions that shape the nature of literacy in our nation's school districts, schools, and classrooms.

Consequently, policymakers at the state (e.g., legislative staff, Department of Education personnel), district, and school levels form one audience for the insights ribboned throughout this book. At the same time, I am very much interested in directing the behaviors of leaders at the district and school levels into channels that will result in high levels of literacy achievement for all students. While the prime audience here is the principal, the work is also designed to inform teacher leadership at the school level and administration at the district office.

About the Author

Joseph Murphy is Professor of Education and Associate Dean at Peabody College of Education at Vanderbilt University. He has also been a faculty member at the University of Illinois and The Ohio State University, where he was the William Ray Flesher Professor of Education.

In the public schools he has served as an administrator at the school, district, and state levels, including an appointment as the Executive Assistant to the Chief Deputy Superintendent of Public Instruction in California. His most recent appointment was as the founding President of the Ohio Principals Leadership Academy. At the university level, he has served as Department Chair and Associate Dean.

He is past Vice President of the American Educational Research Association and is the Chair of the Interstate School Leaders Licensure Consortium (ISLLC). He is co-editor of the *AERA Handbook of Research on Educational Administration* (1999) and editor of the National Society for the Study of Education (NSSE) yearbook *The Educational Leadership Challenge* (2002).

His work is in the area of school improvement, with special emphasis on leadership and policy. He has authored or co-authored thirteen books in this area and edited another eleven. His most recent authored volumes include *The Quest for a Center: Notes on the State of the Profession of School Administration* (1999), *The Productive High School* (2001), and *Understanding and Assessing the Charter School Movement* (2002).

Dedication

Linda C. Holste of
Covered Bridge Farm

Epigraphs

Education, finally, is recognized as the central question for our country's future. The nation now is coming to grips with the need for a more literate society.

—(Richardson, 1991, p. l)

While science continues to discover more about how children learn to read and how teachers and others can help them, the knowledge currently available can equip our society to promote higher levels of literacy for large numbers of American schoolchildren.

—(Snow, Burns, & Griffin, 1998, p. l3)

* *

One frequently finds a strong administrative leader associated with the exemplary reading programs.

—(Samuels, 1981, p. 266)

Principal leadership is deemed to be critical for programmatic development of early reading.

—(Fisher & Adler, 1999, p. 25)

PART I

Laying the Foundations for Success

1

Exploring the Foundations of Leadership for Literacy

The knowledge is now available to make worthwhile improvements in reading throughout the United States. If the practices seen in the classrooms of the better teachers in the best schools could be introduced everywhere, the improvements would be dramatic. (Anderson, Hiebert, Scott, & Wilkinson, 1985, p. 3)

We have good evidence that most children can become literate alongside their peers. Not just a majority, but virtually all. Not someday, but along with their peers. (Allington, 1995, p. 2)

Setting the Stage

The knowledge exists to teach all but a handful of severely disabled children to read well. (American Federation of Teachers, 1999, p. 5)

We know much about how to design reading activities that promote a solid and successful start in reading and literacy for every child in America. (Kameenui, Simmons, Baker, Chard, Dickson, Gunn, et al., 1998, p. 47)

In this introductory chapter, I establish the framework for an exploration of literacy leadership. Following some initial comments about the focus of the book, I summarize the four areas that were mined to create it: effective schools, quality instruction, successful reading programs, and leadership in schools in which all students master literacy. I feature a comprehensive design for strengthening literacy at the primary grades. I attend, in particular, to the importance of consistent efforts across all levels of the educational system—from classroom, to school, to district, to state. Some key insights from this nested perspective for successful literacy education are enumerated. In Chapters 2 through 4, I extend this introductory material by framing the concepts of literacy and leadership that are at the heart of this book, by discussing the current state of literacy in the United States, and by reviewing foundational principles of high-quality reading programs.

Focus

We know how to give students a good start and a proper foundation, and we should do it. (Williams, 1991, p. 17)

While I illuminate many facets of the concept of literacy in this volume, the spotlight shines most brightly on the early years of schooling. I focus here because a consensus has emerged over the last twenty years about the critical nature of the primary grades (preK–3) in terms of literacy development (Snow, Burns, & Griffin, 1998). As Taylor and her colleagues (1999) remark, "our number one priority for funding research should be to improve classroom reading instruction in kindergarten and the primary grades" (p. 1). Taylor and Traxis (n.d.) make a parallel argument in terms of resource deployment in education. Much of this consensus emanates from data revealing that many youngsters arrive in kindergarten with literacy backgrounds that place them at significant risk of school failure (Hart & Risley, 1995; Smith, 1997). This knowledge, coupled with our inability until now to develop successful post-primary interventions for students with low literacy achievement (Pikulski, 1994) and the growing recognition that students who remain behind after the second or third grade face very long odds in the race for school success (Honig, 1997; Juel, 1988), forcefully directs our attention to the literacy of young children.

While I cover the spectrum of students defined by ability and family background, I also provide space to investigating ways to ensure high levels of literacy for youngsters who historically have not fared well in our schools, that is, those children on the wrong side of the achievement gap (Spiegel, 1995). As Snow and her colleagues (1998) remind us, the group includes:

> (1) children living in low-income communities; (2) children with limited English proficiency; (3) preschool children slated to attend an elementary school where achievement is chronically low; (4) children suffering from specific cognitive deficiencies, hearing impairments, and early language impairments; and (5) children whose parents have a history of reading problems. (p. 137)

Given the moral imperative of addressing the underachievement of these children, as well as the shifting economic and political landscape that heightens both the problem and the demand for its resolution, it seems especially appropriate to target strategies that promise to strengthen literacy outcomes for students at risk. In understanding this endeavor, the featured mechanism is prevention of problems rather than their remediation, as recommended by a host of reading analysts (Clay, 1994; Duffy-Hester, 1999; Slavin & Madden, 1989). Throughout, however, the focus is on reading and writing for purpose, not as ends in themselves. In addition, I am concerned with explaining success as well as describing it.

Finally, it is important to note that the material in this book is constructed from the best available knowledge—"a productive interplay among research and application" (Jones & Smith-Burke, 1999, p. 263)—about policies, practices, and behaviors that promote literacy achievement. Following Allington's (1997a) advice, my aim is to build up a "generally compelling basis for modifying current practice" (p. 34). While I am cognizant of the ways that answers to literacy questions have been informed by "polemics" (Stanovich, 2000, p. 388), "half-baked philosophy" (p. 411), and "political" rather than "scientific" criteria (p. 401), the touchstone here is "the basic research on reading that has allowed the community of reading scientists and educators to agree on what needs to be done" (American Federation of Teachers, 1999, p. 7). How far we have progressed in developing that knowledge can be gleaned by reviewing the state of the art in reading research in 1960, 1980, and 2000.

> The purpose of the [1959] meeting was to map out programs of needed research. Participants agreed that the problem of beginning reading, although acknowledged to be a difficult one, desperately needed more attention from researchers. They felt that the research then available provided evidence so vague, contradictory, and incomplete as to encourage conflicting interpretations. No serious research could state with any degree of certainty, on the basis of such evidence, that either one or another approach to beginning reading was indeed the best or the worst. (Chall, 1983, p. 4)

> If one is willing to accept the standardized reading achievement test score as a criterion for effective instruction, then there is now sufficient evidence to say that some of the variables associated with successful instruction in reading at the elementary grades are known. (Berliner, 1981, p. 203)

> No one could come away from reading this book without appreciating the enormous amount that has been learned in the past two decades about literacy development in the preschool and elementary years. (Pressley, 1998b, p. 274)

Audience

Morris, Shaw, and Perney (1990) assert that the struggle to ensure high levels of literacy achievement for all youngsters "will ultimately involve mobilizing societal and political support to change present educational policy" (p. 148). I concur, and I agree with Stanovich (2000) that "we have an obligation . . . to make sure that policies are informed by the best, most current, and most convergent knowledge we can provide" (p. 386). It is my aim, therefore, to influence political actions that shape the nature of literacy in our nation's school districts, schools, and classrooms. Consequently, policymakers at the state (e.g., legislative staff, Department of Education personnel), district, and school levels form one audience for the insights ribboned throughout these chapters. At the same time, I am very much interested in directing the behaviors of leaders at the district and school levels into channels that will result in high levels of literacy achievement for all students. While the prime audience here is the principal, the work is also designed to inform teacher leadership at the school level and administration at the district office.

A Comprehensive Framework for Action

We need evidence from many different levels of analysis. This is as true when trying to understand literacy as it is for any other complex behavior. (Stanovich, 2000, p. 158)

The great challenge for reading educators, therefore, is one of understanding the parts of the system and their interrelations. (Adams, 1990, p. 6)

In the pages that follow, I describe the significance of a comprehensive approach to strengthening literacy, an approach that provides the scaffolding for the material in Chapters 5 through 12. I then explore the four realms of knowledge that were harvested to form the comprehensive design.

The Framework

Indicators [of success] concern home conditions of each student, the community in which the school is located, the organizational features of each school, the resources in each school, the reading program initiative the school takes, the school principal's activities, the teaching experience of the reading teacher, and each teacher's activities and strategies in teaching reading, and his or her views about reading. (Postlethwaite & Ross, 1992, p. 13)

Having a significant effect on literacy achievement will require operating in several domains: effecting changes in homes and schools, encouraging communication between parents and teachers, working to reform curriculum and school management, and enlisting community, state, and federal support for education. (Snow, Barnes, Chandler, Goodman, & Hemphill, 1991, p. 164)

The architecture I develop assumes that "the more elements of good parenting, good teaching, and good schooling that children experience, the greater the likelihood that they will achieve their potential as readers" (Anderson et al., 1985, p. 117). The design, therefore, attends to the multiple actors in the literacy script and to the multiple levels in the system. Throughout, coherence and integration across actors and levels is of critical concern. Finally, within this coherent pattern, the viability of strategies is highlighted. Underlying everything in the framework is the belief that knowledge should backward map from our best understanding of student learning. Center stage is occupied by "the learner and the 'academic work' the learner is engaging in" (Hoffman, 1991, p. 946).

The central idea here is that since "district policies, school level decisions, approaches used by individual teachers [and] other factors determine . . . reading achievement" (Armor, Conroy-Osequera, Cox, King, McDonnell, Pascal, et al., 1976, p. 20), what is critical is coordinated action on many fronts and across many levels of the educational system. Literacy interventions that appear as "isolated phenomena" (Gaffney & Paynter, 1994, p. 26) are rarely successful. In many places, state policies, district frameworks, school actions, and classroom work are only loosely aligned. "Practice[s] based on widely differing theoretical assumptions" (Pinnell, Lyons, DeFord, Bryk, & Seltzer, 1994, p. 10) are often thrown together. The power of coherence is absent. Teachers and pupils are often pulled by conflicting goals. There are often frequent shifts in programmatic direction. The benefits of action from multiple levels reinforcing common objectives are lost (Creemers, 1994; Murphy, 1992).

On the other hand, mastery of literacy skills is associated with comprehensive designs that weave levels of the schooling enterprise into a common tapestry (Slavin & Madden, 1989; State of New York, 1974). "The process of learning and development at every level of the education system" (Lyons & Pinnell, 1999, p. 197) is attended to. Each level (e.g., the school) is carefully nested within the next level (e.g., the district). Features do not exist in isolation. Rather, they can be viewed "as a set of interrelated components" (Samuels, 1981, p. 256). Influence moves in both directions through the levels (Samuels, 1981). The home and the school are linked and employ the same playbook to ensure that all children learn to read well (Snow et al., 1991). And this same systems ideology is applied within each of the levels as well. For example, there is a "comprehensive literacy framework in classrooms" (Williams, Scharer, & Pinnell, 2000, p. 27); teaching itself is a system. What is important is not so much the individual elements but "how the features fit together to form a whole . . . individual features make sense only in terms of how they relate with others that surround them" (Stigler & Hiebert, 1999, p. 75).

So far, I have shown that my framework underscores (1) the influence of the actors at multiple levels of the educational enterprise, that is, "school-level change is as important as change within classrooms" (Taylor, Pearson, Clark, & Walpole, 1999, p. 43) and (2) the importance of a comprehensive approach to action, with its essential requirement that each piece of the system perform in a coherent, coordinated, and consistent manner. My final point guides us to the road map needed to formulate an integrated design. Much of the literature on school improvement reads like the quest for the Holy Grail, the search for the single variable that will guarantee success. The position taken here is quite different. As Fraser (1989) reports:

> The educational productivity research highlights that we should not expect any single factor to have an enormous impact on student learning; rather, the key to improving student learning and enhancing school effectiveness lies in simultaneously optimizing several different factors each of which bears a modest relationship to achievement. (p. 716)

Specifically, in the area of reading "a combination of factors, rather than one or two, makes the critical difference in raising the reading achievement level in a school" (Williams, Scharer, & Pinnell, 2000, p. 28; see also Fletcher & Lyon, 1998; Phi Delta Kappa, 1980; Sanacore, 1997).

> There are so many important elements in a good reading program, that simple, "quick fix," single element approaches usually cannot produce a significant impact on achievement. To produce a significant impact, a comprehensive approach operating on a student over time is required. (Samuels, 1981, p. 271)

Or, as Armor and his research team (1976) state, "the separate effects of the school inputs we found to be important for reading are small compared with their combined power" (p. 30).

A corollary of the combined variable story line is "that there is more than one route to successful reading performance" (Konold, Juel, McKinnon, 1999, p. i). Because the learning context matters a good deal (Au & Mason, 1981; Williams, Scharer, & Pinnell, 2000), because "children take varied routes to common outcomes"

(Askew & Gaffney, 1999, p. 79), because "different approaches are better to teach different goals" (Stahl, 1997, p. 21), and because effect variables can be mixed in many ways, "there is no single way to improve the teaching-learning process" (Clay, 1994, p. 139), "there are many different routes to literacy development" (Neuman, Caperelli, & Kee, 1998, p. 250), and "no one model explains school effectiveness" (Edmonds, 1979, p. 32). Not surprisingly, within the framework of high coordination and integration, "there are many different patterns that effective schools might assume" (Hoffman & Rutherford, 1984, p. 83) and "there are numerous models of effective reading programs" (Patty, Maschoff, & Ranson, 1996, p. 2).

The Four Knowledge Pillars

The answer . . . then seems to be that *both* individual schools *and* individual classrooms are affecting students' reading achievement levels. (Armor et al., 1976, p. 21)

The implication is that to improve reading achievement, we must improve both programs and classroom delivery. Each seems to contribute separately and significantly to children's progress. (Adams, 1990, p. 43)

A combination of school and teacher factors, many of which were intertwined, was found in the most effective schools. (Hiebert & Pearson, 1999, p. 10)

Effective Instruction

As can be seen in Figure 1.1, I conducted reviews in four broad domains of research to gather the raw material needed to construct my comprehensive portrait of leadership for literacy. Working from the classroom outward, the first domain is the research on effective instruction (see Table 1.1). I began with studies and research reviews in the general area of literacy. I also analyzed studies in specific areas of literacy such as tutoring, comprehension, family literacy, repeated reading, and so forth. Table 1.1 contains examples of work in two of these areas: studies and reviews on oral reading, and research in the field of silent reading. In building the knowledge base in the area of instruction, I also examined a number of studies that focused on literacy instruction for specific groups of learners, in particular for students at risk of school failure. Again, in Table 1.1 some examples of the type of work on which I relied are listed. To leaven the product,

Figure 1.1   Domains of Research Informing the Leadership for Literacy
Platform

Characteristics of Effective
Instruction

Characteristics of Effective
Reading Programs

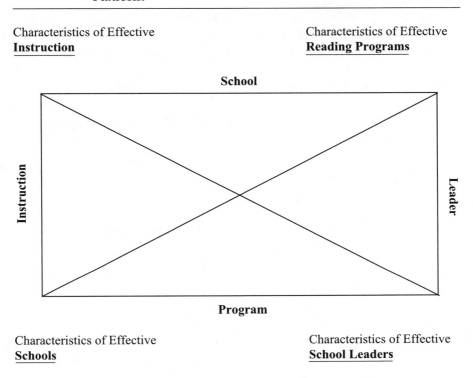

Characteristics of Effective
Schools

Characteristics of Effective
School Leaders

I also incorporated findings from general studies of effective instruction, that is, those that did not focus explicitly on literacy. The investigations here were of two types: general studies of instructional effectiveness; and research on effective instruction for children of color, pupils from low-income homes, and youngsters from culturally and linguistically diverse families. Finally, despite "a lack of systematic study of effective teachers, a lack of understanding of their practices and perspectives" (Wharton-McDonald, Pressley, & Hampston, 1998, p. 102), I unearthed a few studies of effective teaching in reading.

Effective Reading Programs

A second major set of readings was undertaken to determine what the literature on effective reading programs could contribute to the narrative on leadership for literacy. Studies and reviews in this domain were clustered into two lines of work. First, I grouped studies that answered the question, What are the characteristics of reading programs that are especially productive in promoting high levels of reading achievement? Six of these natural harvest types of studies can be seen

Table 1.1 Examples of Studies on Effective Instruction

General Area of Literacy

Adams, M. J. (1990). *Beginning to read: Thinking and learning about print.*

Chall, J. S. (1983). *Learning to read: The great debate.*

Knapp, M. S., & Needels, M. (1991). Review of research on curriculum and instruction in literacy.

Morrow, L. M., et al. (1999). Characteristics of exemplary first-grade literacy instruction.

Pflaum, S. W., et al. (1980). Reading instruction: A quantitative analysis.

Pressley, M. (1998). *Reading instruction that works: The case for balanced teaching.*

Snow, C. E., et al. (1998). *Preventing reading difficulties in young children.*

Specific Area of Literacy (e.g., Oral & Silent Reading)

Allington, R. L. (1984). Oral reading.

Collins, C. (1980). Sustained silent reading periods: Effects on teachers' behaviors and students' achievement.

Hoffman, J. V. (1987). Rethinking the role of oral reading in basal instruction.

Koskinen, P. S., & Blum, I. H. (1984). Repeated oral reading and the acquisition of fluency.

Leinhardt, G., et al. (1981). Reading instruction and its effects.

Moore, J. C., et al. (1980). What we know after a decade of sustained silent reading.

Reutzell, D. R., Hollingsworth, P. M., & Eldredge, J. L. (1994). Oral reading instruction: The impact on student reading development.

Wilkinson, I., et al. (1988). Silent reading reconsidered: Reinterpreting reading instruction and its effects.

Literacy Instruction for Specific Students (e.g., Students Placed at Risk)

Allington, R. L. (1991). Effective literacy instruction for at-risk children.

Foorman, B. R., et al. (1998). The role of instruction in learning to read: Preventing reading failure in at-risk children.

Garcia, G. E., & Pearson, P. D. (1991). Modifying reading instruction to maximize its effectiveness for all students.

Harris, A. J., & Serwer, B. L. (1966). The CRAFT project: Instructional time in reading research.

Taylor, B. M., et al. (1999). Beating the odds in teaching all children to read.

Studies of Effective Teachers

Haberman, M. (1995). *Star teachers of children in poverty.*

Pressley, M., et al. (2000). A survey of instructional practices of primary teachers nominated as effective in promoting literacy.

Ruddell, R. B. (1997). Researching the influential literacy teacher: Characteristics, beliefs, strategies, and new research directions.

Wharton-McDonald, R., et al. (1998). Literacy instruction in nine first-grade classrooms: Teacher characteristics and student achievement.

Table 1.2   Examples of Studies on Effective Reading Programs

Natural Harvest Programs

     Armor, D., et al. (1976). *Analysis of the school preferred reading program in selected Los Angeles minority schools.*

     Briggs, K. L., & Thomas, K. (1997). *Patterns of success: Successful pathways to elementary literacy in Texas Spotlight Schools.*

     Fisher, C., & Adler, M. A. (1999). *Early reading programs in high-poverty schools: Emerald Elementary beats the odds.*

     Hallinger, P., & Murphy, J. (1985). Characteristics of highly effective elementary school reading programs.

     Hoffman, J. V., & Rutherford, W. L. (1984). Effective reading programs: A critical review of outlier studies.

     Samuels, S. J. (1981). Characteristics of exemplary reading programs.

     Wilder, G. (1977). Five exemplary reading programs.

Specially Developed Reading Programs—Regular and Remedial

     Askew, B. J., et al. (2000). A review of Reading Recovery.

     Pikulski, J. J. (1994). Preventing reading failure: A review of five effective programs.

     Pinnell, G. S., et al. (1994). Comparing instructional models for the literacy education of high-risk first graders.

     Ross, S. M., et al. (1995). Increasing the academic success of disadvantaged children: An examination of alternative early intervention programs.

     Slavin, R. E., et al. (1994). Success for All: A comprehensive approach to prevention and early intervention.

in Table 1.2, including my own 1985 research report and recent work from the Center for the Improvement of Early Reading Achievement. A second cluster of work focuses on specially developed reading programs—both regular and remedial or preventative—that are effective in promoting student achievement in the area of literacy. Again, examples from this area, including research from Pinnell and her colleagues at The Ohio State University and Slavin and his collaborators at Johns Hopkins University, can be seen in Table 1.2.

Effective Schools

Over the last three decades, investigations of effective schools have grown into a robust area of research (see, e.g., Teddlie and Reynolds, 2000). These studies sometimes connect conditions at the school level to reading achievement. Illustrative studies from this line of research, including classic studies from the 1970s, can be seen in

Table 1.3   Examples of Studies on Effective Schools

Reading Achievement

Ellis, A. B. (1975). *Success and failure: A summary of findings and recommendations for improving elementary reading in Massachusetts city schools.*

Postlethwaite, T. N., & Ross, K. N. (1992). *Effective schools in reading: Implications for educational planners.*

Rowe, K. J., (1995). Factors affecting students' progress in reading: Key findings from a longitudinal study.

State of New York. (1974). *School factors influencing reading achievement: A case study of two inner city schools.*

Venezky, R. L., & Winfield, L. F. (1979). *Schools that succeed beyond expectations in teaching reading.*

Weber, G. (1971). *Inner-city children can be taught to read: Four successful schools.*

General Achievement

Brookover, W., & Lezotte, L. W. (1979). *Changes in school characteristics coincident with changes in student achievement.*

Fraser, B. J. (1989). Research syntheses on school and instructional effectiveness.

Frederiksen, J., & Edmonds, R. (n.d.). *The identification of instructionally effective and ineffective schools.* Unpublished manuscript, Harvard University, Cambridge, MA.

Phi Delta Kappa. (1980). *Why do some urban schools succeed? The Phi Delta Kappa study of exceptional urban elementary schools.*

Rutter, M. (1983). School effects on pupil progress: Research findings and policy implications.

Wellisch, J. B., et al. (1978). School management and organization in successful schools.

Table 1.3. More often, studies of highly productive schools uncover organizational characteristics that are related to achievement in both reading and mathematics. Examples of work reviewed for this category can also be seen in Table 1.3, including examples of foundational work by Brookover and Lezotte and by Edmonds.

Instructional Leadership

Finally, I reviewed the growing body of research that links the activities of school leaders to student performance, the instructional leadership literature. Important examples from that body of work for

Table 1.4   Examples of Studies on Effective Educational Leadership

Hallinger, P., et al. (1996). Social context, principal leadership, and student reading achievement.

Murphy, J. (1990). Principal instructional leadership.

Murphy, J., & Hallinger, P. (1986). The superintendent as instructional leader: Findings from effective school districts.

the principalship and the superintendency can be seen in Table 1.4, although it is important to note that rather than being investigated directly, our knowledge of effective leadership tends to be culled primarily from studies of program and school effectiveness.

Summary

In this first of four introductory chapters, I laid some of the groundwork that helps the reader see into the chapters that follow. I also argued for the importance of a comprehensive framework for strengthening literacy in the primary grades (preK–3), one that acknowledges that success is a mixture of what unfolds at the classroom, reading program, and school levels—and one that is dependent on leadership and policy at the district and state levels as well. I suggested that consistency, coordination, and integration around a common vision are the hallmarks of that framework. In the next chapter, I examine the two concepts that define this volume, literacy and leadership.

2

Framing Literacy
and Leadership

In this chapter, I unpack the two concepts that form the axes of this book—literacy and leadership. In subsequent chapters, specific ideas for leading schools where all youngsters master important literacy skills are located along these coordinates.

Framing Literacy

> In the last ten years or so a major shift has occurred in research in the field traditionally called "reading." An emblem of this shift is the adoption of the term "literacy" to refer to the phenomenon under study. The term "literacy" signals a recognition of the complex relationships among reading, writing, ways of talking, ways of learning, and ways of knowing. Literacy is not just a cognitive achievement on the part of the child: it is also participation in culturally defined structures of knowledge and communication. (Snow et al., 1991, p. 175)

> Literacy-related research constitutes one of the most vital, vigorous, diverse, complex, and problematic domains of educational and psychosocial inquiry. (Rowe, 1995, p. 60)

Definitions

> With the multitude of experts and published books on the topic, one would suppose that there would be a fair amount of agreement as to how to define the term "literacy." On the one hand, most specialists would agree that the term connotes aspects of reading and writing; on the other hand, major debates continue to revolve around such issues as what specific abilities or knowledge count as literacy, and what "levels" can and should be defined for measurement. (Wagner, 1999, p. 6)

It is not my intention to review the literature on the meaning of literacy in great detail. However, it is necessary to establish the boundaries of the subject in question, to provide a definition of literacy and reading, to expose key elements of the concept, and to describe the reading process. Since "reading literacy" (Postlethwaite & Ross, 1992, p. 8), which is the focus of this book, nests within the concept of literacy more generally, I begin with a few insights about the larger construct. While there is growing agreement on a "componential view of literacy" (Snow et al., 1991, p. 5), that is, that literacy is composed of reading, writing, and language skills, "no one definition of literacy . . . is generally accepted" (Harris & Sipay, 1990, p. 5). Because "major debates continue to revolve around such issues as what specific abilities or knowledge counts as literacy and what 'levels' can and should be defined for measurement" (Wagner, 1999, p. 6), "definitions of literacy are highly problematic" (Graff, 1995, p. 46). In short, what counts as literacy is open, and "what it means to be literate . . . remains a matter of contention" (Johnston, 1999, p. 29).

The more expansive conception of literacy encompasses two subcomponents, "literacy skills as they are taught and measured in schools (usually called 'reading achievement') and literacy skills that are practiced outside of schools (usually called 'functional literacy')" (Kaestle et al., 1991, p. 78). Functional literacy is generally defined as the ability "to engage effectively in all those activities in which literacy is normally assumed in [one's] culture or group" (Wagner, 1999, p. 5)—"the ability to read common texts such as newspapers and manuals and to use the information gained, usually to secure employment" (Resnick & Resnick, 1977, p. 383), and the ability "to understand and use the printed material one normally encounters in work, leisure, and citizenship" (Kaestle et al., 1991, p. 92).

Methods to assess functional literacy have shifted over time (Graff, 1995; Wagner, 1999), although completion of a set number of years of schooling has held the high ground for some time. In a similar manner, the literacy criterion has been recalibrated from time to time (Resnick & Resnick, 1977).

> The Civilian Conservation Corps seems to have coined the term "functional literacy" in the 1930s. They defined it as three or more years of schooling, reasoning that a person with that much schooling could read the essential printed material of daily life. The level of education considered necessary to be functionally literate has risen steadily since then. During World War II the army used the term to refer to a fourth-grade educational level and, until manpower demands became overwhelming, rejected recruits with less schooling. In 1947, the Census Bureau applied the term "functional illiterates" to those with fewer than five years of schooling and ceased questioning those with more schooling about rudimentary literacy. In 1952, the bureau raised the functional-literacy definition to the sixth grade, and by 1960, the U.S. Office of Education was using eighth grade as the standard. Finally, by the late 1970s, some noted authorities were describing functional literacy in terms of high-school completion. (Kaestle et al., 1991, p. 92)

Finally, the proportion of citizens expected to reach functional literacy has increased throughout the last two centuries (Resnick & Resnick, 1977).

Reading, in turn, has been defined in a number of ways. For example,

> Reading is the process of constructing meaning from written texts. It is a complex skill requiring the coordination of a number of interrelated sources of information. (Anderson et al., 1985, p. 7)

> Reading is about constructing meaning from text. (Pressley, 1998b, p. 52)

> Reading is the process of constructing meaning through dynamic interaction among reader, the text, and the context of the reading situation. (Michigan State Board of Education, cited in McGill-Franzen, 2000, p. 898)

> Reading is the meaningful interpretation of written language. In short, reading is comprehending. (Harris & Sipay, 1990, p. 10)

> Reading is an interactive process in which readers interact with the text as their prior experience is activated. Using prior experience as a channel, readers learn new information, main ideas, and arguments. Most important, readers construct meaning from the text by relying on prior experience to parallel, contrast, or affirm what the author suggests. (Carter, 1997, pp. 65-66)

The Commission on Reading, in the highly influential report *Becoming a Nation of Readers,* provided this helpful analogy:

> Reading can be compared to the performance of a symphony orchestra. This analogy illustrates three points. First, like the performance of a symphony, reading is a holistic act. In other words, while reading can be analyzed into subskills such as discriminating letters and identifying words, performing the subskills one at a time does not constitute reading. Reading can be said to take place only when the parts are put together in a smooth, integrated performance. Second, success in reading comes from practice over long periods of time, like skill in playing musical instruments. Indeed, it is a lifelong endeavor. Third, as with a musical score, there may be more than one interpretation of a text. The interpretation depends upon the background of the reader, the purpose for reading, and the context in which reading occurs. (Anderson et al., 1985, p. 7)

And the National Reading Panel (National Institute of Child Health and Human Development, 2000b) portrays the difficult task that confronts beginning readers as follows:

> Learning to read is a complex task for beginners. They must coordinate many cognitive processes to read accurately and fluently. Readers must be able to apply their alphabetic knowledge to decode unfamiliar words and to remember how to read words they have read before. When reading connected text, they must construct sentence meanings and retain them in memory as they move on to new sentences. At the same time, they must monitor their word recognition to make sure that the words activated in their minds fit with the meaning of the context. In addition, they must link new information to what they have already read, as well as to their background

knowledge, and use this to anticipate forthcoming information. When one stops to take stock of all the processes that readers perform when they read and comprehend text, one is reminded how amazing the act of reading is and how much there is for beginners to learn. (2:99)

These various windows into reading help us see that while there are multiple goals in reading (Stahl, 1998), comprehension or the construction of meaning is the central aim (Kuhn & Stahl, 2000; Pressley, 1998b; Torgesen, 1997). They also reveal how much deeper this concept is than is the construct of functional literacy (Johnston, 1999; Pressley, Ranking, & Yokoi, 2000). According to Knapp and Needels (1991), the definition of reading "goes beyond the set of functional skills required by routine life to include the capacity for thinking and reasoning that has come to be associated with highly developed literate behavior" (p. 86). These definitions also honor the cognitive, inquisitive, and cultural dimensions of reading work (Purcell-Gates, 1998). As well, they underscore the relative nature of reading (Graff, 1979; Harris & Sipay, 1990), that is, reading literacy "involves skills at using print and language in ways that change as skills develop" (Snow et al., 1991, p. 5). Reading literacy "is a process, different for different roles and . . . its requirements change with individual and social changes" (Graff, 1995, pp. 46-47).

In terms of design, the reading process can be decomposed into "two basic cognitive tasks" (NICHHD, 2000b, 3:8) or "two primary components: *decoding*, or word recognition, and language *comprehension*" (Fletcher & Lyon, 1998, p. 57); that is, both "good word reading skills and good general language comprehension are the most critical skills required for effective comprehension of written material" (Torgesen, 1998, p. 33). As a host of literacy scholars have shown, instruction begins with "the encoding and decoding aspects of print" (Purcell-Gates, 1998, p. 60) and progresses to issues of comprehension, especially after the primary grades (Pressley, 1998a; 1998b). On the first issue, there is a growing consensus "that learning to break code is a critical part of primary-level reading" (Pressley et al., 2000, p. 11) and that "learning to break the code of written text is dependent on . . . phonemic awareness" (Juel, 1988, p. 437). On the second issue, Juel (1988) defines comprehension as "the process by which the meanings of words are integrated into sentences and text structures" (p. 438). And Snow and her colleagues (1998) remind us that "mature readers construct meaning at two levels . . . literal understanding of what the author has written [and] . . . reflective, purposive understanding [that] goes beyond literal understanding" (p. 216). I take up the topics of decoding and comprehension in considerable detail in later chapters.

Stages of Reading Development

> Reading development can be viewed as a series of qualita-
> tively different stages through which learners proceed.
> Development in each stage is dependent upon the concepts
> learned in previous stages; likewise, each stage is prerequisite
> for the learning that follows. (Kuhn & Stahl, 2000, p. 1)

While the spotlight in this book is on reading in the early years, especially the primary grades, it is important to couch one's understanding in the knowledge that "reading is a continuously developing skill" (Anderson et al., 1985, p. 16) and that learning to read is a developmental process; that is, "literacy development is not a childhood thing but rather a lifespan development" (Pressley, 1998b, p. 271). It is also necessary to begin with the knowledge "that much literacy acquisition occurs outside school and a considerable amount might occur before school entry" (Snow et al., 1991, p. 175). Finally, the understanding that reading is not a single-stage phenomenon, that it changes at different developmental levels, is essential to my narrative (Chall, Jacobs, & Baldwin, 1990; Ehri, 1995). Thus, "the process of learning can be conceptualized as a series of qualitatively different stages through which learners progress as they become increasingly proficient with print" (Kuhn & Stahl, 2000, p. 1).

Chall has crafted the best known stage model of reading development, one that features six levels of maturation.

> These changes fall into six stages—from Stage 0 (prereading)
> to Stage 5 (the most mature, skilled level of reading, in which
> readers construct and reconstruct knowledge from their own
> reading). Generally, in Stage 0 (from birth to about age 6) the
> child learns some simple concepts of reading and writing—
> reading of signs, giving the names of the letters, writing one's
> name, and pretending to read books. Stages 1 and 2 (typically
> acquired in Grades 1, 2, and 3) can be characterized as the
> time of "learning to read." In Stage 1 (Grade 1), children learn
> the alphabetic principle—how to recognize and sound out
> (decode) words in print—and they read simple texts. In
> Stage 2 (Grades 2 and 3), children acquire fluency and become

automatic in reading simple, familiar texts—those that use language and thought processes already within their experience and abilities. Stages 3 to 5 can be characterized roughly as the "reading to learn" stages—when the texts read in school go beyond what the readers already know, linguistically and cognitively. (Chall et al., 1990, pp. 10-11)

It is helpful to divide Chall's stages into two clusters. Stages 0, 1, and 2 can be thought of as the period of beginning reading, the primary grades, and Stages 3, 4, and 5 can be characterized as the time of mature reading, Grade 4 through college. It is the first cluster that holds our attention here. At this phase of development, "the major learning task for reading . . . is recognition and decoding of words seen in print" (p. 44).

In the course of developing sight word reading—Chall's first three stages—Ehri (1995) has distinguished four distinct phases "characterized by the involvement of the alphabetic system—pre-alphabetic, partial alphabetic, full alphabetic, and consolidated alphabetic" (p. 117).

During the pre-alphabetic phase, beginners remember how to read sight words by forming connections between selected visual attributes of words and their pronunciations or meanings and storing these associations in memory. . . . We have called this visual cue reading. . . . This phase is called pre-alphabetic because, in contrast to subsequent phases, letter-sound relations are not involved in the connections. When pre-alphabetic phase readers are observed to read print in their environment, such as stop signs and fast food restaurant signs, they do this by remembering visual cues accompanying the print rather than the written words themselves.

During the next phase, partial alphabetic, beginners remember how to read sight words by forming partial alphabetic connections between only some of the letters in written words and sounds detected in their pronunciations. Because first and final letters are especially salient, these are often selected as the cues to be remembered. We have called this phonetic cue reading.

During the full alphabetic phase, beginners remember how to read sign words by forming complete connections between letters seen in the written forms of words and phonemes detected in their pronunciation. The ability of full phase readers to retain complete information about the spellings of sight words in memory makes it possible for their print lexicons to grow rapidly as they encounter many different words in their reading. As fully connected spellings of more and more words are retained in memory, letter patterns that recur across different words become consolidated. Repeated experience reading a letter sequence that symbolizes the same phoneme blend across different words yields a consolidated unit. Consolidation allows readers to operate with multiletter units that may be morphemes, syllables, or subsyllabic units such as onsets and rimes. These letter patterns become part of a reader's generalized knowledge of the spelling system. (pp. 118-121)

For my purpose in this book, the important message from this work on stages of reading is twofold. First, as noted above, the process of learning to read is developmental. Second, there "appears to be no one set of best practices for teaching reading that applies to all grades and all aspects of reading" (Chall et al., p. 148). Reading requires "different instructional emphases for different stages of development. Beginning reading may look the same as mature reading but it is quite different. Beginning reading has much to do with phonology" (Chall, 1991, p. 24), and phonology in all of its complexity is the major support structure in the framework I create in this book.

Comments on Reading Failure

Many studies have been conducted to answer the question of why some children fail to learn to read and write as well as others their age. Conclusions of these studies have implicated inappropriate teaching methods, low academic standards in schools attended by poor children, insufficient language stimulation at home and at school, and a variety of individual child characteristics. (Snow et al., 1991, p. 2)

Before I move into the chapters on the programmatic and instructional dimensions of leading for high levels of literacy, a few preliminary comments on the causes of reading difficulties in young children are in order. Reading failure is generally traced to one of three sources: the learner himself or herself, the organization charged with educating the child (i.e., the school and the classroom), or the environment surrounding the learner—the home and the larger cultural, economic, social, and political milieus. For example, child-anchored explanations for reading failure rest at the heart of special education solutions to low reading achievement, while compensatory education programs are rooted in a belief that environmental conditions account for school failure (Allington & McGill-Franzen, 1989b; McGill-Franzen, 1987).

Environmental explanations for reading success and failure are of two types. Some investigators point to "the home as the main cause of poor literacy skills" (Snow et al., 1991, p. 7). These analysts tend to cite factors such as "a low level of parental literacy, a low level of parental aspirations for children's achievement" (p. 7), and the general absence of a supportive literacy environment in the home. Other reviewers highlight the larger milieu surrounding families. Areas of interest here include political matters—the absence of political support for children at risk of school failure; economic issues—disadvantage and poverty; and social and cultural topics—a mismatch between the culture of the youngster and his or her home and the culture of the school, changing family structure, immigration, and so forth.

Organizational conditions in two domains are also presented to account for reading failure. School-level topics are often raised. For example, the use of organizational arrangements such as pull-out programs, homogeneous grouping, and retention are targeted as explanations for inadequate reading performance. Failure is also linked to the absence of adequate resources in schools and to "the questionable quality of administrative leadership" (Snow et al., 1991, p. 7). In addition, failure is often connected to actions in classrooms. For example, low teacher expectations; low teacher efficacy; and poor, inappropriate, and watered-down programs have all been implicated in reading failure.

Finally, "assumptions about [children's] physiological deficits, especially neurological impairments underlie explanations" (Allington & McGill-Franzen, 1989b, p. 530) of inadequate reading achievement. Disability is highlighted in this explanatory framework. Biology is also often implicated, and neurological and intelligence problems are raised (McGill-Franzen, 1987; Pressley, 1998b).

Two final points merit attention. First, the reading success and failure equation is quite complex. It is unlikely that problems can be connected to a single cause, or as Snow and her colleagues (1991) phrase it, "patterns of literacy success and failure are too complex for one or a few variables to explain them" (p. 10). Second, there has been a shift in emphasis over the last quarter century. During the 1980s, as McGill-Franzen (1987) reports, "reading failure [was] redefined from one of socioeconomic disadvantage to one of [student] disability"

(p. 477). More recently, I aver, there has been another shift—one that features the organizational elements of our explanatory framework.

Framing Leadership

Schools that are especially effective in teaching children to read are characterized by vigorous instructional leadership. (Anderson et al., 1985, p. 112)

The findings suggest that elementary school principals who are perceived by teachers as strong instructional leaders promote student achievement through their influence on features of the schoolwide learning climate. (Hallinger, Bickman, & Davis, 1996, p. 543)

In this section, I provide a comprehensive framework for examining instructional leadership. The framework presented in Table 2.1 contains four major dimensions: (1) developing mission and goals, (2) managing the educational production function, (3) promoting an academic learning climate, and (4) developing a supportive work environment. Each dimension is divided into specific functions that administrators perform. Functions, in turn, are composed of policies that principals develop and specific practices and behaviors that they carry out. It is this general model that gives meaning to instructional leadership in reading detailed in later chapters.

Developing Mission and Goals

Numerous studies support the contention that one aspect of the principal's role as an instructional leader is to define and communicate a mission or purpose for a school. As Powell, Farrar, and Cohen (1985) point out, "the existence of a common purpose has an educational force of its own, quite independent of the skills of individual teachers" (p. 316). Instructional leaders are often said to have a "vision" of what a school should be trying to accomplish. For example, studies of highly effective and less effective principals find that highly effective principals have a clear sense of direction for their schools and are able to articulate it clearly. Less effective principals seem to possess little sense of direction for their schools; they focus on maintaining tranquility in the here and now. Defining or developing homogeneity of values or consensus involves communicating a vision to the staff and students in such a way that a sense of shared

Table 2.1   A General Model of Instructional Leadership

Developing Mission and Goals
  framing school goals
  communicating school goals

Managing the Educational Production Function
  promoting quality instruction
  supervising and evaluating instruction
  allocating and protecting instructional time
  coordinating the curriculum
  monitoring student progress

Promoting an Academic Learning Climate
  establishing positive expectations and standards
  maintaining high visibility
  providing incentives for teachers and students
  promoting professional development

Developing a Supportive Work Environment
  creating a safe and orderly learning environment
  providing opportunities for meaningful student involvement
  developing staff collaboration and cohesion
  securing outside resources in support of school goals
  forging links between the home and the school

purpose exists, linking together the various activities that take place in classrooms throughout the school or district. Research shows that the principal is pivotal in creating this mission. The administrator's role in defining the mission involves framing schoolwide goals and communicating these goals in a persistent fashion to the entire school community.

Framing School Goals

Although many schools are characterized by vague goals that provide little direction to staff, schools with more effective principals often have goals that look quite different. To begin with, schools with high levels of instructional leadership often have well-defined aims; effective principals set specific learning goals, while less effective principals do not. Instructional goals and goals stressing student achievement have the highest priority in schools with active instructional leadership. Goals in these schools are also more directly focused on students. As Wimpelberg (1986) notes, the generalizable difference between effective and less effective schools "is the centrality of children in their mission. The less effective schools tended to have adult needs or value systems in mind. In the more effective schools, principals responded as though they 'saw' the children first" (p. 7). Instructionally effective schools have goals that place considerable emphasis on student achievement. Their goals also apply to *all* the children served by the school. They emphasize a few goals around which staff energy and other school resources can be mobilized. A few coordinated objectives, each with a manageable scope, appear to characterize schools with active instructional leaders. At the same time, effective principals formulate ambitious goals for student performance, while the goals of less effective principals focus more on ensuring that the school runs smoothly. Effective principals actively coordinate school goals with the goals of the larger organization. Goals incorporate data on past and current student performance and include staff responsibilities for achieving the goals. Effective principals rely on a greater number of sources in developing goals and more public (and fewer private) sources. Staff and parent input during the development of the school's goals are deemed to be important. Performance goals are expressed in measurable terms. Effective principals use goals for planning and decision making, while less effective leaders do not.

Communicating School Goals

Communicating school goals is a function concerned with the ways in which school administrators communicate goals to teachers, parents, and students. Instructional leaders ensure that the importance of school goals is understood by discussing and reviewing them with staff periodically during the school year, especially in the context of instructional, curricular, and budgetary decisions. Both formal communication (e.g., goal statements, staff bulletins, articles in the principal or site-council newsletter, curricular and staff meetings, parent and teacher conferences, school handbook, assemblies) and informal interactions (e.g., conversations with staff) are used to communicate the school's mission. "Highly effective principals, in contrast to their less effective peers, seek out opportunities to clarify goals with staff, students, parents and other members of the school community" (Leithwood & Montgomery, 1984, p. 31).

Not only do instructional leaders spend more energy than their peers on communicating goals, they also appear more successful in getting their messages through. For example, teachers in schools with active instructional leaders are much more aware of and can clearly communicate the school's mission and goals. Their counterparts in schools with less effective instructional leadership lack a common understanding of schoolwide goals and expectations. Teachers in instructionally effective schools tend to refer to instructional competencies when describing their areas of expertise. Their peers in less effective schools, on the other hand, emphasize competencies in personal, social, and managerial domains. Teachers in instructionally effective schools share a common language of teaching and learning to a much greater extent than do their colleagues in less effective schools.

Managing the Educational Production Function

Managing the educational production function involves working with teachers in areas specifically related to curriculum and instruction. It consists of the following related job functions: promoting quality instruction, supervising and evaluating instruction, allocating and protecting instructional time, coordinating the curriculum, promoting content coverage, and monitoring student progress.

Promoting Quality Instruction

Significant progress has been made in the last twenty-five years in our understanding of the factors that promote high levels of student achievement at the classroom, school, and district levels. Studies of effective principals reveal that these administrators seem to be aware of this knowledge and to ensure that it is translated into management practices and behaviors that are supportive of learning. At the broadest level, managers in effective schools are more active than their colleagues in planning and evaluating the total instructional program. They spend more time on program-related issues. They ensure greater consistency and coordination of instruction programs. Methods of instruction tend to be more clearly defined and focused. Interactive teaching strategies are often emphasized in instructionally effective schools. There is also evidence that instructional leaders infuse routine school activities with greater educational meaning than do their less effective colleagues. That is, while regular decisions, such as teacher assignments, are often made with a bureaucratic perspective in schools, instructional leaders often use these decision points to promote student learning.

Supervising and Evaluating Instruction

A central task of school administrators is to ensure that system-wide goals are translated into practices at the classroom level. This involves coordinating the classroom objectives of teachers with those of the school and monitoring classroom instruction through numerous classroom observations, in short, supervising instruction. We know from a variety of observers that the supervision and evaluation of staff in schools often is little more than a symbolic ritual. Instructional leaders, however, do tend to be more actively engaged than their peers in supervising and providing evaluative feedback to teachers. Nonetheless, a close reading of the school effects and school improvement literature provides little support for those who argue for direct and formal approaches to administrative supervision of teachers, especially for advocates of clinical supervision programs. Rather, the preponderance of evidence indicates that instructional leaders rely less on formal classroom observations and teacher conferences, and emphasize more indirect methods of supervision such as informal classroom visits and meetings with staff members. There are, however, important differences between more and less effective administrators in the area of teacher evaluation. More effective principals have been found to engage in the following activities to a greater extent than their less effective colleagues: studying and reading about classroom instruction, visiting classrooms, participating in classroom activities, providing specific feedback to teachers about the teaching-learning process, offering assistance for improvement, and counseling poor instructors to leave the classroom.

Allocating and Protecting Instructional Time

Research conducted over the last quarter century indicates the substantial effects of time on student learning. Although the relationship between total relevant instructional time and student achievement is less clear, there is strong evidence that allocated, engaged, and academic learning time are related to achievement. In the area of time allocations, research shows that effective principals improve time usage in four ways: setting time allocations for instruction in all classes, ensuring coordination of time usage among teachers (e.g., all teachers teach reading first period), allocating more time for instruction (and less time for noninstructional activities), and providing more time for instruction in basic skills. Instructional leaders are also active in protecting instructional time. Studies report that these administrators stress policies that provide teachers with uninterrupted blocks of instructional time, ensure that reading and language arts are taught at times least likely to be disturbed by school events such as assemblies, and buffer teachers from outside interruptions of classroom learning time. Instructional leaders also pay attention to faculty punctuality and establish and enforce procedures that reduce student absenteeism and tardiness.

Coordinating the Curriculum

Effective leaders tend to be thoroughly grounded in the technology of their organizations. This appears to be especially true for educational leaders. Principals in high-achieving schools have more knowledge about technical core operations (curriculum and instruction) than their less effective colleagues. Effective principals translate this knowledge into active involvement with the specification, alignment, and coordination of curricular programs. In many schools, the match between learning objectives, curriculum materials, and standardized tests is rather poor. Principals in effective schools, on the other hand, often ensure that school objectives are closely aligned with the content taught in classes and with achievement tests. In addition, effective schools are often characterized by a high degree of continuity in the curriculum across grade levels. This aspect of curriculum coordination is often supported by high levels of interaction among teachers, within and across grade levels, on instructional and curricular issues. Instructional leaders also work to ensure that instructional support services are coordinated both among themselves and with the regular program.

Promoting Content Coverage

A number of influential studies at both the elementary and secondary levels have affirmed that exposure to academic content is a key variable in explaining student learning. Unfortunately, the role of principals in promoting content coverage has been largely unexplored.

Monitoring Student Progress

Instructional leaders actively monitor student progress. They promote a serious attitude toward test taking among staff and students. Instructionally effective schools emphasize both standardized and criterion-referenced testing. Tests are used to diagnose program and student strengths and weaknesses, to evaluate the results of changes in the school's instructional program, and to make classroom assignments. Researchers have discovered that the principals who lead these schools practice a wide variety of monitoring behaviors: they encourage the establishment and use of testing programs; they provide teachers with test results in a timely and useful fashion; they discuss test results with the staff as a whole and with grade-level and specialty-area staff and individual teachers; they provide interpretive analyses that describe the test data in a concise form for teachers; and they underscore the use of test results for setting goals, assessing the curriculum, evaluating instruction, and measuring progress toward school goals. Instructional leaders also ensure that student progress is regularly and precisely reported to parents.

Promoting an Academic Learning Climate

School learning climate refers to the "norms, beliefs and attitudes reflected in instructional patterns and behavioral practices that enhance or impede student achievement" (Lezotte, Hathaway, Miller, Passalacqua, & Brookover, 1980, p. 4). Studies of schooling show that teaching performance and student outcomes are as much a function of this ethos or environment as they are of the personal qualities and abilities of teachers. They also demonstrate that for both teachers and parents, the principal is a central element in the school climate equation.

The principal's functions in this dimension of the framework deal with those elements of the school learning climate that are most directly related to the teaching-learning process in classrooms. These functions are heavily task oriented. The functions in the supportive work environment dimension, on the other hand, have more of a maintenance orientation, affect learning tasks only indirectly, and often require the principal to operate in a boundary-spanning role with the larger school environment. Principals foster the development of a school learning climate conducive to teaching and learning by establishing positive expectations and standards, maintaining high visibility, providing incentives for teachers and students, and promoting professional development.

Establishing Positive Expectations and Standards

Studies in classrooms have shown that teachers often hold inappropriately low expectations for low-ability students and for low-ability instructional and curricular groups. These reduced expectations, in turn, are often translated into teacher behaviors that disadvantage these students in terms of academic performance. Studies of administrators at schools with particularly high and low levels of student achievement affirm these conclusions at the school level as well—inappropriately low expectations are often held for schools with high concentrations of minority and poor students and for low-ability tracks within schools.

In contrast to these findings, researchers have discovered that principals in schools with high levels of student achievement are actively involved in defining high academic and behavioral expectations for their students, and are less likely to base expectations on adult beliefs about the biosocial characteristics of students. Research shows that instructional leaders translate this attitude into school policies and practices that reflect and define positive expectations for students in the following ways: they place more instructional demands on teachers; they communicate their concern for and interest in student achievement; they establish clearly defined schoolwide academic standards; they develop standards that apply to *all* students; they hold more specific expectations than their less effective peers; they create policies that encourage students to pursue more rigorous academic goals; they hold adults responsible for learning outcomes; they couple success with performance; and they require student mastery of grade level skills prior to entry in the following grade.

Maintaining High Visibility

Visibility refers to the presence of the principal on the school campus and in classrooms. High visibility by executives has been called management by touring around (Mintzberg, 1973). In schools, this touring has been associated with positive effects on students' and teachers' attitudes and behaviors. Although the evidence is not conclusive, researchers generally find that instructional leaders spend more time in classrooms and on the school campus than does the average school administrator.

Providing Incentives for Teachers and Students

Another aspect of the instructional leadership role in creating a positive learning climate involves setting up a work structure that rewards and recognizes teachers for their efforts. Principals have few discretionary rewards to use with teachers. The single salary schedule and the tenure system severely limit principals' ability to motivate teachers. However, research has begun to show that money is not the only way to reward high levels of performance. Specifically in schools, principals have identified the following activities that can provide recognition to teachers: distributing leadership, lending discipline support, showing personal interest, providing public acknowledgment before colleagues and parents, and giving private praise and encouragement.

Although there has not been much work done in this area, there is evidence that instructional leaders use rewards and recognition of students to help establish a school learning climate where academic achievement is valued. Instructional leaders institute schoolwide recognition systems. They are the key actors in linking classroom and school reward systems, ensuring that they are mutually supportive. They are also actively involved in providing personal recognition to individual students. Principals in effective schools make sure that rewards are given frequently and that they reach a high percentage of students. Although rewards are distributed for a variety of reasons, in schools led by effective administrators, special emphasis is placed on recognizing academic excellence. Finally, effective principals often establish student reward programs that are both public in nature and closely connected in time to the behavior for which recognition is given.

Promoting Professional Development

A number of researchers find that principal support for and involvement in teacher professional development activities characterizes effective schools. Administrator attention and support has also been linked to more effective implementation of professional development activities, and institutionalization of improvement efforts generally. Principals in effective schools are committed to helping teachers improve their skills and teaching strategies. They focus staff development activities on the entire staff and on the specific goals and curriculum programs of the school. They are especially adept at using informal coalitions of teachers in implementing new programs. They take an active role in planning, participating in, and evaluating professional development activities with their staffs. Research also reveals that instructional leaders provide both direct aid (e.g., concrete technical assistance and materials) and indirect support (e.g., encouragement) to teachers as they attempt to integrate skills learned during staff development programs into their repertoire of instructional behaviors. Effective principals facilitate opportunities for professional growth by enabling teachers to attend conferences, establishing mechanisms that facilitate the exchange of professional dialogue, and personally sharing ideas and materials with staff.

Developing a Supportive Work Environment

Studies of school effectiveness and program improvement have shown that especially effective schools establish important organizational structures and processes that support the teaching-learning process. In these organizations, administrators are actively engaged in creating safe and orderly learning environments, providing opportunities for meaningful student involvement, developing collaboration and cohesion among staff, securing outside support for school goals, and forging links between the school and the larger community. As I noted earlier, the functions in this dimension of the framework are less directly connected to the teaching-learning process occurring in classrooms; that is, they are less directly task oriented. In addition, they often require the principal to work with actors (e.g., parents, business leaders) in the larger school environment.

Creating a Safe and Orderly Learning Environment

Effective schools are characterized by learning environments that are safe and orderly without being oppressive, and by physical environments that are clean and well maintained. It is also clear that the development of the learning environments in these schools is due in large part to the leadership of the principal. Instructional leaders seem to be more concerned than their colleagues with the management and disciplinary tone of their schools. They work with individual teachers to ensure the use of effective classroom management practices. More importantly, they create consistency and coordination in the school discipline program. This last point is of particular consequence because studies of effective schools find that "the particular rules and approaches to discipline may be less important than the existence of some generally recognized and accepted set of standards" (Rutter, Maughan, Mortimore, & Ouston, 1979, p. 121).

Studies show that effective principals work with their staffs to ensure that school rules and consequences are clearly defined, communicated, and understood by students, teachers, and parents; rules are fairly and consistently enforced; and classroom and school rules are integrally connected. They (1) model appropriate behavior by personally enforcing discipline with students; (2) often involve teachers and students in the development of school rules; (3) secure support for school rules; (4) see that all staff members support and enforce discipline procedures; (5) confront problems quickly and forcefully; (6) provide support for the management system (e.g., student detention and recognition programs); and (7) support teachers with discipline problems in their classrooms.

Providing Opportunities for Meaningful Student Involvement

The opportunity for students to be meaningfully involved in school activities has been noted in some effective school studies. This finding receives support from studies of the effects of extracurricular

activities on student learning, and from independent work in the area
of juvenile delinquency prevention. The components of this factor are
opportunities for students to (1) learn responsibility and practice
leadership behavior, (2) form ties to the school and to appropriate
adult role models, and (3) develop the skills necessary to participate
successfully in activities.

Successful schools are adept at bonding students to important
adult academic and social values and norms. This bonding helps
prevent the development of student cultures that are often inimical to
the goals of the school. Instructional leaders operate in these schools
to promote meaningful opportunities for student involvement by
establishing system-wide activity programs; encouraging teachers
and students to become involved in these activities; providing
rewards and recognition for successful student participation; and
promoting the widespread use of school symbols (e.g., school jackets
and t-shirts) that both distinguish the school from the larger community
and clearly mark students as members of the school.

Developing Staff Collaboration and Cohesion

Collaborative organizational processes that bring staff together
to plan, make decisions, and resolve conflicts about instruction and
curriculum are often found in effective schools and successful
improvement programs. While principals in effective schools promote
staff collaboration, teachers working with less effective instructional
leaders function more as individuals than as members of a school
team—"in the less successful schools, teachers were often left completely alone to plan what to teach, with little guidance from their
senior colleagues and little coordination with other teachers" (Rutter
et al., 1979, p. 136). Collaborative activities that do occur in these less
successful schools are more socially based and less professionally
oriented than the exchanges that occur in schools with more effective
instructional leaders.

Research shows that instructional leaders employ the following
structural activities to facilitate the development of staff collaboration: developing schoolwide goals and objectives and clearly articu-
lating the rationale and foci of new programs; establishing and using
formal mechanisms for professional interchanges (e.g., staff meetings,
professional development activities, common planning periods);
promoting staff stability; providing resources and a supportive work
milieu for cooperative planning; giving faculty a formal role in
communication and decision making; and using a variety of methods

of decision making. On a less formal level, instructional leaders promote staff collaboration by discussing instructional issues regularly in informal exchanges with teachers, by soliciting teachers' opinions, by showing respect and consideration for staff and their ideas, and by encouraging direct, informal communication among staff.

Securing Outside Resources in Support of School Goals

More effective schools often have administrators that are skilled in obtaining supplemental resources for teachers and students. To begin with, these schools are more adept in attracting additional funds and materials from the community. Instructional leaders are also often more powerful in their districts. They use the formal and informal channels at their disposal to influence district-level decision making and to better the competitive position of their schools in the distribution of power and resources. Effective principals seem to be more active than their peers in obtaining resources—an outcome consistent with the findings of the general body of research on educational organizations. For example, while their less effective colleagues often follow standard procedures in hiring and transferring staff, effective principals take assertive action to shape their staffs according to the philosophy and objectives of the school. Finally, instructional leaders allocate money and other resources based on school goals. This goal-directed administrative behavior is often conspicuous by its absence in less effective schools.

Forging Links Between the Home and the School

Many highly successful schools have high levels of parental involvement and support. Although almost all forms of parental involvement and support have been shown to have some positive effects on student achievement, the most effective type is that which focuses attention on the primary mission of educating students, that is, in which parents support at school and at home the academic activities that are occurring in the classroom. In addition to improved academic performance, parent interest has been linked to increased political support and maintenance of legitimacy in the larger environment surrounding the school. Specific activities in the area of home-school relations that have been attributed to instructional leaders include communicating with parents on a regular basis and informing parents of programs and activities; obtaining human resources for both regular and extracurricular programs; establishing programs that promote contact between teachers and parents; interacting personally to promote the school to important community groups; providing educational activities and other programs for parents to learn about the curriculum used to teach their children; and developing systems that parents can use to work with their children at home on the academic skills being stressed in the school program.

Summary

In this second introductory chapter, I continued building the foundation that supports Chapters 5 through 12. I did this by unpacking the two concepts at the heart of the book—literacy and leadership. In framing literacy, I examined definitions, reviewed stages of reading development, and began a discussion on the causes of reading failure. In framing leadership, I crafted a model of instructional leadership featuring four domains: developing mission and goals, managing the educational production function, promoting an academic learning climate, and developing a supportive work environment.

3

Examining Reading Performance

The reality is that many of our children are not reading well enough to keep up with the demands of school, let alone the demands of our society or their personal dreams. (Taylor et al., 1999, p. 1)

The devastating effects of reading failure are widely acknowledged. (Pikulski, 1994, p. 38)

The good society depends on a highly literate citizenry. (Lyons & Pinnell, 1999, p. 197)

In Chapters 1 and 2, I established a framework for thinking about literacy. The bulk of attention was devoted to exposing the foundations on which the material in subsequent chapters will be built. I also provided an in-depth analysis of the two variables that define this book, literacy and leadership. In this chapter, I discuss the critical nature of literacy in the school improvement equation. I review the current state of literacy achievement in the United States, documenting concerns about the condition of reading performance in our schools.

I also explore the changing conditions in the United States (and the world) that enhance the importance of well-developed literacy skills. I close by analyzing the foundational nature of literacy for the health of the nation.

The State of Reading Achievement

> The most basic expectation for children attending school is that they will learn to read and write. Sadly, this expectation is not always fulfilled for schoolchildren in the United States, far too many of whom fail at the basic school task of literacy acquisition. (Snow et al., 1991, p. 1)

> Far too many children have trouble reading and writing. About 20 percent of elementary students nationwide have significant problems learning to read; at least another 20 percent do not read fluently enough to enjoy or engage in independent reading. (American Federation of Teachers, 1999, p. 9)

The Story Line

> Go into a city, find where the poor people live, visit one of the elementary schools their children attend, and the overwhelming likelihood is that you will be in a school that is failing to teach its students to read. (Ellis, 1975, p. 4)

In spite of the rather large infusion of resources into our schools, "many children are now not learning to read and many other children are learning so little, so slowly, that they will never be good readers" (Williams, 1991, p. 17). Across the spectrum of analysts, this conclusion has been labeled in recent years as a "serious literacy problem" (Kaestle et al., 1991, p. 121), an "epidemic of reading failure" (McGill-Franzen, 1987, p. 481), and as "a crisis in American reading education" (Hall & Moats, 1999, p. 3). The recurring finding "that there is little evidence that many children are reading and writing as well as they need to if they are to become contributing members of American society" (Allington, 1995, p. 10), "that large numbers of young people cannot read well enough to do what school and society require of them" (McGill-Franzen, 1987, p. 477), suggests "that schools, even our most effective schools, have a long way to go in improving reading instruction" (Taylor et al., 1999, p. 50).

This recognition of reading problems has cascaded across various levels of society to produce a "great national concern for literacy" (Chall, 1991, p. 20) and sparked a "growing discontent among the general public with the state of reading instruction in America" (Anderson, 1998, p. 1). It has touched the health community, prompting "the National Institutes of Health to regard reading development and reading difficulty as a major public health concern" (American Federation of Teachers, 1999, p. 9). It has become the preeminent weapon in the political arsenal of school reform (Allington, 1997b; McGill-Franzen, 2000) and a critical factor in the corporate agenda for school improvement. And it is increasingly occupying the attention and energy of the education community.

The Data

> Approximately 25 percent of elementary school students are not adequately learning to read [and] write. (McGill-Franzen, 1987, p. 484)

Before I illustrate the narrative chronicled above, the "reading problem" needs to be placed in perspective. It is important to note that the educational system is not experiencing a catastrophic meltdown (Murphy, 2001). To begin with, "most children learn to read adequately" (Brown & Felton, 1990, p. 225) and many learn to read quite well. Also, as Harris and Sipay (1990) remind us, "the status of reading achievement in the U.S. is not as bad as some would have us believe" (p. 4), especially when we compare the reading skills of our youngsters to those in other nations (Taylor, Hanson, Justice-Swanson, & Watts, 2000). Third, to say that children cannot read well, for example at the basic level on the National Assessment of Educational Progress (NAEP) reading test, "is not to say that they cannot read in absolute terms" (McGill-Franzen, 2000, p. 904) but only that they have problems reading well enough (Foertsch, 1992). Finally, and most importantly, the problems that reviewers discern are not the result of a decline in the reading abilities of youngsters (Klenk & Kibby, 2000; National Center for Educational Statistics, 1999, 2000), nor can they be attributed to a worsening state of schooling in the nation (Graff, 1995). As a number of analysts have demonstrated, "the overall level of reading achievement in the U.S. has remained fairly stable since 1970" (Taylor et al., 2000, p. 267). Or more broadly, "it is an irrefutable fact that children in grades K–8 today read as well or better than children at any time in the history of the United States" (Klenk & Kibby, 2000, p. 667; see also Kaestle et al., 1991).

The real issue here is "change in the criterion of literacy" (Resnick & Resnick, 1977, p. 382), what Snow and her colleagues (1998) portray as "rising demands for literacy" (p. 1) caused by "profound changes in the United States—changes in economics, technology, and culture" (Chall, 1991, p. 20): "Levels of literacy that were once held—even very recently held—to be satisfactory will be marginal by the year 2000" (Adams, 1990, p. 26). Beginning with the publication of *Becoming a Nation of Readers* (Anderson et al., 1985) and continuing throughout the 1990s, reviewers consistently held that a central element of the reading problem is that "society is demanding higher reading levels than ever before" (Hall & Moats, 1999, p. 4). This "inflation in literacy skills" (Samuels, 1981, p. 255) coupled with the newly emerged criterion of "zero tolerance of literacy failure" (Jones & Smith-Burke, 1999, p. 275)—the inability of many of our students to reach the higher standard, to read advanced materials—casts the literacy problem in stark relief. For, as Kaestle and his team (1991) reveal, "even if schools today are performing about as well as they have in the past, they have never excelled at educating minorities and the poor or at teaching higher order skills" (p. 218).

Given these caveats, the data do reveal a portrait of reading achievement that leaves much to be desired. To begin with, there seems to be a professional consensus that places reading failure in the schools in the 20–25 percent range (Foorman, Fletcher, Francis, & Schatschneider, 1998; Hall & Moats, 1999; Stein, Johnson, & Gutlohn, 1999). That is, one in five elementary students "do not read fluently enough to enjoy or engage in independent reading" (American Federation of Teachers, 1999, p. 7)—"at least 10 million school-age children in the United States are poor readers" (Fletcher & Lyon, 1998, p. 52).

Data from studies of adult literacy and from the NAEP provide more texture to the narrative on reading performance. On the adult literacy front, even factoring in "difficulties in definition and measure-ment" (Graff, 1995, p. 45), measures of functional illiteracy are signif-icant, ranging from 20 to 33 percent (Hall & Moats, 1999). For example, in perhaps the most scholarly analysis on the topic, Kaestle and his research group (1991) argue as follows:

> Based on these studies, we find it reasonable to estimate that about 20 percent of the adult population, or around 35 million people, have serious difficulties with common reading tasks. An additional 10 percent are probably marginal in their functional-literacy skills. (p. 109)

More tangibly, they conclude that "18 percent of those aged eighteen to twenty-three read below the seventh-grade level" (Kaestle et al., 1991, p. 114). As is the case with school-aged youngsters, substantial discrepancies exist between functional literacy scores for different ethnic groups and different races, with black adults lagging significantly behind their white peers (Kaestle et al., 1991).

Turning to the data from the NAEP, and consistent with the leitmotif teased out above, we discover that many students possess only minimal reading skills. Results from the 1980s revealed that nearly 45 percent of fourth graders were unable to read at even the basic level of performance (Hall & Cunningham, 1996; Slavin, Madden, Karweit, Dolan, & Wasik, 1991). At the high school level, reading scores held steady, at best, throughout the 1980s (National Center for Educational Statistics, 2000). Data from the 1990s mirror results from the 1980s. Two-fifths of the 1994 fourth-grade test takers failed to reach the basic level (Stein et al., 1999; Vadasy, Jenkins, Antil, Wayne, & O'Conner, 1997); that is, "more than 40 percent of American 4th graders read too slowly to understand what they were reading" (Honig, 1997, p. 8). In 1998, 38 percent of fourth graders, 26 percent of eighth graders, and 23 percent of twelfth graders were reading below the basic level (Donahue, Voelkl, Campbell, & Mazzeo, 1999, p. 2). In another NAEP study examining reading fluency, 44 percent of fourth grade students were found to be "disfluent even with grade-level stories that the students had read under supportive testing conditions" (NICHHD, 2000b, 3:5). Fletcher and Lyon (1998) remind us that "regardless of whether the rate is changing, the inability of such a large portion of our students to reach basic levels of achievement should be a cause for alarm" (p. 53).

Coming at the issue of reading performance from another angle reveals that the literacy problem is being borne disproportionately by children from low-income homes and by pupils of color, "that black and Hispanic children perform considerably poorer than their Anglo counterparts" (Garcia & Pearson, 1991, p. 32), and that "a substantial proportion of those who fail to achieve adequate levels of literacy are from financially disadvantaged families" (Snow et al., 1991, p. 1). Not surprisingly, this makes the literacy problem an urban issue (Ellis, 1975; Snow et al., 1991). In its influential report, the American Federation of Teachers (1999) documents that "for poor, minority children who attend low-performing urban schools, the incidence of reading failure is astronomical" (p. 9). Using NAEP data, analysts point out that the failure rate, that is, the inability to read at the basic level, is over 60 percent for these youngsters (Hall & Cunningham,

1996, p. 195). Equally distressing is the fact that "while the typical disadvantaged urban students at age 9 are about one year below the overall national average, they are four to five years behind at age 17" (Chall et al., 1990). Although there was some progress in narrowing the achievement gap in reading between white and black students from 1971 to 1988 (Kaestle et al., 1991), more recently progress has leveled off (Taylor et al., 2000).

Non-NAEP data reinforce the conclusions outlined above. As Ellis (1975) and others have observed over the last thirty years, in urban schools reading failure is often "the norm" (Foorman et al., 1998, p. 37). Indeed, Allen (2000) and Honig (1997) assert that as many as 70 to 80 percent of inner city pupils in some schools "fail to meet grade level reading standards" (Allen, 2000, p. 2).

Summary

In closing this first section, it is fair to summarize findings in the area of literacy as follows. Many of the adults in society, perhaps as many as one fourth, do not read well. Many others show little proclivity for reading. A roughly equal percentage of school-aged children do not read well; like their parents, these youngsters are not inclined to read much. Measures of reading achievement, both national and international, reveal considerable room for improvement.

Exploring more deeply, we discover that a minority of our youngsters read quite poorly. These are overwhelmingly children of color and youngsters from low-income homes. They often begin their formal education with impoverished language and reading skills. Our lack of attention to very early intervention with these learners ensures fairly predictable patterns of school failure and truncated opportunities for financial well-being. Even when these pupils begin the literacy journey on equal footing, they often fall increasingly behind their peers.

While the reading problem in the United States can, to a large extent, be explained by reference to the minority of children who read very poorly, it is much deeper than that. The movement into the information age has raised the bar for what counts as literacy. Thus, while absolute levels of literacy have held up well over time, it is growing increasingly clear that achieving old targets will not ensure success in a more demanding technological society. While many of our students handle basic reading tasks well, their ability to read for meaning and to address higher order assignments leaves a good deal to be desired. And the widespread problem of "aliteracy"—the fact "that relatively few students become avid, interested readers" (Guthrie, McGough, Bennett, & Rice, 1996, p. 165) is especially troubling.

I agree with Kaestle and his colleagues (1991) that our vision for literacy needs to be based not on "alleged declines in literacy skills" (p. 127) but rather "on an assessment of our current conditions and on the basis of our ideals" (p. 127). Starting from here, whether we view reading through the prism of our standing on extant measures of success or through the lens of aspirations for the future, there is significant room for improvement. Whether one discerns a landscape of crisis or arrives at more muted findings of alarm, the information described in this book leaves little doubt that we must do a better job in the area of literacy education in school, especially in the early years. As Chall (1991) reminds us, while the reasons for our "very serious literacy problem are broad and deep in socioeconomic, cultural, and neurological factors, there is much that is in our hands" (p. 24): "Reading failure can be prevented or ameliorated for all but a small percentage of children. Interaction, however, must begin early" (Moats, 1996, p. 88).

Literacy as the Calculus for Success

Reading is the most important skill for success in school and society. (Hall & Moats, 1999, p. 6)

Reading is a basic life skill. It is a cornerstone for a child's success in school and, indeed, throughout life. Without the ability to read well, opportunities for personal fulfillment and job success inevitably will be lost. (Anderson et al., 1985, p. 1)

Although there is not unanimity of support for this position, nor does everyone accept uncritically its egalitarian, progressive, and meritocratic assumptions (see Dudley-Marling & Murphy, 1997; Graff, 1979, 1995; Hymes, 1999; Shannon, 1996; and Wagner, 1999 for discussions), there is growing consensus in the reading community that "proficiency in reading is the essential key to success both in school and in life" (Briggs & Thomas, 1997, Foreword)—and to the health of the country. Or, phrased alternatively, "the failure to develop basic reading abilities during the first few years of schooling portents a host of later academic and economic . . . difficulties" (Wharton-McDonald et al., 1998, p. 101).

Foundations for School Success

There is no skill more basic to success in school than reading ability. (Taylor, Short, Frye, & Shearer, 1992, p. 592)

Teaching children to read is the key to subsequent educational success. (Honig, 1997, p. 6)

Success in *reading* is the essential basis for success in school. (Slavin & Madden, 1989, p. 8)

Literacy researchers and school reform analysts have been arguing for some time that "reading is the most important skill . . . children learn in school and that all other education depends on it" (Chall, 1983, p. 3). In addition to uncovering "the central importance of reading in the educational process" (Postlethwaite & Ross, 1992, p. 21), these reviewers have also developed a robust case for the importance of early literacy (Taylor et al., 2000), for the fact "that learning to read early in life is fundamental to later school success" (Kameenui et al., 1998, p. 47). Or, examined from the opposite vantage point, "the consequences of failing to learn to read in first grade are enduring and pervasive" (Steinet al., 1999, p. 275). Early failure has, as I describe below, "grave and cascading effects" (Vadasy et al., 1997) over the long term. Or, to borrow a phrase from Rutter (1983), failure "sets in motion a train of events that result in persistent sequelae" (p. 14).

If learning to read well is at the core of school achievement, then early success is essential. A good start in reading appears critical primarily because it "opens windows of opportunity" (Sherman, 2001, p. 3). In particular, there is "persuasive evidence that children who get off to a slow start rarely become strong readers" (Beck, 1998, p. 15). In perhaps the best known study on this issue, Juel (1988) concluded that "the poor first-grade reader was almost invariably still a poor reader by the end of the fourth grade. The good first-grade reader almost invariably remained a good reader at the end of the fourth grade" (p. 444). Other analysts have reached the same conclusion from their own studies (Torgesen, 1997) or through reviews of the research (Adams, 1990; Honig, 1997; Morris et al., 1990). Still others have demonstrated the critical nature of early reading achievement through analyses of large-scale data sets. For example, Juel (1991) chronicles NAEP data showing "that good 9-year-old readers from previous assessments were likely to remain good readers through secondary school" (p. 775). The message from all this research is fairly clear, "those who are not on track by third grade have little chance of ever catching up" (Snow et al., 1998, p. 212). In fact, the evidence is relatively straightforward, "once a child falls behind in reading . . . deceleration is likely to increase with each succeeding grade" (Chall et al., 1990, p. 159).

The upside to the narrative is that "the case for early intervention is strong" (Hiebert, Colt, Catto, & Gury, 1992, p. 546), both in terms of need and impact. Indeed, "early intervention is a key factor in [providing] a good start in reading" (Taylor et al., 2000, p. 267): "If low achieving students can be brought up to grade level within the first three years of school, their reading performance tends not to revert but to stay at grade level thenceforth" (Adams, 1990, pp. 27-28).

Reading success or lack thereof in the primary grades has a dramatic effect on nearly every facet of the schooling career of a youngster: "For those children who do not catch on, the disadvantages tend to spread themselves broadly and profoundly from reading to every other aspect of their schooling" (Adams & Bruck, 1993, p. 131). "To begin with, a poor start leads to dire consequences on later reading development" (Juel, 1991, p. 759). Specifically, "difficulty with the first steps of reading eventually undermines vocabulary growth . . . mastery of language, and skill in writing" (American Federation of Teachers, 1999, p. 9). Students "who struggle in vain" (Snow et al., 1998, p. 172) with early reading often develop "a negative attitude toward reading" (Torgesen, 1997, p. 32); they conclude that "they neither like nor want to read" (Snow et al., 1998, p. 172). As a consequence, they not only fall behind their peers but they become "outsiders" in their own classrooms (Durkin, 1978–1979, p. 527). Because "reading ability becomes both an instrument and badge of stratification" (Kaestle et al., 1991, p. 123), "stigmatization and labeling" (Brown, Palincsar, & Purcell, 1986, p. 105) often follow. Access to "higher level literature" (Hiebert & Taylor, 1994, p. 204) is often precluded. A variety of reading problems materialize in later grades (Juel, 1996). The development of comprehension skills is jeopardized (Juel, 1991; Torgesen, 1998). Reading at subsequent levels of schooling is compromised (Chall, 1991). Reading achievement (Juel, 1991) and verbal intelligence (Stanovich, 2000) are negatively impacted.

Since "reading is the cornerstone of academic success" (American Federation of Teachers, 1999, p. 11), "reading disability threatens a child's entire education" (Adams & Bruck, 1993, p. 133) and students who fail to reach mastery early are "apt to meet academic failure" (Harris & Sipay, 1990, p. 7) as they progress through school. According to Brown and her colleagues (1986), students who "get off to a bad start in school run the risk of cumulative decline in their academic status" (p. 105). Reading problems at the start "spiral the child into a pattern of ever increasing scholastic achievement problems" (Stanovich, 2000, p. 201; see also Jimerson, Egeland, & Teao, 1999). Not unexpectedly, "because most subsequent school learning (science, social studies, and even math) depends on the ability to read" (Morris et al., 1990, p. 133), youngsters who cannot read well "experience difficulties in most other school subjects" (Ross, Smith, Casey, & Slavin, 1995, p. 774)—"excellence in high school and beyond is unattainable" (Anderson et al., 1985, p. 1).

Maladjustment at school and delinquency are not infrequent accompaniments to failure to master literacy skills (Jones & Smith-Burke, 1999). Indeed, "low achievement in reading is implicated in virtually all profiles of children in trouble" (McGill-Franzen, 1987, p. 477). Lack of early success in reading is highly correlated with placement in remedial and special programs and with retention at grade level (Slavin et al., 1991; Stein et al., 1999) and with "traumatic emotional consequences from which [poor readers] never fully recover" (Blachman, 1996, p. 66). In short, "early reading failure causes major damage to children" (Slavin et al., 1991, p. 405) and places considerable burdens on the educational system (Jones & Smith-Burke, 1999). Children who fail to learn to read are much more likely to drop out of school than are peers who read well (Slavin et al., 1991; Snow et al., 1991). Poor early reading follows youngsters into adulthood (Kaestle et al., 1991; Pressley, 1998b). As I elaborate in the next section, occupational career options are truncated for these readers (State of New York, 1974) and unemployment rates are higher (Blachman, 1996).

Foundation for Economic and Social Success

> We must do as much with reading. In our society, their lives depend on it. (Adams, 1990, p. 91)

> To say that not learning to read limits life's possibilities, both personally and professionally, is to understate the problem. (McGill-Franzen, 1987, p. 477)

According to an assortment of analysts, "beginning reading instruction is the key to an individual's success in life" (Richardson, 1991, p. 6) and to success in our society. Reading ability is seen as "essential to economic and social success" (Purcell-Gates, 1998, p. 54) and as an indispensable ingredient in one's ability "to participate fully in American . . . political life" (Snow et al., 1991, p. 1). Indeed, if anything, "the social and economic values of reading . . . are multiplying in both number and importance as never before" (Adams, 1990, p. 26) and children with low reading achievement in early grades face greater risk of "negative . . . social and economic outcomes" (Kameenui et al., 1998, p. 47).[1]

As noted above, reading mastery is associated with the completion of high school, with "disadvantaged third-graders who are significantly behind in reading . . . hav[ing] little chance of ultimately graduating" (Wasik & Slavin, 1994, p. l44). Since low reading skills often take applicants "out of the running for jobs" (Harris & Sipay, 1990, p. 7), the "success or failure in a child's career often hangs upon success or failure in the first grade" (Richardson, 1991, p. 6). Low reading ability and unemployment and underemployment are well known bedfellows (American Federation of Teachers, 1999; Harris & Sipay, 1990). The place of reading as the keystone of economic and social success has been reinforced as we have moved into a post-industrial, technological society (Purcell-Gates, 1998). Opportunities to partake of higher levels of education are also dependent on possessing a robust portfolio of reading skills (Snow et al., 1991). Finally, there is considerable evidence that the inability to read well is linked to low income (Hall & Moats, 1999), and that "literacy is . . . a key factor in the attack on poverty" (Chall, 1983, p. 2).

Although I do not examine the issue in detail herein, it is important to note that "reading is important for the society as well as the individual" (Anderson et al., 1985, p. 1; see also Pinnell et al., 1994). Reading achievement is associated with "responsible citizenship" (Chall, 1991, p. 20) and with the economic well-being of the nation (Anderson et al., 1985). And, as Adams (1990) reminds us, beginning reading instruction is an essential pillar in the democratic infrastructure of the country: "we shall need much better reading if we are to survive and improve as a democratic society in an increasingly complex age, quite apart from workplace demands for more literacy" (Kaestle et al., 1991, p. 128).

Summary

In this chapter, I examined the state of the nation in terms of reading achievement. I reported that there is room for considerable improvement in the literacy performance of both adults and youngsters in the United States. I also linked reading achievement to the success of children in school and in life after formal education. Throughout, the critical nature of reading achievement in the early years was highlighted.

Note

1. Remember, however, as I reported in the introduction to this chapter, the line of argument that reading achievement equals success is not universally accepted. See especially Graff (1979, 1995) and Kaestle and his team (1991) for insightful analyses on the range of conditions that weaken or override this progressive line of thought.

4

Reviewing the Principles of High-Quality Reading Programs

What star teachers do is inextricably interwoven with their ideology. (Haberman, 1995, p. 76)

Attempting to get teachers to teach, or even plan instruction against their instructional belief system, is next to impossible. If the belief system can be altered, then the reorganization of instruction can be simplified dramatically. (Johnston & Allington, 1991, p. 1006)

At the heart of any effective program is a set of underlying principles that give meaning to and shape policies, practices, and behaviors. These principles are cobbled together from beliefs and values and from assumptions and predispositions. Collectively, they provide the architecture for work, or as Nespor (1987) captures it, they "serve the means of defining goals and tasks" (p. 319). Focusing on principle-anchored change leads to some important deductions. First, to understand what is unfolding in a school, especially in the area of teaching, we need "to understand the beliefs with which [educators] define their work" (Nespor, 1987, p. 323). Second, as Rutter (1983) observes, a focus on underlying principles "suggest[s] the importance of some kind of schoolwide set of values and norms of behavior" (p. 24).

In the balance of this chapter, I discuss six guiding principles needed to ground schooling in an era where a commitment to high levels of literacy for all children holds center stage. The insights flow from the research on schools that are especially efficacious in promoting mastery of important literacy skills. They also derive from substantial work that helps us understand that to create a school in which all pupils are literate, it will be necessary to replace the core beliefs about teaching reading that have dominated the profession for the last seventy-five years. Or, as Allington (1995) phrases it, "to make literacy for all children a reality . . . will require a dramatic shift in the conventional wisdom that has dominated the educational profession since the turn of the [20th] century" (p. 2).

Literacy Is the Top Priority of the School

> Those objectives of education receiving high priority by society ought to be the objectives receiving emphasis in the curriculum within the classroom. (Berliner, 1981, p. 221)

> In all of the most effective schools, reading was a priority at both the building and classroom level. Teachers and administrators gave their reading program the time, energy, and resources to bring all students under its umbrella. (Hiebert & Pearson, 1999, p. 11)

From the earliest studies of schools that are successful in helping all students learn to read well (e.g., Armor et al., 1976; Edmonds, 1979; Ellis, 1975; State of New York, 1974; Venezky & Winfield, 1979; Weber, 1971) to the more recent investigations of effective literacy programs (e.g., Briggs & Thomas, 1997; Fisher & Adler, 1999; Pressley et al., 2000; Rowe, 1995), research consistently confirms that a strong emphasis on reading at the school level and "an operational priority in the classroom" (Taylor et al., 1999, p. 47) on reading combine to form the first principle of literacy achievement.

> Across the four most effective schools in this study, reading was clearly a priority. The teachers and principals considered

reading instruction their job and they worked at it. They worked together, worked with parents, and worked with a positive attitude to reach the goal of all children reading well before they left the primary grades. They set personal preferences aside in order to reach consensus on schoolwide monitoring systems, curriculum, and professional development, with the constant goal of improving an already effective reading program. (Taylor et al., 1999, pp. 29-30)

Vision and Goals

Excellent reading programs are founded on a strong vision and goals. (Patty et al., 1996, p. 9)

The improving schools are clearly different from the declining schools in the emphasis their staff places on the accomplishment of the basic reading objectives. The improving schools accept and emphasize the importance of these goals and objectives while declining schools give much less emphasis to such goals and do not specify them as fundamental. (Edmonds, 1979, pp. 29-30).

Although in later chapters I disclose in detail how reading achievement becomes a top priority and how "the successful reading achievement of all children [becomes] a common goal" (Fisher & Adler, 1999, p. 22), here I outline a few ways by which we can identify literacy as a central pillar in elementary schools. Many schools lack systematic and well-developed strategies for addressing literacy. Effective schools, by contrast, have articulated plans for maintaining high levels of student performance equitably distributed (State of New York, 1974). They engage the reading mandate more comprehensively and with more vigor (Postlethwaite & Ross, 1992). They have more challenging aims (Patty et al., 1996; Venezky & Winfield, 1979), more explicit program goals (Hoffman & Rutherford, 1984; Samuels, 1981), and more targeted objectives (Phi Delta Kappa, 1980). They place more emphasis on meeting these goals than do less effective schools (Edmonds, 1979; Hallinger & Murphy, 1985). They are less satisfied with the status quo (Hoffman & Rutherford, 1984) and are more likely to be engaged in a process of continuous renewal (Taylor et al., 1999). Effective schools have outstanding reading programs—"programs that are founded on strong vision and goals" (Patty et al., 1996, p. 9).

Resources

All five of the schools described in this paper (and indeed all of the schools felt by observers to have effective reading programs) had defined reading as an important instructional goal. In all of the five schools, reading was accorded top priority among the school's activities. By virtue either of the time spent in reading activities, the money spent for reading materials, or the quality of the resources devoted to reading, the schools indicated clearly that they considered reading important. (Wilder, 1977, p. 275)

Priority in effective programs is also "made evident through the time spent in reading activities and money spent on materials and resources" (Samuels, 1981, p. 264). Professional development aligns with reading objectives (Briggs & Thomas, 1997; Murphy, Hallinger, & Mesa, 1985). Schoolwide events (Taylor et al., 1999) and displays throughout the school reinforce the central place of literacy in effective schools (Briggs & Thomas, 1997; Murphy, Weil, Hallinger, & Mitman, 1985). Researchers looking in effective classrooms, examining successful programs, and studying productive schools regularly report that the priority enjoyed by reading is reflected in the amount of time devoted to literacy activities (Ivey, 2000). In short, more time is devoted to reading in schools where literacy is a priority—for example, twenty minutes more a day for all students in the study conducted by Taylor and her colleagues (1999), and considerably more for students experiencing difficulties in reading in other investigations (e.g., Weber, 1971). Schools with a strong literacy focus are also more sensitive to protecting reading time by eliminating competing activities (Murphy, 1990; Taylor & Taxis, n.d.) and by "diverting school energy and resources when necessary in furtherance of fundamental objectives" (Edmonds, 1979, p. 32).

Leadership

All of the principals in effective programs believe that teaching reading is one of the most important things they do. (Briggs & Thomas, 1997)

The model indicates a strong relation between the degree of instructional leadership provided by the principal and the existence of a clear school mission. (Hallinger, Bickman, & Davis, 1996, p. 543)

Leadership is consistently shown to be linked to the ability of a school to spotlight literacy in its education program (Sherman, 2001). Successful principals "place the development of literacy as a priority" (Licktieg, Parnell, & Ellis, 1995, p. 306) for themselves and their schools (Phi Delta Kappa, 1980). Leaders are at the center of efforts to "establish reading improvement as a program priority and [to] set explicit goals in terms of pupil achievement" (Hoffman & Rutherford, 1984, p. 88). They are active in communicating expectations, allocating needed resources, and "creating a school environment where reading and writing are a priority in teaching and learning" (Briggs & Thomas, 1997, p. 40).

Educators Are Committed to Making a Difference

There are several important assumptions or beliefs held by staff in exemplary reading programs which seem to be associated with student academic growth. The first assumption one often finds is that the school can have a significant impact on the academic achievement of its students. (Samuels, 1981, p. 266)

The more efficacious teachers felt, the more their students advanced in reading achievement. (Armor et al., 1976, p. 23)

Efficacy and commitment are forged to form the second principle that supports effective literacy programs. Teachers in schools that excel in educating all students well are "confident that their teaching [will] yield positive results" (Armor et al., 1976, p. 38). They have a "strong sense of personal efficacy" (p. 38) or, in common vernacular, "an attitude of 'it can be done'" (Walmsley & Allington, 1995, p. 27). Studies from all four domains of the framework I presented in Chapter 1 demonstrate that while "high achieving teachers [are] likely to believe that they [can] foster literate behaviors" (Wharton-McDonald et al., 1998, p. 113), educators in unsuccessful schools are "pessimistic about their impact on students" (Samuels, 1981, p. 260).

Teachers in schools where learners perform well in reading not only believe that they have "the power to influence a child's maturation" (Wharton-McDonald et al., 1998, p. 120), they also have "the will . . . to teach all students to read well" (Duffy-Hester, 1999, p. 492). In effective schools, "teachers and administrators . . . have a strong commitment to giving the maximum so that all children have a chance to learn and succeed" (Danridge, Edwards, & Pleasants, 2000, p. 660). They are "committed to the successful implementation of the reading program in their school" (Hoffman, 1991, p. 934). Less effective programs tend to have educators who do "not have a feeling of commitment" (Samuels, 1981, p. 271) and are "pessimistic about their ability to have an impact" (State of New York, 1974, p. vi).

Educators Hold High Expectations for Student Achievement

> It seems that teachers' beliefs and expectations, particularly about individual differences between learners, have direct and indirect, positive and negative, influences on children's learning. (Johnston & Allington, 1991, p. 996)

> One generalization can be made about the elements of a successful reading program; in practice, these factors reflect a belief on the part of principals and teachers that children can be taught to read, regardless of motivation or background. (Armor et al., 1976, p. 40)

> Good first teaching begins with a belief that all children can learn to read and write. (Fountas & Pinnell, 1999, p. 165)

Teachers and administrators in effective schools connect their personal sense of efficacy and commitment to beliefs about the educability of youngsters (Fountas & Pinnell, 1999). This is important because the literature on expectations and investigations of effective schools consistently reveals the central place of adult expectations in students' sense of academic efficacy and pupil performance (Brookover & Lezotte, 1979; Fraser, 1989; Pressley, 1998b). The core message is that "improvement depends on faculties' beliefs" (Patty et al., 1996, p. 55).

Studies that unpack expectations in *classrooms* regularly report that high-achieving students are taught by instructors who "display consistently high expectations for all students" (Wharton-McDonald et al., 1998, p. 119). In short, "classrooms with outstanding [reading] teachers [are] filled with the message that students can and will learn" (Pressley, 1998b, p. 165). Anderson and his colleagues (1985), in the influential report *Becoming a Nation of Readers*, captured the findings as follows:

One characteristic that distinguishes effective classrooms from ineffective ones is the teacher's commitment to the belief that all children can learn to read. Effective teachers strive to see that every child masters basic skills and then goes as far beyond this basic level as possible. (p. 87)

Drilling down more deeply into these studies exposes the mechanisms by which expectations influence student reading achievement. Specifically, "teachers' beliefs play a major role in defining teaching tasks and the knowledge and information relevant to these tasks" (Nespor, 1987, p. 324), or as Smith (1980) succinctly observes, "teaching behavior varies in relation to teacher expectations" (p. 54). Because "teaching . . . is highly determined by belief" (Stigler & Hiebert, 1999, p. 103; see also Otto, Wolf, & Eldridge, 1984), teachers allocate key resources such as time, amount of material, feedback, and so forth—resources that collectively constitute access to knowledge (Murphy & Hallinger, 1989)—based on those beliefs and expectations (Hiebert, 1983; Johnston & Allington, 1991; Knapp & Needels, 1991). Thus teacher expectations are the starting point in a cascade of actions that can smooth or burden children's voyage to mastering literacy skills (Allington, 1995; Purcell-Gates, 1998).

Similarly, research into *schools* that are instructionally effective in the area of literacy locate adult expectations at the center of the student success equation, with "high and appropriate expectations" (Anderson et al., 1985, p. 113) powering student achievement and low expectations "creating an environment in which children fail because they [are] not expected to succeed" (State of New York, 1974, pp. vi-vii). Thus according to a host of school improvement scholars, educators in "improving schools hold decidedly higher and apparently increasing levels of expectations with regard to the educational accomplishment of their students. In contrast, staffs of declining schools are much less likely to believe that their students will complete high school or college" (Edmonds, 1979, p. 30).

In effect, the research suggests many students fail because their "school has shaped them to expect academic failure" (Pressley, 1998b, p. 243); "children who are treated as if they are uneducable invariably become uneducable" (Ellis, 1975, p. 5). Many others perform well because "instructional staff and the leadership of the school believe that the students they face will be successful in learning to read if they do their job" (Hoffman, 1991, p. 934). These youngsters learn to read well because for their teachers "failure [is] unacceptable" (Samuels, 1981, p. 257). They are also successful because their teachers embed our best knowledge of "linguistic principles in a larger perspective that recognizes these children as intelligent, well-adjusted products of their own culture" (Snow et al., 1998, pp. 241-242) and that "conveys great respect for the knowledge and culture that they bring to the classroom" (Pearson, 1996, p. 272).

Decisions and Actions Backward Map From Learning and Children

> The best classrooms we observed were decidedly student centered. (Pressley, 1998b, pp. 174-175)

As Taylor and Taxis (n.d.) remark, a key to effective literacy education is the consistent ability of staff to "put the children first" (p. 12), to ensure that classrooms and schools are student centered. However, researchers document that in the average classroom the literacy spotlight is directed toward methods of instruction and curriculum frameworks with their prescribed scope and sequence of skills (Allington, 1997b; Duffy-Hester, 1999; Pressley, 1998b). When students experience difficulty in these schools, the response is often to assume "that something must be wrong with the children" (Klenk & Kibby, 2000, p. 668), "to categorize and label children" (Allington, 1995, p. 7), and "to repeat the same treatment" (Fisher & Adler, 1999, p. 20).

In contrast, in schools that bring all learners to mastery of literacy skills, "student learning [is] the highest priority when compared with curriculum and instruction" (Fisher & Adler, 1999, p. 20). Faculty in these schools are "not satisfied with presenting a particular method of reading; they allow student learning to dictate how to proceed" (p. 20). The penchant of more productive schools to plan backwards from learning encourages educators to adjust their methods of instruction and their curriculum when students are not reading well (Fountas & Pinnell, 1999), and "to be responsible to [learner] needs" (Duffy-Hester, 1999, p. 489). Educators in these learner-centered schools "continually work to find ways for students to learn rather than assign blame or accept failure" (Fisher & Adler, 1999, p. 20).

Staff Maintains a Strong Academic Press

> At any given ability level, children's scholastic achievement tends to be higher in schools (or classes) with a strong academic emphasis and high expectations. (Rutter, 1983, p. 21)

Overall, the strongest gains in reading were associated with the two programs that had the strongest academic focus. (Hoffman, 1991, p. 928)

Since the earliest teacher effects and school effectiveness studies, researchers have been documenting the connections between a focused and coordinated academic orientation and student mastery of literacy skills (Murphy, Weil, Hallinger, & Mitman, 1982; Murphy, Weil, & McGreal, 1986). As Weber (1971) discovered over three decades ago, success in beginning reading has much to do with "the stress that is placed on reading achievement" (p. 24). In schools that promote high levels of literacy, there is (1) a strong academic emphasis and a climate of challenge, (2) a powerful "achievement orientation" (Venezky & Winfield, 1979, p. 11) in the administrative ranks, and (3) a framework of "product-oriented management" (Becker, 1977, p. 530) at the school level.

In many schools, a confluence of beliefs (e.g., in the non-educability of certain students) results in practices (e.g., slowing down instruction, watering down curriculum) that undercut academic focus (Allington, 1995; Manning, 1995) and dilute the "density of academic activities" (Pressley, 1998b, p. 181). Since "the amount of challenge" (Stahl, Duffy-Hester, & Stahl, 1998, p. 350) goes a long way to explain student achievement, this state of affairs can have devastating effects on the reading performance of youngsters. As I describe in some detail in subsequent chapters, low academic task focus undermines student success directly by reducing opportunity to learn (Murphy & Hallinger, 1989), and indirectly by damaging students' sense of efficacy and "effort attribution" (Pressley, 1998b, p. 236)—the understanding that hard work rather than chance or natural endowments leads to mastery.

Educators Assume
Responsibility for Student Learning

Teachers who . . . accept responsibility for children's learning • are more likely to teach, and teach well. (Allington, 1991, p. 22)

The staffs of declining schools . . . tend to displace the responsibility for skill learning on the parents or the students themselves. (Edmonds, 1979, p. 30)

In his seminal work on the organizational dynamics of schools, Weick (1976) concluded that these institutions were characterized by a discernable absence of accountability for outcomes. Although a framework of compliance accountability had been built up around adherence to regulations and a type of symbolic accountability had been established around categories such as grade promotion and graduation, historically, school personnel shouldered little responsibility for their failure to bring significant numbers of their charges to mastery of academic skills in reading. Thus in average and declining schools, the failure of students is viewed as "human pathology" (Skritic, cited in Duffy-Hester, 1999, p. 492) or an environmental/social pathology, rather than as a condition of the school organization or a consequence of the actions of the adults who work there (Allington & McGill-Franzen, 1995; Haberman, 1995). School staff attribute pupil failure to "out-of-school" (Hoffman & Rutherford, 1984, p. 82) or "nonschool" (State of New York, 1974, p. vi) factors—an attribution that shifts responsibility for failure to society at large, to parents, and to the children themselves (Haberman, 1995; Murphy, 1992; Slavin & Madden, 1989) and ensures that "educators are not responsible for student achievement" (Kameenui, 1998, p. 334). Especially disheartening is the well-oiled reflex—what Haberman (1995) labels the "active pastime of schools and educators" (p. 51)—to explain reading failure through reference to problems with the learner, to blame the victim.

Schools that excel in helping youngsters master literacy skills operate from a different mind-set: "teaching failure is not excused. . . . When students fail to learn, the school assumes the major responsibility" (Samuels, 1981, pp. 262-266). Educators in schools where learning for all is the norm tend to look inward to the school, rather than outward to society and the family when seeking explanations for students' problems in mastering literacy skills (Edmonds, 1979; Ellis, 1975; Murphy, 1992). The source or cause of failure in learning to read is viewed not so much in terms of pupil background as in terms of shortcomings in the school program, and by reference to the "instructional strategies employed to help children learn to read" (Fisher & Adler, 1999, p. 24).

There is collaborative or community accountability in schools where all students reach rigorous literacy goals (Taylor & Taxis, n.d.). In effect, "responsibility for student success in reading [is] shared among several teachers" (Fisher & Adler, 1999, p. 22) and stretched across the entire adult community (Allington & Broikou, 1988; Walmsley & Allington, 1995). Or, as Askew, Fountas, Lyons,

Pinnell, & Schmitt (2000) describe it, "there is recognition that everyone is responsible for every child" (p. 293).

Summary

In this final introductory chapter, I laid out six guiding principles that support the portrait of leadership for literacy contained in Chapters 5 through 12: (1) literacy is the top priority of the school, (2) educators are committed to making a difference, (3) educators hold high expectations for student achievement, (4) decisions and actions backward map from learning and children, (5) staff maintains a strong academic press, and (6) educators assume responsibility for student learning.

PART II

Leading for
Literacy

5

Promoting Quality Instruction

An indisputable conclusion of research is that the quality of teaching makes a considerable difference in children's learning. Studies indicate that about 15 percent of the variation among children in reading achievement at the end of the school year is attributable to factors that relate to the skill and effectiveness of the teacher. (Anderson et al., 1985, p. 85)

Ultimately, children's early literacy achievement will depend on the quality of good first teachers. (Fountas & Pinnell, 1999, p. 184)

In the end, there will be excellent primary-level education in American classrooms when there are excellent primary-level teachers delivering such instruction. (Pressley, 1998b, p. 186)

The leitmotif for the remainder of this book is that "to improve reading achievement we must improve both programs and classroom delivery. Each seems to contribute separately and significantly to children's progress" (Adams, 1990, p. 43). Or, using Chall's (1983) terminology, we need to attend to both the "method factor" and the "teacher factor." In a broad sense, my focus here and in Chapter 6 is on the instructional dimension of this two-sided framework.

In Chapters 7 through 10, I spotlight the curricular or method aspects of leadership for literacy.

Within this broad design, however, because it is often difficult and sometimes inappropriate to disentangle curriculum and instruction, I also commit considerable space to the teacher factor in our discussion of the literacy program in later chapters. In particular, a number of critical dimensions of the effective literacy portfolio that could be located here under instruction are taken up in chapters devoted to program. The importance of phonics instruction and the imperative of providing balanced skill and language instruction, for example, are explored in great detail in Chapters 7, 8, and 9. In a similar vein, instruction related to program integration and coordination is examined in Chapter 10. Finally, the teacher role in creating a literate classroom environment is discussed in Chapter 8, and some of the instructional aspects of home-school connections are postponed until Chapter 12.

The essential message from the research at the outset of my work on the teacher factor is "that learning to read depends on certain insights and observations that, for many children, are simply not forthcoming without some special guidance" (Adams & Bruck, 1993, p. 122; Allington, 1991; Hiebert & Pearson, 1999). That is, "many children do not discover reading strategies without help" (Spiegel, 1995, p. 93; Foorman et al., 1998; Honig, 1997); "skills . . . do not just develop—they must be taught" (Snow et al., 1991, p. 114); "students who are at the beginning stages of reading need to be taught *how* to read" (Leinhardt, Zigmond, & Cooley, 1981, p. 358). Specifically, "instruction seems to set in motion vectors for achievement in reading that are powerful" (Hoffman, 1991, p. 938); "thus, whether children will make rapid or slow progress in becoming skilled readers depends upon the content and method of instruction" (Anderson et al., 1985, p. 71). Indeed, it is likely "that teacher quality is more critical to early literacy success than curriculum" (Allington, 1997a, p. 32). Weber (1971) expresses this idea nicely when he concludes that "outstanding teachers can teach beginning reading successfully with *any* materials and under a wide range of conditions. At the other extreme, poor teachers will fail with the best materials and procedures" (p. 129). Or, as Duffy-Hester (1999) asserts, "I am convinced that the teacher is more important and has a greater impact than any single, fixed, reading program, method, or approach" (p. 492).

What this means, of course, is that a "key to understanding differences in classroom products lies in identifying what happens in different classrooms" (Hiebert, 1983, p. 233), that "what is done instructionally during [learning] time is what makes the difference" (Pikulski, 1994, p. 35). High-quality literacy instruction—"that offered by teachers who have expertise in how literacy develops (and what impedes its progress) and in how to facilitate literacy development" (Walmsley & Allington, 1995, p. 33)—is tightly linked to enhanced student achievement performance; it has "strong positive effects on students' attitudes, behaviors in the classroom, and achievement" (Rowe, 1995, p. 91).

At the outset, it is appropriate to acknowledge that our "stock of information [about] quality teaching" (Allington, 1997b, p. 5) is considerably less than might be expected (Allington, 1997b; Pressley, Wharton-McDonald, Ranking, Mistretta, Yokoi, & Ettenberger, 1996). There is still a good deal of empty space in the vault on "high-craft" (Askew & Gaffney, 1999, p. 82) or highly "successful" teachers. Or as Ruddell (1997) succinctly notes, "research on highly effective teaching and teachers is very limited" (p. 50). More troubling still are "the enormous discrepancies between the instruction offered in most classrooms and the kind of instruction that basic research suggests would most benefit learners" (Hoffman, 1991, p. 944), especially the children of the poor (Edmonds, 1979). It is disheartening that the knowledge that we do have "on prerequisites and requisites of beginning reading acquisition fails to find its way into the instructional strategies of classrooms and schools" (Kameenui et al., 1998, p. 65).

In the balance of this chapter, I stitch together the research on effective literacy instruction in the early grades—keeping in mind that the four major instructional issues noted above (e.g., phonics) are held over for discussion in Chapters 7 through 12. I collect findings in two major sections, a short analysis of the learning environment and a more extended discussion of the teaching function itself—or in Hoffman's (1991) model, "the role teachers play in organizing and managing the instructional environment . . . [and] the role teachers play in presenting academic content" (p. 930). In undertaking this work, I sought commonalities and regularities that distinguish instruction in classrooms where youngsters excel in reading, language usage, and writing from those in which children languish academically. That is, I attempted to tease out "shared . . . instructional routine" (Hiebert & Taylor, 2000, p. 480). My gaze was directed toward studies of effective teachers and productive classrooms.

My search and the resulting narrative were shaped by two conclusions from the literacy literature. First, "quality instruction involves many elements. Strengthening any one element yields small gains. For large gains, many elements must be in place"

(Anderson et al., 1985, p. 4). Thus, there is no silver bullet in the quest for high levels of literacy success for all youngsters. Second, while the routines are important, "the key is helping teachers flexibly adapt their instructional actions to fit particular situations" (Roehler & Duffy, 1991, p. 877). "One size does not fit all when it comes to beginning reading instruction" (Hiebert & Pearson, 1999, p. 15); there is no single best approach. Rather, there are "multiple routes to learning" (McNaughton, 1999, p. 5). Neither is there a fixed set of ideas that hold the high ground regardless of context. Situational demands are important: "effective teachers . . . alter their instructional actions based on their purpose, task and text demands, student responses, and situational context" (Dole, Duffy, Roehler, & Pearson, 1991, p. 256). This knowledge is particularly relevant in this discussion because certain practices are "more highly correlated with children's literacy development in the earlier than in the later grades" (Chall et al., 1990, p. 139). The central theme here is nicely encapsulated by Bereiter and Scardamalia (cited in Askew & Gaffney, 1999, p. 82) who remind us that "the expert addresses problems whereas the nonexpert carries out practiced routines." Thus, "there are many paths to successful reading and hence many paths to successful reading instruction" (Van den Broek, 1996, p. 193).

This prelude leads us away from the search for "a single critical variable in defining outstanding instruction" (Wharton-McDonald et al., 1998, p. 122) and away from the development of a "simple series of prescribed steps to be undertaken in a rote manner" (Fountas & Pinnell, 1999, p. 166) and toward "cluster[s] of practices and beliefs" (Wharton-McDonald et al., 1998, p. 122), to a "common menu of instructional strategies" (Hiebert & Pearson, 1999, p. 11) and a system or a common "instructional framework to foster reading activity" (Guthrie et al., 1996, p. 185) by "support[ing] a variety of learning approaches" (Hall & Cunningham, 1996, p. 204). My focus throughout is on general principles of quality literacy instruction and on the broader instructional activities (Anderson, 1999; Lyons & Pinnell, 1999) and "teaching functions, rather than teaching methods and skills" (Berliner, 1981, p. 223). When all is said and done, it is these bundles of practice or teaching functions that need to be "met for successful classroom experiences to occur" (p. 223).

Managing the Learning Environment

How teachers structure the learning environment make[s] a difference in how students spen[d] their time. (Leinhardt et al., 1981, p. 352)

Classroom atmosphere affects the reading gains of all the students in a class. (Armor et al., 1976, p. 32)

Evidence is accumulating to suggest that more structured learning environments produce better student achievement. (Otto et al., 1984, p. 821)

All instructional activity occurs within the context of the classroom learning environment. The environment can facilitate or hinder accomplishment of the instructional task. There are at least six learning environment variables or functions that are under the control of the teacher and that have been shown to be associated with reading achievement in the primary grades: teacher centrality, task orientation, positive expectations, student cooperation and accountability, positive affect, and established structure. Each of these factors is important because it helps establish the methods and procedures that the teacher uses to manage the learning task itself. That is, each variable suggests that certain behaviors are more likely than others to promote literacy achievement as the teacher provides instruction (Guthrie et al., 1996).

Teacher Centrality

The quality of adult-child discourse is important, as is the amount of such interaction. (Snow et al., 1998, p. 148)

The management-effectiveness literature suggests that elementary reading instruction is more effective when students are directly supervised by an adult. (Otto et al., 1984, p. 815)

Contrary to popular educational folklore, teacher centrality, or strong teacher direction and control, is highly associated with student success in learning to read. Effective teachers "organize and guide most of the reading instruction that students receive" (Briggs & Thomas, 1997, p. 11). Conversely, an emphasis on student freedom and control is negatively related to learning. The greater amount of learning that occurs when the teacher maintains a central role is due to two factors: greater involvement and more on-task behavior on the part of students.

Teacher direction and control occur when the teacher does the following: maintains a prominent role in the classroom, controls discussion and maintains a central role in class discussions, structures and selects academic tasks on which students will work, assigns children to seats and learning groups, arranges the learning environment so that children do not have to get up to secure materials, and organizes instruction around teacher questions and uses questions that require specific answers in a recitation format.

Task Orientation

The most effective teachers were businesslike with a strong sense of task and direction for themselves and their students. (Taylor et al., 1999, p. 4)

Another variable that is associated with student success in mastering important literacy skills is "task orientation" (Murphy et al., 1986, p. 84). A learning environment characterized by a task orientation is one in which the teacher's primary emphasis is the assignment and completion of academic tasks. A strong academic focus does not exclude attention to affective needs, but it does place the two areas of interest in a certain perspective—one in which attention to academic learning is clearly the more important of the two. Numerous studies confirm that teachers who maintain a strong task orientation obtain greater student engagement in learning tasks, and significantly more student learning, than do teachers who maintain a strong affective orientation (Pressley, 1998b).

Challenging and Appropriate Expectations

Effective reading teachers convey by word and deed that everyone can learn to read. (Anderson et al., 1985, p. 16)

Stars think in terms of maximum—not minimum—standards. (Haberman, 1995, p. 28)

A third learning environment variable that is highly correlated to student achievement is positive teacher expectations. Teachers who show concern for the academic progress of each student produce youngsters who learn more than pupils of teachers who are not as concerned with academic progress. Positive teacher expectations and concern for academic progress are reflected both in demands for academic excellence per se and in expectations for behavior conducive to academic progress. Teachers who maintain "appropriate and high expectations for learning" (Ruddell, 1997, p. 50) demand more of their students in terms of both quantity and quality of work (Haberman, 1995; Taylor et al., 1999).

Student Cooperation and Accountability

> Students' conceptual knowledge develops more completely when they work together in communities of learners. (Pressley, 1998b, p. 256)

> Thoughtful teachers . . . help students learn to be active members of literacy communities . . . communities filled with real live persons with whom to exchange oral and written communications. (Pearson, 1996, p. 273)

Student cooperation on academic tasks and accountability for work compose a fourth learning environment variable that is correlated with student achievement. Effective teachers recognize "the importance of the social character of learning" (Moll, 1991, p. 76) and the social nature of literacy (Young & Beach, 1999). They "encourage social collaboration" (Gambrell & Morrow, 1996, p. 126), "social interaction" (Morrow, Tracey, Woo, & Pressley, 1999, p. 464) and "collaboration over literacy tasks" (Pressley, 1998b, p. 255; Briggs & Thomas, 1997). They promote the development of learning communities (Guthrie et al., 1996). Teachers who expect students to cooperate in the accomplishment of academic tasks, who hold students accountable for their work, and who use well-thought-out reward systems for cooperating student groups contribute more to student learning than do teachers who do not emphasize student cooperation and accountability. As Kuhn and Stahl (2000) remind us, "if students are not held responsible they probably will not practice, and thus will not make gains" (p. 18).

Positive Affect

> These [effective] teachers were able to redirect students' behavior in a positive way without resorting to criticism or punishment. (Wharton-McDonald et al., 1998, pp. 120-121)

> The trust that stars build with children enables them to serve as successful models. (Haberman, 1995, p. 56)

A fifth learning environment variable that influences student achievement is positive affect. Although there is still disagreement about the influence on student learning of an environment characterized by strong positive affect, there is substantial evidence that negative affect inhibits student achievement. Teachers who control learning and emphasize academic achievement and who avoid such negative practices as criticism of student behavior, screaming, sarcasm, scolding, and ridicule facilitate student learning. Their classrooms are well run, but are "not stern or oppressive" (Taylor et al., 1999, p. 4).

We are also learning that while a positive environment is often marked by warmth, this is not the indispensable element in the climate mosaic. Rather, the critical factors here are (1) caring—effective teachers "exhibit a strong sense of personal caring about the student" (Ruddell, 1997, p. 40; Morrow et al., 1999; Pressley, 1998b) and "seek to establish in-depth caring relationships in the course of their day-to-day teaching activities" (Haberman, 1995, p. 5), and (2) trust—productive teachers "establish a bridge of trust and personal contact with students" (Ruddell, 1997, p. 41). Accomplished teachers employ this framework of caring and trust to create "a positive atmosphere in their rooms" (Morrow et al., 1999, p. 464). Their classrooms are "business-like but supportive and friendly" (Anderson et al., 1985, p. 15). They model respect for children (Haberman, 1995), enthusiasm for the work at hand (Briggs & Thomas, 1997), "personal commit[ment]" (Samuels, 1981, p. 259), "personal responsibility for helping every student learn" (Briggs & Thomas, 1997, p. 30), and a "willingness to expend considerable energy" (Armor et al., 1976, p. 38) even in the face of long odds—a characteristic that Haberman (1995) calls "irrepressibility" (p. 73).

In other venues, this positive environment is referred to as personalization. What is critical here is that "relationships with students are established around learning activities" (Haberman, 1995, p. 4). Positive affect is not an end in itself. Effective teachers connect caring to an equally strong sense of academic press. The relationship between these two essential dimensions of student literacy achievement has also come more clearly into focus in the last twenty years. In short, the old paradigm—which posits the creation of a warm, positive environment to help build self-esteem, which in turn enhances academic performance—might not be the most accurate model. A more precise sequence may be the creation of an academically oriented environment where children experience success that leads to the enhancement of self-esteem, which in turn promotes a positive environment (Singer & Balow, 1981).

Established Structure

> Good classroom management underlies all other principles and makes it possible to implement them in instruction. (Anderson, Evertson, & Brophy, 1979, p. 222)

The outstanding teachers are terrific managers. Their behavior management of students is superb and always positively toned. (Pressley et al., 1996, p. 265)

A final learning environment variable that is associated with increased learning is established structure. According to Soar and Soar (1979), established structure "represents internalization by pupils of limits of behavior, patterns of behavior that are carried out, and sequences of activities that have been established in the past" (p. 101). Teachers who establish class rules and procedures and subsequently work to ensure that students learn those procedures and adhere to them accomplish the following: they create a sense of academic press; they increase the on-task behavior of students; they reduce the need for ongoing behavioral interactions with students, which are negatively associated with student achievement; and they promote student literacy development (Snow et al., 1998).

Presenting Academic Content

Excellent teachers more often blend perspectives, intermeshing a variety of methods. (Pressley et al., 1996, p. 266)

The exemplary teachers used both transmission and constructivist models of learning. (Morrow et al., 1999, p. 475)

In this section, I target research about the teacher's role in presenting content and working with students to master that content. I review the evidence in three sections: organizing for engagement, motivating students for learning, and providing explicit instruction and scaffolding.

Organizing for Engagement

Common sense suggests that some ways of grouping students and teachers should be more effective than others. (Otto et al., 1984, p. 802)

How children are classified and grouped for reading instruction at the school level has a direct impact on children's experiences. (McGill-Franzen & Allington, 1990, p. 151)

Statistically significant school factors in the most effective schools include a collaborative model for the delivery of reading instruction. (Taylor et al., 1999, p. i)

Organizing for engagement is about two issues: appropriately grouping students in classrooms and crafting a collaborative model of instruction that deepens student engagement in literacy activities. I examine both of these issues in this section.

Grouping Strategies

The research on grouping for student engagement champions an emphasis on the extensive use of individual and small group instruction for mastering beginning literacy skills, especially in reading (Hoffman, 1991; Taylor et al., 1999). This conclusion is particularly relevant when addressing the education of students at risk of reading failure and for "the lowest SES students" (Taylor et al., 1999, p. 4; Snow et al., 1991). Indeed, for these youngsters "to be successful readers, individual or very small group (i.e., no more than 4 or 5 students) instruction is essential" (Pikulski, 1994, p. 38).

In their work at the Center for the Improvement of Early Reading Achievement, researchers found that children in the classrooms of more accomplished teachers spend nearly twice as much time in small group instruction—48 minutes vs. 25 minutes with the whole group—as do youngsters being instructed by the least accomplished teachers—25 minutes in small groups vs. 48 minutes with the whole group (Taylor & Taxis, n.d., p. 8). This focus on small group instruction "provides the opportunity for instruction and practice in all aspects of reading" (Anderson et al., 1985, p. 49). It facilitates youngsters "spend[ing] more school time under the direct instructional guidance of adults working on learning tasks appropriate to the particular child" (Phi Delta Kappa, 1980, p. 206), a condition that, as I noted earlier, has consistently been found to be "highly related to reading achievement" (Hiebert, 1983, p. 235; Taylor et al., 1999).

After one acknowledges that the portfolios of effective teachers of beginning reading are filled with a variety of instructional formats, that is, whole group, small group, one-on-one tutoring (Taylor et al., 1999), and that intensive teacher-directed small group instruction occupies a privileged place in that portfolio, the story line becomes more complex. This is the case because the criteria employed to organize these small groups is contested, and the findings on the use of the nearly universal organizing criterion, ability grouping, are annoyingly difficult to interpret at times; they are, "for the most part, equivocal and inconsistent" (Barr & Dreeben, 1991, p. 895). For example, we learn from schools that promote high levels of literacy and from effective reading programs that teachers often "create programs that recognize this need for differentiation" (Hiebert & Pearson, 1999, p. 16), that they "place students into groups primarily based on ability" (Briggs & Thomas, 1997, p 20). In short, "successful schools strongly emphasize homogeneous grouping for reading" (Venezky & Winfield, 1979, p. 23; Taylor et al., 1999), and most teachers in these effective schools "organize students by ability" (Briggs & Thomas, 1997, p. 20). At the same time, an assortment of very thoughtful analysts conclude that using ability or achievement to assign youngsters to class (Slavin, 1994) or to forge small learning groups is at best not especially efficacious and at worst harmful to the denizens of low-ability groups. *Becoming a Nation of Readers*, for example, documents "serious problems inherent in ability grouping" (Anderson et al., 1985, p. 91). The authors of the report encourage teachers to "explore other options for reading instruction" (p. 91). Allington (1995), in turn, argues that the "conventional wisdom about [the benefits of] homogeneous instructional groups is simply misguided" (p. 7).

How is it that homogeneous ability grouping is often found in schools where students are quite successful in mastering reading skills, but seems to be suspect in the general population of schools? The answer can be traced to the fact that, in many cases, being assigned to a low-ability group is a sentence to an inferior education (Allington, 1995; Murphy & Hallinger, 1989). Specifically, almost all of the organizational and classroom conditions (e.g., access to high status peers, time, content covered, teacher feedback) that explain high achievement are consistently allocated in an inequitable manner among groups (Hoffman, 1987; Murphy & Hallinger, 1989). That is, "the child in the group designated as low-ability will receive less instruction and qualitatively different [and less robust] instruction than the child would in a group designated high ability" (Anderson et al., 1985, p. 90).

Thus my reading of the research tells me that organizational arrangements in and of themselves have not, do not, and never will predict organizational performance (Murphy, 1991). Or as Barr and Dreeben (1991) capture the dynamic, "a social arrangement, in and of itself, does not lead directly to achievement or attitudinal outcomes; rather, it is the activities and knowledge that students experience as part of instruction that bear directly on what they learn and how they feel about their learning" (p. 895). The decisive issue is what unfolds in the learning group. We need to "examine the instructional events that mediate the influence of grouping (heterogeneous versus homogeneous) on achievement" (Barr & Dreeben, 1991, p. 896; Hiebert, 1983). Where homogeneous grouping by ability works, students in all groups are advantaged by the instruction. Where it is ineffective or pernicious, children in some groups—almost always the low-ability groups—are systematically harmed.

A number of analysts help us see how to use small groups organized by ability to the best advantage of children. This is the path I recommend in this book. I agree with Anderson and his team (1985) that "the problems with ability grouping can be alleviated, if not eliminated entirely" (p. 91). Specifically, I support capturing the benefits of targeted, teacher-directed instruction provided to small groups of students organized by ability or skill, while overcoming the negatives often associated with this instructional format. Helpful strategies include ensuring that this form of instruction is directed at skill development, that students are grouped heterogeneously for other literacy activities and for study in other curricular domains (Hiebert & Taylor, 2000), that a criterion other than ability (i.e., interest) is employed to form groups at times (Anderson et al., 1985), and that there is a reasonable portion of whole group instruction in the literacy block of time.

Another important element of my design is to ensure that the groups do not become "rigid and inflexible" (Taylor et al., 1999, p. 45; Fisher & Adler, 1999; Hoffman & Rutherford, 1984). To guarantee that ability grouping is not a permanent appointment to low group membership (Hiebert, 1983), "the assignment to groups should be reviewed periodically and children switched around" (Anderson et al., 1985, p. 91). Accomplished instructors of primary-age children "appear especially adept at moving students up so that near the end of the school year high-ability groups are relatively larger, while low groups are smaller" (Barr & Dreeben, 1991, p. 898). The research in this area shows that "systematic assessment" (Taylor et al., 1999, p. 45), or continuous monitoring of student progress, is a hallmark of flexible ability-based reading groups (Slavin, 1994; Venezky & Winfield, 1979). Indeed, Taylor and her colleagues (1999) assert that "the importance of schoolwide monitoring cannot be underestimated in this [flexibility] regard" (p. 33).

An especially powerful strategy to secure the benefits of homogeneous ability grouping is to employ cross-class and cross-grade learning clusters, rather than simply relying upon within-class groupings (Barr & Dreeben, 1991; Pikulski, 1994; Slavin, 1994). Finally, for ability grouping to be a productive instructional arrangement, it is essential that the critical elements that explain student achievement (e.g., allocation of time, content coverage) are distributed equitably across groups—remembering that equity will often necessitate that the lower-ability groups receive more of these critical learning variables.

A Collaborative Model of Instruction

Effective reading programs often mount a schoolwide effort to provide literacy instruction, "a collaborative model for reading instruction" (Taylor et al., 1999, p. 28), and overall "strong teacher collaborations" (Taylor & Taxis, n.d., p. 20). By carefully "coordinat[ing] support personnel toward student needs" (Hoffman & Rutherford, 1984, p. 86), these programs demonstrate considerable "instructional efficiency" (p. 86). Accomplished teachers, in turn, are "skillful managers of the human resources available to them" (Pressley, 1998b, p. 165).

Primary programs in which students master literacy skills often mass personnel to facilitate maximum engagement and achievement in reading (Sherman, 2001; Van Vleck, Fritzsche, Joiners, Lorvig, & Lentz, 1994). They employ what Samuels (1981) labels a pattern of "intensive staffing" (p. 260). They utilize "additional personnel in the form of teacher aides and/or reading specialists" (p. 259). All school employees—"librarians, resource teachers, instructional assistants, guidance counselors, reading specialists, and administrative staff" (Sherman, 2001, pp. 17-18)—and "as many parents as possible are involved in teaching students to read" (p. 5).

Specialist teachers "bring expertise and concentration to the reading program" (Weber, 1971, p. 27). They work collaboratively with regular classroom colleagues to enhance their instructional expertise. They provide a "multiplier effect" (Samuels, 1981, p. 258) by working with teachers and teacher aides "to upgrade teacher skills and to provide teachers with needed materials" (p. 258).

This pattern of intensive staffing in conjunction with the thoughtful engagement of these additional personnel (Wharton-McDonald et al., 1998) creates an organizational context that "allow[s] the pupil-adult ratio to be reduced during reading instruction" (Weber, 1971, p. 27)—a condition "associated with positive school performance" (Phi Delta Kappa, 1980, p. 205). In particular, this collaborative model facilitates extensive use of small group instruction and targeted individualization (Slavin, Madden, Karweit, Dolan, & Wasik, 1994; Taylor et al., 1999, 2000). It helps guarantee that existing time is used productively while adding blocks of learning time for youngsters (Taylor et al., 1999). It often limits the number of groups with which teachers must work to a manageable number . And it has the power to redirect energy currently flowing into modes of instruction that do not receive high marks for enhancing literacy performance (e.g., uncoordinated use of paraprofessionals, pull-out resource instruction) into more productive channels (Pressley, 1998b; Samuels, 1981; Slavin, 1994). It moves personnel resources into contact "with students in instructional situations" (Wharton-McDonald et al., 1998, p. 121), as opposed to placing them on the periphery of the core activity of the school (Durkin, 1978–1979).

Motivating Students for Learning

> Literacy instruction that provides opportunities for challenge, choice, and collaboration supports children in acquiring the motivation to develop into active, engaged literacy learners. (Gambrell & Morrow, 1996, p. 134)

> Teachers attempt to motivate literacy by reducing risks for attempting literate activities, positive feedback, setting an exciting mood, encouraging students to believe they can be readers and writers, and so on. (Pressley et al., 1996, p. 274)

Snow and her colleagues (1998) remind us of a central dynamic in the literacy development process; that is, that "the strategies chosen to engage children's interest and attention in . . . activities and materials determine their effectiveness" (p. 195). Or, examining the issue from a slightly different angle, "reading . . . depends . . . heavily on motivation for reading" (Guthrie et al., 1996, p. 167) while the "absence or loss of initial motivation to read . . . is a stumbling block that [will] throw children off the course on the journey to skilled reading" (Snow et al., 1991, pp. 4-5). The subtext here underscores the "important role of the teacher in creating an . . . instructional context . . . related to motivation" (Gambrell & Morrow, 1996, p. 134) and exposes the fact that highly productive teachers are "clearly concerned with motivating their students to do literate things" (Pressley, 1998b, p. 160).

A diverse group of literacy scholars note functions and activities that have been found to motivate learning. According to Guthrie and his research team (1996), a motivational classroom is one "that supports the development of active reading and creates contexts that satisfy the students' needs for curiosity, aesthetic involvement, challenge, competitiveness, and social exchange. The most central of these needs is curiosity, the desire to know more about something" (p. 167). For Gambrell and Morrow (1996), "motivation is viewed in terms of three critical dimensions of the instructional context" (p. 116): "presenting some challenge to the learner, providing opportunities for choice, and encouraging and supporting social collaboration in learning" (p. 135). Turning from functions to activities, Pressley and his colleagues (2000) disclose that accomplished teachers make "intensive efforts to make literacy and literacy instruction motivating" (p. 27), including employing the following practices: (a) creating a risk-free environment in the classroom; (b) giving positive feedback; (c) conveying the importance of reading and writing in life; (d) setting an exciting mood for reading, adding color and humor, and so on; (e) encouraging an "I can read, I can write" attitude; (f) accepting where the child is right now and working to improve literacy from that point; (g) conveying the goal of every lesson and why the lesson is important to students; (h) encouraging students to find and read stories and books that they like, as part of the literacy program (i.e., self-selection of materials that are read); (i) encouraging students' ownership of their reading by having them make decisions about what to read; (j) encouraging personal interpretations of text; (k) selecting class reading materials on the basis of students' interests; and (l) encouraging student ownership of writing (e.g., students' selection of writing topics) (p. 27).

Morrow and Tracey (cited in Stahl, 1998) furnish the following list of activities that motivate student learning:

1. Activities that promote choice of materials and experiences for learning

2. Activities that challenge but can be accomplished

3. Activities that give the learner responsibility and some control over the learning process, such as self-direction, selection and pacing of learning activities, and materials

4. Activities that involve social collaboration with peers or adults

5. Activities that are facilitated by teachers who model, guide, and scaffold information to be learned

6. Activities that are meaningful and functional by using authentic materials and settings

7. Activities with conceptual orientations that add interest to what is being learned

8. Activities that offer time for practicing skills learned in settings that are independent of the teacher

9. Activities and materials that are easily accessible

10. Activities that offer the child a feeling of success (pp. 52-53)

I expand on and extend some of these factors below. Before I execute that assignment, however, it is important to emphasize that matters treated in other sections of this volume have strong motivational elements. In particular, creating a literate school and classroom environment (a topic taken up in Chapter 8) is highly motivational. So too are teacher efforts to ensure that classroom "activities connect with one another" (Pressley, 1998b, p. 165), that the pieces of the literacy program are tightly linked, and that they are integrated with other sections of the curriculum (an idea explored in detail in Chapter 10). The focus on guaranteeing that all youngsters, especially children at risk of reading failure, are successful goes a long way to offset the usual decay in student interest and excitement in literacy activities (a set of activities reviewed in Chapter 9). Finally, much of the framework explored in the first section of this chapter under the heading "Managing the Learning Environment" is ribboned with motivational elements.

Over the last two decades, research has affirmed that instruction that "incorporates children's prior knowledge . . . and beliefs" (Ruddell, 1997, p. 49) and their experiences and interests nurtures motivation, engagement, and literacy learning. As Anderson and his team (1985) aver, children construct meaning based on both "background knowledge [and] . . . information in the text" (p. 51). Thus background knowledge is critical to "the meaning negotiation and construction process" (Ruddell, 1997, p. 49). Because youngsters may not have sufficient background knowledge, or do not "see relationships between what they are reading and what they already know" (Anderson et al., 1985, p. 55), successful teachers motivate by helping "build background knowledge" (p. 50) and by tapping into prior knowledge, that is, by "focus[ing] on materials that connect with students' experiences and backgrounds" (Adelman, 1995, p. 64). Teachers assist students in "us[ing] the everyday to make sense of classroom content and the use of classroom activities" (Moll, 1991, p. 74), both everyday classroom experiences and everyday personal experiences.

Throughout this book, I expound on the significance of student collaboration in the learning process. Here I register the conclusion that "collaboration is viewed as a critical dimension" (Gambrell & Morrow, 1996, p. 118) in motivating students to master important literacy skills. According to Guthrie et al. (1996) and Gambrell and Morrow (1996), there are three important motivation facets to this collaboration: (1) the opportunity to "interact socially" (Guthrie et al., 1996, p. 171), (2) the chance for children "to teach and learn from each other" (Gambrell & Morrow, 1996, p. 127), and (3) the occasion to "communicate . . . understanding to genuine audiences" (Guthrie et al., 1996, p. 186). Various types of this shared literacy activity are described in the literature, almost all of which are clustered under the broad headings of peer collaboration, in which youngsters "help each other equally" (Gambrell & Morrow, 1996, p. 131), and peer teaching, in which "one child takes the role of teacher" (p. 130).

Throughout this volume, I also examine the importance of balancing teacher direction and control with student choice and ownership. My position from my review of the literature is that the proportion between these variables needs to shift over the learning period, with the teacher factor heavily weighted as new skills are presented or new concepts introduced, and the student factor highlighted as lessons unfold and learning solidifies. Successfully navigating this transitional path is a key to effective literacy instruction. Within this dynamic, producing appropriate choice or what I label "controlled choice" seems to be an especially motivating instructional strategy (Gambrell & Morrow, 1996): "enabling students to pursue and extend their interests through continuous selection of topics and materials is at the heart of the motivating classroom content" (Guthrie et al., 1996, p. 185).

> When students are provided with opportunities to make choices, they feel that they have some control over their own learning. Student choice promotes involvement, commitment, and engagement in learning, and there is evidence from several studies that suggests a strong correlation between choice and intrinsic motivation. Clearly, there is ample support for the contention that intrinsic motivation is increased when children are afforded opportunities to make genuine choices about their learning; therefore, choice is viewed as a critical dimension of the motivating instructional context. (Gambrell & Morrow, 1996, p. 118)

Selecting material that is "personally relevant" (Ruddell, 1997, p. 41), providing projects that interest children, "bas[ing] instruction on intrinsically interesting content" (Guthrie et al., 1996, p. 168), and "identifying the activities with which children are familiar and providing understandings of their situated expertise" (McNaughton, 1999, p. 13) are dimensions of teaching employed by accomplished teachers to motivate youngsters to engage in literacy activities. This notion of connectedness—"connecting subjects with children's backgrounds and experiences" (Haberman, 1995, p. 86)—or pattern of providing relevant instruction is motivating because it stimulates active involvement and it helps children see the usefulness of reading, that is, that it "is not merely a cognitive exercise" (Guthrie et al., 1996, p. 186).

Providing challenge is another instructional plank in the establishment of "a motivating . . . context that supports children in developing positive capability beliefs with respect to their reading ability" (Gambrell & Morrow, 1996, p. 117). In such an environment, children should be "challenged but not overwhelmed" (Spiegel, 1995, p. 91). Because "children are capable of learning little from text that is beyond their independent [reading] level [and] there is little new for them to learn from text that is beneath their instructional level" (Snow et al., 1998, p. 214), "tasks are motivating when they are appropriately challenging, rather than too easy or too hard" (Pressley, 1998b, p. 254). Thus according to Gambrell and Morrow (1996), "challenging learning tasks involve an investment of effort and awareness on the part of the learner that if effort is expended, there is a reasonable chance of success" (p. 117).

Research on student engagement and achievement in the area of literacy reveals a variety of additional motivational strategies in the instructional repertoires of accomplished teachers. One that links to the earlier discussion of developing cooperative learning tasks is the establishment of a non-competitive work environment. As Pressley (1998b) concludes after an extensive review in this area, student competition undermines motivation rather than fosters it, although "the competitive classroom model thrives in contemporary America" (p. 241). He documents that "in competitive classrooms, many more students are going to feel like losers than winners" (p. 255).

Consistent with this line of analysis, motivation seems to be enhanced when teachers emphasize "internal reader motivation" (Ruddell, 1997, p. 49) and downplay extrinsic rewards. Effective teachers "seek to convince their students that learning itself is the reward" (Haberman, 1995, p. 18); "they use sparingly any external student motivation, such as using achievement pressure 'to please the teacher'" (Ruddell, 1997, p. 40) and they regularly "tap internal student motivation" (p. 40). Instead of promoting competition among youngsters, influential teachers "reward students for improving on their past performances . . . and consistently send the message that improvement is what matters" (Pressley, 1998b, p. 255). They "reward children for growth, not for outperforming others" (p. 243).

Providing Explicit Instruction and Scaffolding

Research supports direct and explicit teacher action associated with planning, motivating, information giving, and mediating student understandings. Conversely, there is no research support for inexplicit teacher actions or for instruction in which teachers assume passive or covert roles. (Roehler & Duffy, 1991, p. 877)

What distinguished the most effective schools from their peers was their use of coaching to help students learn how to apply word recognition strategies to real reading. (Taylor et al., 1999, p. 46)

Effective instruction for mastery of literacy skills in the primary grades is best captured by two analogies: "teacher as explicit instructor" (Raphael, 1998, p. 140) and teacher as scaffolder. I examine the research on both of these roles below. Before I pursue that charge, however, I want to foreshadow my discussion in Chapter 10 on the place of the portrait of teacher knowledge in the gallery of literacy achievement. I begin with the research conclusion that good teachers "need . . . the *skill* to teach all students to read well" (Duffy-Hester, 1999, p. 492) and that "the development of teachers' knowledge and skills" (Lyons & Pinnell, 1999, p. 197) and "teacher competence" (Hoffman, 1991, p. 920) are key "characteristic[s] found to be significantly related to pupil reading achievement at the end of the first grade" (p. 920). "Teacher's prior knowledge . . . is critical to effective literacy instruction in the classroom" (Ruddell, 1997, p. 39) and "expert teaching of reading requires knowledge of language structures at all levels" (American Federation of Teachers, 1999, p. 17). In short, "teaching reading is a job for an expert" (p. 11), and star teachers "bring expertise to their work" (Haberman, 1995, p. 36).

Teacher as Explicit Instructor

Research has shown that children's learning is facilitated when critical concepts or skills are directly taught by the teacher. (Anderson et al., 1985, p. 71)

It is better to teach the code system of written English systematically and explicitly than it is to teach it randomly, indirectly, or incidentally. (American Federation of Teachers, 1999, p. 22)

The significance of direct, systematic, explicit instruction is examined in considerable detail in Chapters 7 and 9. Here I provide the foundation for those extended discussions. As a point of commencement, we know from the literature that, contrary to prevailing belief, there is not an overabundance of explicit instruction in many classrooms, especially special classrooms. Or as Durkin (1978–79) nicely discloses, although "our study assumed that at least some of the time [teachers] are teaching reading . . . the data . . . do anything but support that assumption" (p. 523). While there is a good deal of teacher talk in classrooms, often this communication is unrelated to providing students with needed skills.

We also know from the corpus of scholarship on literacy in the primary grades that beginning readers need explicit instruction "for reading and writing, both in the context of 'authentic' and 'isolated' practice" (Snow et al., 1998, p. 196). As Singer and Balow (1981) observe, "if you want pupils to learn a particular skill or knowledge, it is more efficient to teach it directly than to expect it to transfer from other learnings" (p. 309). In explicit instruction, "the teacher explains, models, demonstrates, and illustrates reading skills and strategies that students ought to be using" (Anderson et al., 1985, p. 56). The goal of direct instruction "is to make explicit those processes to which we do not typically attend. The strategies previously described make explicit the implicit strategies that good readers use to recognize sounds in words, relate sounds to letters, and blend sounds into words" (Kameenui et al., 1998, p. 59).

"Focused instruction" (Snow et al., 1991, p. 145), "direct instruction" (p. 159), "strategy instruction" (Kameenui et al., 1998, p. 57), or "direct explanation instruction" (Roehler & Duffy, 1991, p. 874) is a prominent factor in explaining literacy gains; that is, "direct instruction produces gains in reading achievement beyond those that are obtained from less direct means" (Anderson et al., 1985, p. 56). "Well-designed, controlled comparisons of instructional approaches have consistently supported direct teaching of decoding, comprehension, and literature appreciation . . . and systematic and explicit instruction in the code system of written English" (American Federation of Teachers, 1999, pp. 7-8). Indeed, direct instruction "is the surest means of developing the strategic processing that [is] a characteristic of skilled readers" (Anderson et al., 1985, p. 72). In classrooms where literacy achievement is routine, "teaching [is] direct, explicit, and systematic . . . much explicit, planned skill development [takes] place" (Morrow et al., 1999, pp. 467, 474). And in schools that are effective in bringing youngsters to high levels of literacy achievement in the early grades, "teachers take most of the responsibility for planning, directing, and guiding reading instruction" (Briggs & Thomas, 1997, p. 13).

Finally, we know that while explicit instruction, "teacher-directed instruction" (Briggs & Thomas, 1997, p. 11), and "close teacher supervision" (Anderson, et al., 1985, p. 91) are necessary for most youngsters to master literacy skills, teacher explicitness does not gainsay student ownership and responsibility, or what Pearson (1996) labels "real engagement and true empowerment" (p. 273). As with all effective instruction, the objective is to transition control of the learning over time from the teacher to the student, to provide "gradual release of responsibility" (Garcia & Pearson, 1991, p. 43) from the instructor to the learner. Each child over time "must become a self-extending reader and writer" (Anderson, 1999, p. vii). This basic principle is not negated in direct instruction simply because teachers take major responsibility for initiating the learning sequence, that is, because they "organize and guide most of the reading that students receive" (Briggs & Thomas, 1997, p. 11). The central message of the research is that the journey to productive skill use and understanding is mediated by the "explicit presentation of information" (Roehler & Duffy, 1991, p. 871).

Teacher as Scaffolder

In addition to planned, explicit instruction, the teachers with high-achieving students were skilled at incorporating skill minilessons into ongoing lessons as opportunities presented themselves. (Wharton-McDonald et al., 1998, p. 114)

The more effective reading teachers were more in tune with students' individual needs and more successful in adjusting instruction to these needs. (Otto et al., 1984, p. 813)

In the introduction to this section, I disclosed that accomplished primary teachers employ both transition and constructivist models of teaching. My introduction to explicit instruction explored the transition model. Here I spotlight the constructivist perspective, acknowledging full well that many elements of instruction find their way into both approaches.

According to Pearson (1996), scaffolding is the function of "interven[ing] in an environment . . . to provide the cueing, questioning, coaching, corroboration, and plain old information needed to allow students to complete a task before they are able to complete it independently and while they gradually gain control of it" (p. 273). It is "the process whereby a teacher monitors students' learning and steps in to provide assistance on an as-needed basis" (Wharton-McDonald et al., 1998, p. 116). Unlike the emphasis on breaking tasks into component skills, or "decomposition" (Garcia & Pearson, 1991, p. 50), which we see throughout our various discussions of direct instruction, scaffolding "requires teachers to observe students while they carry out a task and to offer feedback, modeling, explanations, and clues designed to help them complete the task" (Roehler & Duffy, 1991, p. 873).

There is a growing body of "evidence that a key ingredient in effective beginning reading instruction is such scaffolding" (Pressley, 1998b, p. 140). That is, that this "coaching-while-reading strategy" (Taylor et al., 1999, p. 41) characterizes accomplished teachers—"the best teachers make scaffolding a centerpiece of the instructional day" (Pressley, 1998b, p. 174)—and is a defining element of effective reading programs in the primary grades: "coaching was found to be a characteristic of teachers in the most effective schools" (Taylor et al., 1999, p. 45). In short, "the best teachers [are] exceptionally active in scaffolding students' learning" (Pressley, 1998b, p. 166).

Scaffolding in effective classrooms is characterized by "learning in social situations" (Garcia & Pearson, 1991, p. 45). It "acknowledges the role of social interaction in the development of language, thinking, and learning" (Gambrell & Morrow, 1996, p. 116). It highlights "the importance of children learning language and literacy as a medium of communication instead of as a static subject" (Moll, 1991, p. 69).

Scaffolding also emphasizes "the construct of gradual release of responsibility" (Garcia & Pearson, 1991, p. 45) I introduced in the last section; that is, it carefully attends to the appropriate transfer of ownership from the teacher to the student as learning deepens. Or, examining this interactive system from a different vantage point, scaffolding fosters "self-regulation through cognitive monitoring strategies" (Snow et al., 1998, p. 196) rather than "depend[ency] on the teacher" (Garcia & Pearson, 1991, p. 37). That is, through scaffolding accomplished teachers "encourage students to monitor the quality of their work" (Wharton-McDonald et al., 1998, p. 118) and to develop the "metacognitive awareness to know when and where to apply the skills they have learned" (p. 117; Pressley, 1998b).

Scaffolding privileges understanding and meaning making (Ruddell, 1997; Snow et al., 1991; Taylor et al., 1999), or what Chall, Jacobs, and Baldwin (1990) label a "thinking approach to learning" (p. 6). In the teacher-as-scaffolder analogy, the fact "that the thinking children do during their academic work is the crux of the matter" (Allington, 1991, p. 13) is acknowledged. Quality teacher scaffolding moves children beyond literal interpretations of their work. It "make[s] children think" (Anderson et al., 1985, p. 86) and it "requires them to . . . reason about what they are doing" (Garcia & Pearson, 1991, p. 37). As such, scaffolding is a kind of "metacognitive instruction" (Haller, Child, & Walberg, 1988, p. 8) that nurtures students' thinking about what they are and are not understanding (Allen, 2000), that is, it promotes "metacognitive thinking" (Wharton-McDonald et al., 1998, p. 117). The goal in the classroom is "the development of a strategy that can be useful elsewhere . . . not the completion of an assigned task" (Spiegel, 1995, p. 91).

The starting point for teacher scaffolding is the careful monitoring of "student thought processes" (Wharton-McDonald et al., 1998, p. 116; McNaughton, 1999) as they teach—what Fountas and Pinnell (1999) call "systematic assessment" (p. 167). It is this thoughtful "monitoring of students' progress in literacy" (Pressley et al., 2000, p. 10) that permits teachers to match instruction to the needs of specific learners (Fountas & Pinnell, 1999) and "that keep[s] children engaged in their assigned tasks" (Berliner, 1981, p. 218). Research shows that this ability to "derive an understanding of the child's mental map by carefully observing behavior" (Lyons & Pinnell, 1999, p. 200) is an essential element of good first teaching. Research in effective schools also reveals that this monitoring includes daily assessments (Wharton-McDonald et al., 1998) as well as periodic stock taking (Morrow et al., 1999; Slavin et al., 1994; Wellisch, MacQueen, Carriere, & Duck, 1978).

Ongoing monitoring leads in turn to "good knowledge of what children know" (Fountas & Pinnell, 1999, p. 167; Otto et al., 1984), to "adaptability of instruction" (Venezky & Winfield, 1979, p. 22), and to what I label "just-in-time teaching." It helps ensure that the focus is "on the child and what the child is learning rather than on what the teacher appears to be teaching" (Juel, 1991, p. 761; Leinhardt et al., 1981). Because effective teachers understand where their young charges are in the learning process, that is, they know what children know well and they can discern where they are struggling, they are able to "modify and adapt instructional approaches" (Armor et al., 1976, p. vi) and to tailor instruction accordingly. Because they have "the ability to adjust instruction to the individual needs of the student" (Ruddell, 1997, p. 40), and to "adjust the mode (grouping) and explicitness of instruction" (Snow et al., 1998, p. 196), excellent teachers are freed up from reliance on "prescriptive curriculum" (Fountas & Pinnell, 1999, p. 167) and they "demonstrate much greater flexibility in directing and orchestrating children's thinking processes" (Ruddell, 1997, p. 44).

In teaching via scaffolding, teachers provide on-the-fly interventions. And because "each student is receiving instruction that he or she needs" (Venezky & Winfield, 1979, p. 22), there is less loss due to collective and undifferentiated consumption of learning. These "high achievement teachers" (Wharton-McDonald et al., 1998, p. 120) are especially adept at using this "sensitivity to students and individual student needs" (Pressley et al., 2000, p. 23) "to insert minilessons when the need becomes apparent" (Wharton-McDonald .et al., 1998, p. 120), and to "target things students need to know at this moment" (Pressley et al., 2000, p. 23). Good scaffolders rarely overlook opportunities for learning. They are also proficient at "continuously monitor[ing] their own behavior and the effects of their instruction" (Lyons & Pinnell, 1999, p. 201).

As described above, in addition to careful monitoring of student learning and just-in-time teaching, which "are indispensable to productive reading" (Guthrie et al., 1996, p. 185), scaffolding is also home to a number of important teaching functions. Effective scaffolders are also skilled at modeling (Pressley et al., 1996), or alternatively, "modeling is an effective teacher action" (Roehler & Duffy, 1991, p. 870; Dole et al., 1991; Kuhn & Stahl, 2000). Indeed, "consistent use of modeling has [a] long-term positive effect on literacy achievement" (Pressley et al., 2000, p. 28) and "demonstrating how strategies are applied in real reading situations" (Garcia & Pearson, 1991, p. 49) is "the most powerful method . . . [to] effectively teach children" (Haberman, 1995, p. 34).

Providing targeted, academically focused feedback is also an essential element of scaffolding, and a practice that "leads to higher engagement and achievement" (Berliner, 1981, p. 218). Particularly useful feedback is specific and helps students clarify misunderstanding while pushing back the frontier of learning (Anderson et al., 1979; Hoffman & Rutherford, 1984). Feedback that affords useful clues about overcoming errors is especially efficacious (Anderson et al., 1985). In a similar vein, feedback that provides reinforcement is correlated with gains in reading achievement (Haller et al., 1988). So too is the use of praise for excellent academic performance (Anderson et al., 1985; Briggs & Thomas, 1997): "in outstanding classrooms, every student [is] reinforced for her or his achievements" (Pressley, 1998b, p. 165). Scaffolding is also about furnishing "connection in the instruction" (Pressley et al., 1996, p. 265), among aspects of the literacy program and between ideas encountered over time.

In closing, it is instructive to note that in classrooms in which teachers are master scaffolders, there is a high degree of interaction between the teacher and the students across an array of instructional arrangements (Briggs & Thomas, 1997). The teacher is a moving maestro and there is a good deal of instruction on the run, or teaching by wandering around. The accomplished teacher never seems to be doing "just one thing at a time" (Wharton-McDonald et al., 1998, p. 115). Overall, more learning activities unfold in the classrooms of good scaffolders. Their classrooms are marked by a "high density of instruction" (Pressley, 1998b, p. 165) or "high treatment intensity" (Samuels, 1981, p. 259).

> One of the most striking characteristics of the outstanding classrooms relative to the more typical ones is the intensity of the literacy instruction, with school days definitely filled with high-quality reading and writing experiences. In contrast, more typical classrooms have large portions of time that is not nearly as intense or literacy-relevant. (Pressley et al., 1996, p. 265)

The take-home message from the research reviewed here is that good first literacy teaching includes copious amounts of direct or explicit instruction and much scaffolding, both "systematic phonics instruction [and] on the job coaching during everyday reading" (Taylor et al., 1999, p. 46).

Summary

In this chapter, I unpacked some of the research on effective literacy in the early grades. Other pieces of the narrative on effective first teaching are also found in later chapters, especially Chapters 7 through 10. I divided my examination into two broad topics, managing the learning environment and presenting academic content. In the latter section I took up the issues of organizing for engagement, motivating students for learning, and providing explicit instruction and scaffolding.

6

Managing Time Productively

Other things being equal, the more time allocated to a content area of reading, the higher the academic achievement in that content area. (Berliner, 1981, p. 206)

Within models of classroom instruction, the variable of time has been identified as a crucial determinant of children's learning. The notion underlying these models is fairly simplistic although very powerful in its implications for instruction: what children learn in school is a function of how they spend their time. What children do during class time, in turn, is a function of how teachers structure their own time as well as that of children. (Hiebert, 1983, p. 235)

The quantity of instructional time can have direct, positive effects on student achievement and school leaders . . . can do much to strengthen and restore it. (Smith, 2000, p. 676)

In Chapter 1, I chronicled how my insights for literacy are drawn from four large fields of study—teacher effectiveness, school effectiveness, program effectiveness, and leadership in high-performing schools. A common and especially robust theme running throughout this collective body of work is that "the learning of reading does not occur unless instructional time is provided, and the students are engaged during that time" (Becker, 1977, p. 530). Or recast in a positive mold, "there are abundant data to support the rather sensible notion that, in general, teachers who allocate more instructional time to reading produce readers with higher achievement" (Allington, 1983, pp. 548-549).

In this chapter, I unfold the research concerning time management in five sections. I begin with a succinct overview of the data linking time and achievement. I then examine the concept of allocated time for reading, detailing what we know about normal arrangements and providing suggestions for the more productive use of time. In the third section, I describe the two related issues of variability in time usage and equity in the distribution of reading time. Section four layers in the critical element of how time is employed, the element that gives power to allocated reading time. I acknowledge that time interacts with quality instruction. Finally, I offer a few comments on the strategy of extending quality time in reading by engaging the home in the learning process.

Reading Time and Student Achievement

Analyses of the amount of time spent in reading time and its relation to achievement yield strong positive findings. (Hoffman, 1991, p. 921)

The first conclusion from the research in this area is that "the amount of time spent reading separates successful from unsuccessful readers" (Ivey, 2000, p. 42); that is, that time has a substantial effect on reading achievement (California State Department of Education, 1984; Denham & Lieberman, 1980; Schneider, 1985; Seifert & Beck, 1984). At the macro level, we understand that "instruction measured in terms of hours of schooling per year is highly related to achievement" (Guthrie, Martuza, & Seifert, 1979, p. 155). This, in turn, informs us that issues such as length of the school year and instructional day and student attendance are important factors in enhancing student learning (Williams et al., 2000).

Attending directly to reading, there is an abundance of evidence that "reading time [is] positively correlated with reading achievement" (Harris & Serwer, 1966, p. 54), and "that time spent reading in school contribute[s] to growth in students' reading achievement" (Taylor, Frye, & Maruyama, 1990, p. 360). In particular, investigations confirm that the total amount of reading work (e.g., reading connected text, working in basal readers, engaging in phonics lessons) is positively related to measures of reading achievement (Harris & Serwer, 1966).

Moving one level deeper in the research, we learn that time spent on certain types of reading activities is particularly fertile. For example, some research has documented "that children's reading achievement can be significantly affected by the amount of free reading done" (Spiegel, 1995, p. 90) while other "studies . . . support the assertion that time engaged in silent reading is an important determinant of elementary students' reading achievement" (Taylor et al., 1990, p. 352). There also is evidence across all levels of analysis that the connections between reading time and student learning are especially sturdy for students historically placed at risk of school failure by society, schools, and families, especially for youngsters from low-income homes (Guthrie et al., 1979).

Before forging ahead, a few caveats are necessary. A great number of studies have examined the issue of instructional time and learning, and while the preponderance of the evidence flows in the positive direction, not all investigations have uncovered significant results (e.g., Armor et al., 1976). Even when positive findings are reported, it is instructive to remember "that it is not time itself that influence[s] achievement, [but rather] the events that occur during that time" (Guthrie et al., 1979, p. 175; see also Yair, 2000). Following that reasoning, I acknowledge that the relationship between time and student achievement becomes more robust the deeper one drills into the terrain of allocated, engaged, and academic learning time (Fisher & Berliner, 1983). Finally, analyses affirm that the same time allocations have different impacts on different types of learners, at least in terms of age and at-risk status (Guthrie et al., 1979).

Allocation of Instructional Reading Time

Increasing the amount of time children read ought to be a priority for both parents and teachers. (Anderson et al., 1985, p. 77)

Giving all students, especially those experiencing difficulty, more time to read in school is the most certain way to help all students become more skilled and engaged and even to be more prepared to achieve on standardized tests. (Ivey, 2000, p. 43)

In several of the successful programs, extra amounts of time were allocated to reading. (Samuels, 1981, p. 269)

When one begins to dissect time as a resource in schools, the conclusion is quickly reached that instructional time in schools is very limited. Even though reading and the related language arts enjoy privileged space in the primary program, consuming anywhere from 30 to 50 percent of the school day, the total amount is somewhat anemic when the numbers are compiled and juxtaposed against other activities, such as watching television. To begin with, Taylor and her team (1990) found that reading simply was not taught on more than 15 percent of the school days investigated in their study. Approximately 90 minutes per day was provided for reading on the other days. Something in the neighborhood of 60 percent of potential allocated time was devoted to reading-related activities, with only about one third given over to actual reading. Using this framework, Taylor and her colleagues found that it was normal for students to receive roughly 25 minutes of reading per day.

Coming at this issue using data from other studies, we learn that roughly 70 percent of allocated reading time is dedicated to independent seatwork in which students perform in their workbooks or on worksheets (Anderson et al., 1985), time that is largely "unrelated to year-to-year gains in reading proficiency" (p. 76). Distributing time in this manner means that less time is provided for more productive reading work. For example, according to Gambrel and colleagues (cited in Stahl, 1998), average readers spend only about 6 minutes per day with connected text. The *Becoming a Nation of Readers* report pegs silent reading—the type of activity that shows especially tight connections with student achievement—at 7 or 8 minutes per day at the primary level and 15 minutes per day in the middle grades (Anderson et al., 1985, p. 76; see also Durkin, 1978–1979; Taylor et al., 1990). In the words of Allington (1997b), "classroom teachers . . . routinely allocate more time to the 'introducing of' and 'following up on' stories and books than they allocate for reading those stories and books" (p. 9).

Oral reading also receives limited attention in the traditional time allocation formula, a deficiency that is "particularly harmful to those low-achieving beginning readers who desperately need practice in a situation where feedback is available" (Morris et al., 1990, p. 134). So too does writing, other than filling in worksheets. Indeed, "opportunities to write more than a sentence or two are infrequent in most American elementary school classrooms" (Anderson et al., 1985, p. 119).

Since "instructional time allocated for literacy instruction is obviously important" (Allington, 1991, p. 10) and since learning to read requires time to read, leadership for literacy means creating carefully structured reading programs (Samuels, 1981) in which a significant block of uninterrupted time is devoted to reading and related language arts (Hallinger & Murphy, 1985; Honig, 1997). Fountas and Pinnell (1999) assert that this type of commitment is required for "good first teaching" (p. 181), while Williams and friends (2000) maintain that it is an essential factor in improving reading performance in the early years. Something in the neighborhood of 2.5 to 3 hours a day of dedicated and protected time for literacy work seems appropriate (Taylor et al., 1999).

Within this "literacy block," considerably more time needs to be consigned to reading text than is the norm in primary classrooms. Concomitantly, "workbook and skill sheet activities should be pared to the minimum that actually provide worthwhile practice in aspects of reading" (Anderson et al., 1985, p. 119). In a similar vein, time assigned to whole group instruction can be scaled back in many classrooms (Taylor et al., 1999). Allington (1980) makes the case when he observes that "contextual reading experiences, as opposed to other reading activities, seem to be the only way the learner can integrate the component processes and create self-monitored reading behaviors" (p. 873). The message for leaders here is "that it is valuable for students to actually read during reading class" (Taylor et al., 1990, p. 359).

Two activities in the reading portfolio should be featured. First, there needs to be a considerable amount of teacher-directed small group instruction (Allington, Stuetzel, Shake, & Lamarche, 1986; Fisher & Adler, 1999), some of which can be devoted to group instruction in decoding skills and some of which should be assigned to oral reading of text (Taylor et al., 1999; Weber, 1971). In order to make this a reality, the school will likely need to employ a collaborative model in which all staff are responsible for small reading groups (Taylor et al., 1999). Second, "since an average of 1 minute per day of additional silent reading time increases post-test performance by one point" (Leinhardt et al., 1981, p. 355), "children should spend more time in [teacher facilitated] independent reading" (Anderson et al., 1985, p. 119). Structured programs in the primary grades might unfold according to the following suggestions for allocated reading time drawn by the Center for the Improvement of Early Reading Achievement from studies of reading in especially effective schools: teacher-directed small-group instruction, 60 minutes; independent reading, 30 minutes; whole-group instruction, 30 minutes; writing in response to reading, 15 minutes; and other independent activities, 10 minutes (Taylor et al., 1999).

Addressing Variability in Reading Time

The amount of time allocated to reading varies enormously from one classroom to another, even within the same school. (Anderson et al., 1985, p. 86)

One striking feature of these observations was the enormous variability in reading time experienced by the observed students. . . . Some students received very little instruction, while others participated in reading instruction for fairly large segments of the school day. (Allington & McGill-Franzen, 1989a, p. 82)

Clearly, over a school year, some children spen[d] a great deal more time in reading instruction than others. (Adelman, 1995, p. 68)

In addition to a trove of information on the general allotment of instructional time for reading and on the partition of that time for various reading-related activities (e.g., time for silent reading), we are also blessed with a good deal of data on how time allocations play out differently across classrooms and across groups of students within those classrooms. On the first topic, analysts have repeatedly reported "great variation between teachers in the amount of time they . . . devote to reading time" (Hoffman, 1991, p. 921) as well as "large variations among students in time spent in instructional [reading] activities" (Leinhardt et al., 1981, p. 351). In one study by Allington and McGill-Franzen (1989a) that focused on individual students, allocated reading time varied from 46 to 132 minutes (p. 82). Berliner (1981) discerned similar patterns in his work targeting classrooms, with some classes receiving an average of 47 minutes per day of reading instruction and others receiving 118 minutes of reading (p. 205).

Deepening the analysis to engaged time and academic learning time reveals concordant contours, with some fifth-grade classes getting 120 hours of engaged time and 60 hours of academic learning time per year in reading, while others received 283 hours of engaged time and 148 hours of academic learning time (Berliner, 1981, p. 209). In the Guthrie, Martuza, and Seifert (1979) study, similar findings surfaced. The bottom quarter of the sample in terms of allocated instructional time received about 80 minutes per week of formal reading instruction (p. 159). About two-thirds of this low group was even further disadvantaged, receiving less than 40 minutes per week of reading instruction, or about 7 minutes per day (p. 159). Approximately half of the upper quartile experienced about 225 reading minutes per week or about 45 minutes per day of reading instruction (p. 162). In still another investigation, Adelman (1995) discovered that some pupils were reading texts for less than 5 minutes per day while others had 48 minutes of interaction with connected text (p. 68). Congruent findings have been uncovered by Anderson and his colleagues (1985) and by Anderson, Evertson, and Brophy (1979).

It is also important to record that these fluctuations are not randomly distributed across children. Rather, the disadvantages that accompany less exposure to reading and less interaction with connected text fall disproportionately on the very youngsters who require additional reading instruction (Hoffman, 1991), that is, "children with reading problems" (Stahl, 1998, p. 34). It is also these students who are oversupplied with worksheet and workbook assignments (Spiegel, 1995). Most troubling of all, as I discuss in detail in later chapters, participation in special programs designed to assist these youngsters does "not seem to increase the quantity of reading instruction compared to the amount that nonparticipating peers receive" (Allington & McGill-Franzen, 1989a, p. 83).

Ensuring That Time Is Well Used

> It is not enough to set aside time for reading instruction . . . it is apparent that how time is used is also important. (Briggs & Thomas, 1997, p. 21)

> The time allocated to reading may or may not be used efficiently. Thus more important than time allocated to reading is 'engaged time'—the time the child is productively involved in reading. (Anderson et al., 1985, p. 86)

> Substantial increases in Academic Learning Time are associated with important increases in achievement. (Berliner, 1981, p. 213)

As the statements above corroborate, although attention to allocated time is an important starting point, how time is deployed in schools and used in classrooms and how students focus during learning activities are considerations of even greater significance (Yair, 2000). Throughout this book, I demonstrate that pupil engagement is a product of an array of overlapping and interacting factors, with some focusing on the home and some on the youngsters themselves. At the heart of time deployment, however, are curricular and management decisions made by school administrators and classroom teachers. Some of the elements in this curricular and management equation were introduced in my treatment of instructional effectiveness in Chapter 5. I recast and augment that work now, with the reminder that policies for enhancing the quality of reading instruction are as important as policies relating to the allocation of time (Armor et al., 1976).

One issue of central importance to using time well is the type of learning activities on which students work. While maintaining high rates of engagement is important, at least as much effort needs to be devoted to ensuring that youngsters are engaged in the right stuff. Or, as Allington and his colleagues (1986) express it, "what a student learns is not merely a function of time on task but is also related to the kinds of tasks he/she is being asked to perform" (p. 18). The point is that "instructional time influences reading achievement only if children are engaged specifically in reading activities" (Guthrie et al., 1979, p. 175). For example, on the negative end of the continuum I have already recorded "that much of the time devoted to workbook pages and skill sheets [has] doubtful value in learning to read" (Anderson et al., 1985, p. 86). In a similar vein, time spent on what Harris and Serwer (1966) describe as supportive reading tasks, such as art, discussions, and dramatizations, are not associated with reading performance. Finally, reading time spent in classroom routines such as "handing out books and giving directions" (Samuels, 1981, p. 261) and in management processes "do not influence reading achievement" (Guthrie et al., 1979, p. 175). Indeed, "when teachers of reading spend substantial amounts of time on activities that involve little or no practice in reading, the results in reading achievement tend to be unfavorable" (Harris & Serwer, 1966, p. 56). On the positive side of the ledger, well-paced tasks that engage students in reading connected texts, learning basic literacy skills such as decoding, and comprehending written text are all correlated with increases in student mastery in reading (D'Agostino, 2000; Snow et al., 1991; Topping & Sanders, 2000).

Expanding the amount of engaged learning time in which students experience high levels of success, or maximizing academic learning time, is a second strand assuring that time is well used. We know that both engaged time and success rate independently and in combination are correlated with reading achievement (Rowe, 1995;

Taylor et al., 1990; Topping & Sanders, 2000). We also have affirmation that high rates of "on task behavior" (Taylor & Taxis, n.d., p. 26), "attentiveness" (Rowe, 1995, p. 66), and engagement are defining features of outstanding classrooms (Pressley et al., 1996; Rowe, 1995) and the product of effective reading instruction (Pressley, 1998b; Taylor et al., 1999). In one study, for example, investigators found that in "outstanding classrooms typically most or all of the students and never less than half of the students are attentive and gainfully employed. In contrast, inattention is much more commonly observed in the more typical classrooms" (Pressley et al., 1996, p. 266). In another study, Taylor and her research team (1999) discovered that "teachers rated as most accomplished were found to have an average of 96% of their students on task. . . . By contrast, the engagement rates were 84% and 61%, respectively, for the moderately accomplished and least accomplished teachers" (p. 38).

The third and final piece of the time usage algorithm for school leaders is protecting available instructional time. As Adams (1990) reminds us, "classroom time is limited—a minute poorly spent . . . is a minute robbed from education" (p. 28). At the school level, "schools that are especially effective in teaching reading maximize the amount of uninterrupted time available for learning" (Anderson et al., 1985, p. 114). They "fiercely protect" (Sherman, 2001, p. 16) instructional reading time.

School staff, especially school leaders, act to guard instructional time first by creating organizational cultures that are conducive to learning (D'Agostino, 2000; Hoffman & Rutherford, 1984; Smith, 2000). Indeed, "the general learning environment is identified as being crucial to understanding school effectiveness" (State of New York, 1974, p. 13), and "good first [reading] instruction takes places in a quality, organized environment" (Fountas & Pinnell, 1999, p. 179).

While the "good atmosphere of these schools is hard to describe . . . it is difficult to escape the conviction that the order, sense of purpose, relative quiet, and pleasure in learning of these schools play a role in their achievements" (Weber, 1971, p 26). So too does an abundance of "supportive, friendly, encouraging . . . constructive teacher-student exchanges" (Snow et al., 1991, p. 159). Research reveals "that the best environment in which to help master academic skills is one in which students find the classroom to be a friendly, warm, and supportive place to work. In other words, when there is a task orientation combined with positive classroom climate, the situation is conducive to academic growth" (Samuels, 1981, p. 258; see also Murphy et al., 1986). Studies of effective programs also unearth learning environments that are characterized as "calm and businesslike" (Hoffman & Rutherford, 1984, p. 88) and are marked by "stability, routine, and orderliness" (Rowe, 1995, p. 89; see also Puma, Karweit, Price, Ricciuti, Thompson, & Vaden-Kiernan, 1997), an "environment that provides structure and stability for children" (Fountas & Pinnell, 1999, p. 179; see also Murphy et al., 1986). At the school level, leaders promote efficient use of time by crafting "schoolwide strategies that help teachers use time more effectively" (Briggs & Thomas, 1997, p. 26). They emphasize nonintrusive school schedules (Briggs & Thomas, 1997) through "careful scheduling of special events, rehearsals, health examinations, classroom visitors, and remedial teachers who pull children out of class" (Anderson et al., 1985, p. 114).

Studies of effective teachers, effective reading programs, and productive schools also attest that management at the classroom level is critical to ensuring that time is used well and that reading achievement is maximized (Fountas & Pinnell, 1999; Samuels, 1981). That is, in classrooms taught by skilled teachers, "more of the time available for learning is spent in activities with academic value" (Anderson et al., 1985, p. 87). To begin with, there are substantial data that show "that time allocated for academic instruction in a school day can easily slip away when a teacher cannot keep the transitional time, wait time, and behavioral problems to a minimum" (Berliner, 1981, p. 204). In "unsuccessful classrooms time [is] wasted because routines [are] not established and there [are] often interruptions brought about by discipline problems" (Samuels, 1981, p. 271). Even in many average classes, "there is a lack of attention to classroom management that results in considerable inefficiency and reduced achievement on standardized tests of reading" (Berliner, 1981, p. 205).

Teachers in schools with high levels of literacy, on the other hand, "maximize every instructional minute" (Briggs & Thomas, 1997, p. 25). Teachers in effective reading programs "are good managers of their classes. Students know and (most of the time) follow classroom rules" (p. 22). The classrooms are characterized as "being orderly because less time [is] wasted on discipline problems and giving instructions on routine matters such as passing out books and transitions from one activity to another" (Samuels, 1981, p. 269) and because there are well-ingrained routines for ensuring that learning activities run smoothly (Anderson et al., 1985; Briggs & Thomas, 1997). The bulk of the lesson time is, therefore, given over to the lesson at hand (Rutter, 1983).

A Note on Time and the Home

> Research also shows that the amount of reading students do out of school is consistently related to gains in reading achievement. (Anderson et al., 1985, p. 77)

In the final chapter of the book, I expose how leadership for literacy operates by fashioning sturdy reading linkages between the school and the family and by crafting strategies for parents to create strong literacy environments in the home. I close this chapter by foreshadowing some of that work as it relates specifically to time. Here is what we can distill from the research. First, reading at home has a modest influence on student achievement (Rowe, 1995; Topping & Sanders, 2000). That is, while some analysts have concluded that "the amount of reading students do out of school is consistently related to gains in reading achievement" (Anderson et al., 1985, p. 77), other investigators have unearthed less robust findings (Taylor et al., 1990). Second, homework that involves youngsters in working with books, that is, reading texts as opposed to completing worksheets and workbook pages, is an influential weapon in the arsenal to improve reading performance. In short, "increasing homework is likely to lead to improvements in student outcomes" (Fraser, 1989, p. 717).

Third, there is abundant information attesting to the conclusion that youngsters do not undertake much out-of-school reading. For example, Greaney and Hegarty (1987) report that the "average fifth grade pupils devoted 7.2 percent of their leisure time to reading . . . [as opposed to] 30.4 percent of available time that was taken up by watching television" (p. 10). Nearly one quarter of the students did no book reading. Anderson and his colleagues (1985) reference another fifth-grade study in which half of the students read books for 4 minutes per day or less and another 30 percent devoted less than 2 minutes per day of their free time to book reading (p. 77). Concomitantly, we are aware that good readers, say the top 20 percent of students, do read a fair amount. Juel (1988) characterizes afterschool reading for this group as quite frequent. And finally, and encouragingly, there is evidence "that the teacher has a significant influence on the amount of book reading children do out of school" (Anderson, Wilson, & Fielding, 1988, p. 296): "research suggests that the frequency with which students read . . . out of school depends upon the priority classroom teachers give to independent reading" (Anderson et al., 1985, p. 79).

Summary

This chapter was devoted to an analysis of five issues. I explored the data joining time and reading performance. I then unpacked the issue of time allocation for reading, with particular attention dedicated to the productive use of time. I also consigned considerable space to the analysis of variability in time usage in classrooms and schools. In the fourth section, I examined the connections between how time is employed and student learning. I closed with some insights on how time can be extended by fashioning productive relations between the school and the family.

7

Focusing
on Phonics

Across the research literature, the value of phonics instruction has been demonstrated across literally hundreds of studies—including small, well-controlled laboratory studies as well as large-scale method comparisons involving hundreds of classrooms and thousands of children. (Adams, 1991, p. 42)

There is indeed considerable evidence that the primary difference between good and poor readers lies in the good reader's ability to use spelling-sound knowledge to identify words. (Juel, 1991, p. 774)

Overall, when you start to review the data seriously, you can't seem to get away from the fact that there is something about phonics and decoding that is very, very important. . . . You cannot get away from a consideration of decoding as a central focus of beginning reading instruction. (Williams, 1991, p. 16)

The next four chapters are devoted to an analysis of ways to build an effective "curricular" program in literacy in the early grades. The current chapter examines the critical role of phonics in such a program. Chapter 8, in turn, explores how to deepen the program by creating strong supporting elements around the featured phonics strategy. Chapter 9 zeroes in on the task of crafting "a well-designed instructional support program" (Allington & Walmsley, 1995, p. 256), or the development of "safety nets for children who need something extra" (Fountas & Pinnell, 1999, p. 182). Chapter 10 addresses coordinating the reading program. Although Chapter 5 spotlighted what Chall (1983) refers to as the "teacher factor," in these four chapters my concern is more with what she labels the "methods factor" (p. 8). Chall defines method as "the particular sequencing, focusing, and pacing of a given set of stimuli to which the learner responds in certain ways to achieve a given objective or set of objectives" (p. 3). Consistent with my focus on the early years of literacy development, my priority is on methods that meet the challenge of helping children learn how to read rather than methods for reading to learn. I turn now to my analysis of the central role of phonics in the curriculum in the early grades.

Understanding the Concept

Phonics instruction entails teaching students how to use letter-sound relations to read or spell words. (National Institute of Child Health and Human Development, National Reading Panel, 2000a, p. 7)

Mature forms of sight word learning are alphabetic and phonological at root. (Ehri, 1995, p. 117)

Phonics, as Foorman (1995) reminds us, "is an educational term that refers to the myriad of methods used to teach beginning readers about correspondences between letters and sounds" (p. 376). Similarly, according to Stahl (1992), "phonics . . . refers to various approaches designed to teach children about the orthographic code of the language and the relationships of spelling patterns to sound patterns" (p. 618). It is an "umbrella term" (Beck, 1998, p. 21) that incorporates a "variety of ways" (p. 21) or "methods to help the beginning reader attend to the sequences of letters and their correspondence to speech patterns" (Adams & Bruck, 1993, p. 113).

Phonics incorporates two concepts: (1) phonemic or phonological awareness—a youngster's "sensitivity to the sound structure of speech" (Foorman, Francis, Winikates, Mehta, Schatschneider, & Fletcher, 1997, p. 256) and (2) the alphabetic principle—"the notion that letters in words may stand for specific sounds" (Stahl et al., 1998,

p. 339). At its core, "phonics is the relationship between letters and sounds in *written* words" (Stahl, 1992, p. 621). That is, it is about "showing young learners how the print-to-speech system works" (Beck, 1998, p. 21). It is about teaching "how to translate print into language—how to decode" (Foorman, 1995, p. 378) written language.

> By making the relationships between spellings and sounds explicit, phonics methods are intended to assist the learning process by providing young readers and writers with a basis both for remembering the ordered identities of useful letter strings and deriving the meanings of printed words that, though visually unfamiliar, are in their speaking and listening vocabularies. (Adams & Bruck, 1993, p. 113)

Phonics holds the key to "the most basic skill in learning to read, word identification" (Vellutino, 1991, p. 442), which, in turn, provides the basis for the construction of meaning, that is, comprehension. Phonics instruction explicitly acknowledges that "the most salient problem in learning to read is learning to decode" (Pressley, 1998b, p. 59), and that "when decoding is poor, students do not learn as much from texts as they would if their decoding were stronger" (Pressley, 1998b, p. 71). Its purpose "is to help children acquire knowledge and use of the alphabetic system to read and spell words" (NICHHD, 2000b, 2:113).

Both chains of the phonics DNA strand—phonemic awareness and alphabetic understanding—are "vitally important to success during the early stages of reading acquisition" (Blachman, Tangel, Ball, Black, & McGraw, 1999, pp. 239-240). Both also are "strong predictors of later achievement in reading" (Vellutino, 1991, p. 440). Indeed, "knowledge of letters and phonemic awareness . . . bear a strong and direct relationship to success and ease of reading acquisition. . . . The harder these two variables are investigated, the stronger the predictive value appears to be" (Adams, 1990, p. 82). In their comprehensive review of the work in this area, the National Reading Panel concluded that "correlational studies have identified PA [phonemic awareness] and letter knowledge as the two best school-entry predictors of how well children will learn to read during the first two years of instruction" (NICHHD, 2000a, p. 7).

Research also confirms that while each piece of the phonics puzzle is individually linked with reading acquisition (Snow et al., 1998), "phonological awareness provides the basis for understanding and utilizing the alphabetic principle" (Torgesen & Hecht, 1996, p. 141), that is, "some level of phonological awareness is necessary for the discovery and exploitation of the alphabetic principle" (Stanovich, 2000, p. 177). Studies also show that "the development of skilled reading depends on the mastery of both the parts of the system and the functional relations among them" (Adams & Bruck, 1993, p. 125), and that "phonological sensitivity training is even more effective when combined with practice in letter-sound correspondences" (Stanovich, 2000, p. 367; see also Blachman, 1991; Hatcher, Hulme, & Ellis, 1994; NICHHD, 2000b).

Phonemic Awareness

Phonemic awareness involves understanding that words are composed of individual distinct sounds, and that these sounds can be manipulated. (Copeland, Winsor, & Osborn, 1994, p. 29)

Phonemic awareness is a type of "metalinguistic awareness" (Castle, 1999, p. 55), a concept that "reflects the ability to play with language and to think about it as a system" (Nicholson, 1999, p. 11)— to be "able mentally to stand back from [one's] own talk and reflect on it" (p. 11). It is "an oral language skill that manifests itself in the ability to notice, think about, or manipulate the individual sounds in words" (Torgesen, 1997, p. 13). Phonological or phonemic awareness is cast in slightly different form by various reading researchers. It is portrayed as consisting of

- the awareness of and ability to manipulate segments in words (Blachman, 1991, p. 29),
- the ability to focus on and manipulate phonemes in spoken words (NICHHD, 2000b, 2:10),
- the ability to segment words into concepts (Pressley, 1998b, p. 97),
- the awareness that words are composed of sequences of meaningless and sometimes distinct sounds (phonemes) (Juel, 1988, p. 437),
- knowledge of grapheme-phoneme correspondence (Iverson & Tunmer, 1993, p. 113) or the ability to reflect on and manipulate the phonemic segments of speech (p. 114),
- the ability to explicitly manipulate speech segments at the phoneme level (Cunningham, 1990, p. 429).

What should be clear here is that phonemic awareness is a "skill that does not involve print" (Nicholson, 1999, p. 11). It deals with "the sound structure of spoken words" (Hatcher et al., 1994, p. 41).

According to these same researchers, phonemic awareness is "the key to the development of the alphabetical principle, word recognition, and invented spelling" (Stahl et al., 1998, p. 340), and to learning to decode in general (Pressley, 1998b). This conclusion has been confirmed by a "massive body" (Hatcher et al., 1994, p. 41) of overwhelming and "converging evidence from both experimental and longitudinal studies . . . that some form of phonemic awareness is necessary to successfully learn to read alphabetic languages" (Juel, 1988, p. 437). Indeed, "one of the most compelling and well established findings in the research on beginning reading is the important relation between phonemic awareness and reading acquisition" (Kameenui et al., 1998, p. 50) and reading achievement (Adams, 1990; Copeland et al., 1994).

To begin with, "good and poor readers are distinguished by their performance on tasks requiring phoneme segmentation of spoken words" (Shankweiler, 1991, p. xvi)—"students who have superior phonemic awareness are better readers than students with low PA" (NICHHD, 2000b, 2:12)—and a lack of phonemic awareness "makes learning to read a difficult task for children from all kinds of social backgrounds" (Nicholson, 1999, pp. 17-18).

> Poorly developed phonemic awareness distinguishes economically disadvantaged preschoolers from their more advantaged peers and has been shown to be characteristic of adults with literacy problems. Indeed, among readers of alphabetic languages, those who are successful invariably have phonemic awareness, whereas those who lack phonemic awareness are invariably struggling. (Adams, 1994, p. 15)

Youngsters "who lack phonemic awareness have a difficult time developing understanding of letter-sound relations as well as learning to spell" (Pressley, 1998b, p. 97). In short, they experience "trouble acquiring the alphabetic principle which, in turn, . . . limit[s] their ability to decode words" (Snider, 1995, p. 446; see also Hall & Moats, 1999; Stahl, 1992). All of this,

> undermines reading a wide range of materials and comprehending what is read. The long-term result is less practice in reading and less exposure to information in text and thus, less development of higher-order reading competencies (e.g., the ability to make sense of complex syntax) and word knowledge that can mediate understanding of text. (Pressley, 1998b, p. 97)

Most tellingly, there is evidence that "the failure to acquire phonemic awareness may [lead to] functional illiteracy" (Snider, 1995, p. 446).

On the positive side of the ledger, phoneme awareness is routinely uncovered as "the most potent predictor of reading acquisition" (Stanovich, 2000, p. 161) and "later reading success" (Nicholson, 1999, p. 14), and "the strongest predictor of children's essential success . . . in reading" (Stahl, 1997, p. 15; see also Adams, 1990, 1994; Lundberg, 1991; Shankweiler, 1991). It is a necessary skill for "successfully learning to read alphabetic languages" (Juel, 1991, p. 778)—"to discover how an alphabet works" (Shankweiler, 1991, p. xvi) and "to productive[ly] use an alphabetic script" (Lundberg, 1991, p. 48). It is directly "linked to the ability to decode" (Juel, 1991, p. 778). It is a "powerful cause of growth in word reading skills" (Torgesen & Hecht, 1996, p. 137). It helps explain reading speed (Snow et al., 1998), and it is related to reading comprehension as well (Juel, 1991; Konold et al., 1999). Most importantly, phonemic awareness is "strongly related to reading achievement" (Cunningham, 1990, p. 429), "to both concurrent reading achievement and future reading achievement" (Snider, 1995, p. 445). And while there is an iterative relationship between phonemic awareness and learning to read (Stanovich, 2000), that is, phonemic awareness facilitates learning to read and, in turn, is enhanced by reading, the evidence suggests "that phonemic awareness seems to contribute more to learning to read than learning to read contributes to phonemic awareness" (Pressley, 1998b, pp. 102-103). Finally, to revisit a point introduced above, phonemic awareness is most effective when it is coupled with work that reveals the relations between phonemes and letters (NICHHD, 2000b), that shows youngsters "how to represent phonemes and letters" (Treiman, 1998, p. 304).

So far, I have tracked support for the importance of phonemic awareness to (1) reports that examine the role of truncated phonemic awareness in poor readers; (2) studies that expose the connections between phonemic awareness and important intermediate variables on the learning-to-read-path, such as word recognition and fluency; and (3) investigations that link phonemic awareness to important outcomes such as comprehension and reading achievement. Additional evidence of the significance of phonemic awareness in the algorithm of reading success is derived from "training studies" (Snider, 1995, p. 447) that focus on the direct instruction of these skills. We know from a number of experiments that phonemic awareness can be taught and that "PA instruction is effective under a variety of teaching conditions with a variety of learners" (NICHHD, 2000b, 2:5) "across a range of grades and age levels" (NICHHD, 2000a, p. 7)—a topic that I address in detail in the final part of this chapter. These studies also document that "phonemic awareness training" (Stahl, McKenna, & Pagnucco, 1994, p. 178) has "discernable effects on reading and learning to read" (Pressley, 1998b, p. 99) and "facilitate[s] reading performance" (Cunningham, 1990, p. 438).

Instruction in phonemic awareness "is effective in teaching children to attend to and manipulate speech sounds in words" (NICHHD, 2000b, 2:5), that is, "successful in promoting phonemic awareness" (Pressley, 1998b, p. 101) itself. This attention and awareness platform is linked in these instructional studies to "subsequent acquisition of reading skills" (Snider, 1995, p. 447), such as the ability to recognize words and spell (NICHHD, 2000b; Treiman, 1998), as well as to "subsequent reading achievement" (Pressley, 1998, p. 101). And, quite significantly, "the effects of PA instruction on reading last well beyond the end of training" (NICHHD, 2000a, p. 7). As the authors of the National Reading Panel conclude, "teaching children to manipulate phonemes in words [is] highly effective across all the literacy domains and outcomes" (NICHHD, 2000b, 2:3).

The take-away message here is that (1) "phonemic awareness is highly implicated in the beginning stages of reading development" (Cunningham, 1990, p. 440) and is a "critical precursor of reading acquisition" (Lundberg, 1991, p. 50) and "success in reading" (Liberman, Shankweiler, & Liberman, 1989, p. 14); (2) "variation in phonological awareness is causally related to the early development of reading skill" (Stanovich, 2000, p. 161); and (3) phonemic awareness is "imperative in learning to read" (Adams, 1990, p. 71). In summary, "the positive effects of developing phonemic awareness on subsequent reading achievement [are] overwhelming" (Pressley, 1998b, p. 101). Its contribution "to beginning reading acquisition cannot be overstated" (Kameenui et al., 1998, p. 51).

The Alphabetic Principle

Another big idea in beginning reading is alphabetic understanding, which is a necessary requirement for operating in an alphabetic writing system. The relationship between phonological awareness and alphabetic understanding is closely linked. (Kameenui, 1998, p. 330)

As I discussed above, phonemic awareness is step one in the decoding process. "The child who is to sound out words needs to know more" (Pressley, 1998b, p. 122); however, he or she needs to go "beyond phonemic awareness" (p. 122) to develop "alphabetic understanding" (Kameenui, 1998, p. 329)—knowledge of letters and an "understanding that [these] letters have a relationship with sounds in words" (Stahl et al., 1998, p. 339). Or in recast form, "phonological awareness [is] prerequisite to alphabetic understanding" (Kameenui, 1998, p. 329) and "the purpose of phonics is to teach children the alphabetic principle" (Anderson et al., 1985, p. 43).

Phonemic awareness and the alphabetic principle are closely aligned.

> The primary difference is that in alphabetic understanding, the importance is linking sounds to letters, whereas in phonological awareness, the importance is in hearing and manipulating sounds that make up words. Thus, alphabetic understanding tasks are focused on print stimuli and are concerned with the "mapping of print to speech." (Kameenui, 1998, p. 330)

The alphabetic principle has been presented in various related forms. According to scholars in the field of beginning reading, it represents knowledge, understanding, or awareness that

- letters code the sounds in words (Pressley, 1998b, p. 159),
- written English maps onto oral language alphabetically (Purcell-Gates, 1998, p. 61),
- letters of words systematically map onto sounds in words (Thompson, 1999, p. 28),
- units of print map onto units of sound (Stanovich, 2000, p. 162),
- letters in words may stand for specific sounds (Stahl et al., 1998, p. 339) or, alternatively, that particular phonemes in words are represented systematically by particular letters (Hatcher et al., 1994, p. 43).

The alphabetic principle comprises three elements: (1) "alphabetic letter knowledge" (Ehri, 1987, p. 11); (2) the ability to link those letters to sounds in print, or what Pressley (1998b) labels "letter-sound associations" (p. 123); and (3) familiarity "with the spelling patterns from which frequent words and syllables are comprised" (Adams, 1994, p. 18). Each piece benefits from explicit instruction (Chall, 1983; Ehri, 1987; Stahl et al., 1998).

As was the case with phonemic awareness, research informs us that the alphabetic principle "is a necessary requirement for operating in an alphabetical writing system" (Kameenui et al., 1998, p. 52), that "it must be acquired for a child to progress successfully in reading" (Stanovich, 2000, p. 162). Indeed, all three elements of the alphabetic principle are connected to reading acquisition. Specifically, the body of work on early reading reveals that (1) "knowledge of the alphabet [is] important for success in beginning to read" (Chall, 1983, p. 23), (2) familiarity with letter-sound associations "is a hallmark of successful beginning readers" (Stahl et al., 1998, p. 339), and (3) "the association of spellings with sounds is a fundamental step in the early stages of literacy instruction" (Adams & Bruck, 1993, p. 124).

Collectively, reading researchers provide a "convergence of evidence of the importance of understanding the alphabet" (Kameenui et al., 1998, p. 53) and "affirm the crucial need for understanding the alphabetic principle for learning to read and write" (Purcell-Gates, 1998, p. 62). "Familiarity with the letters of the alphabet is a powerful determinant" (Adams, 1994, p.16) of reading success, for, as Ehri (1987) avers, "knowledge of letters provides children with the foundation for beginning to process graphic cues in printed words" (p. 13). On the negative end of the spectrum, we know that "the ultimate source of the difficulties in learning to read an alphabetic system is a failure to grasp the alphabetic principle" (Shankweiler, 1991, p. xvi). When children's "alphabetic reading skills do not develop . . . they will be inaccurate readers and poor spellers" (Torgesen & Hecht, 1996, p. 140). In particular, poor letter knowledge "is coupled with extreme difficulty in learning letter sounds" (Adams & Bruck, 1993, p. 123).

On the positive end of the spectrum, analysts affirm that it is through mastery of the alphabetic principle that "a seemingly unending world of books" (Pearson, 1996, p. 270) is opened. "Word identification" (Vellutino, 1991, p. 441) becomes automatic and "reading vocabulary jumps to nearly the number of words [children] can comprehend orally" (Snider, 1995, p. 445). "The groundwork for the comprehension of text" (Brown & Felton, 1990, p. 223) is laid. In short, stronger understanding of the alphabetic principle is linked with a "significant advantage in reading" (Blachman et al., 1999, p. 264) in the primary grades (Adams, 1990; Chall, 1983; Pressley, 1998b) as well as with long-term benefits.

The summative message on the alphabetic principle mirrors the one crafted for phonemic awareness: "finding ways to induce young readers to attend to and to assimilate spellings and spelling-sound connections are of irreplaceable importance" (Adams & Bruck, 1993, p. 132). Consequently, the alphabetic principle must be an "instructional priority . . . in beginning reading instruction" (Kameenui, 1998, p. 331): "finding ways to ensure that all children are developing a comfortable knowledge of letters must be a priority concern" (Adams, 1994, p. 17) and "the early growth of alphabetic reading skills must be fostered" (Torgesen & Hecht, 1996, p. 140).

Phonics and Reading

> Unless readers become automatic with the alphabetic code, the time and attention required to identify a "word" directly limits the cognitive resources available to process the meaning of the sentence in which the word appeared. (Kameenui et al., 1998, p. 54)

> There are strong associations between decoding skills and knowledge gained through reading of text. (Pressley, 1998b, p. 64)

In a subsequent section on caveats regarding phonics, I reinforce the fact that phonics is a means to an end, the goal being the comprehension of text and the construction of meaning. The pathway to that goal, however, begins with decoding and the componential skills of phonemic awareness and alphabetic understanding, or as Pressley (1998b) avers, "getting meaning from text very much depends on efficient lower-order processing" (p. 55). The reader cannot "process sentences and paragraphs" (p. 45) unless he or she "can recognize individual words reliably and efficiently" (p. 45). Decoding is thus about learning to recognize words, and to do so fluently (Chall et al., 1990; Richardson, 1991; Stahl, 1992).

In addition, research helps us see "that word identification is the central sub-process of the complex act of reading" (Kameenui et al., 1998, p. 47), and that "the active processing of sentences and paragraphs cannot occur unless the reader can recognize individual words reliably and efficiently" (Pressley, 1998b, p. 45). Thus "the first goal of instruction should be to ensure that children can read words fluently and accurately" (Torgesen & Hecht, 1996, p. 140). Since decoding skills are intricately connected to the capacity of the learner to recognize words, that is, since "productive word learning in alphabetic orthographies ultimately depends on viewing words as a sequence of letters and associating their spellings with sounds" (Adams & Bruck, 1993, p. 124), the lack of these skills interferes with reading at the word level (Stahl, 1992) and with the development of a "rich orthographic reading vocabulary" (Torgesen, 1997, p. 21). This, of course, is why phonics or "learning to decode is so important"

(Pressley, 1998b, p. 45), that is, why phonemic awareness and the alphabetic principle are so critical, and why "activities that engender automaticity in word identification should be a central component of the child's instructional program" (Vellutino, 1991, p. 438).

Word recognition in turn "is basic to reading comprehension" (Chall, 1983, p. 27), that is, there is a "strong relation between word recognition and higher-order comprehension processes" (Kameenui et al., 1998, p. 48)—or, alternatively, "there is a strong relationship between comprehension skills and the efficiency of lower-level word recognition processes" (Brown & Felton, 1990, p. 224). Specifically, weak word identification skills "are strongly coupled with poor reading comprehension in both children and adults" (Adams & Bruck, 1993, p. 119). Indeed, deficient word reading capacity is "the primary bottleneck to the development of reading comprehension" (Torgesen, 1997, p. 20). Absent strong decoding skills, "increasing demand [is placed] on a reader's ability to remember and process information" (Kameenui et al., 1998, p. 54). If children are "devoting too much energy sounding out words, they will not be able to direct enough of their attention to comprehension" (Stahl, 1992, p. 624). On the other hand, "when decoding becomes automatic, requiring little attention, more attention may be allocated for comprehending text" (Reutzel & Hollingsworth, 1993, p. 325): "readers with fast and accurate word recognition skills have greater cognitive resources to direct attention to the meaning of text" (Adams & Bruck, 1993, p. 124).

In summary, phonemic awareness is central to the development of the alphabetic principle. Together, they allow the reader to decode words. Decoding words accurately and quickly, in turn, frees up capacity to comprehend and construct meaning from text: "phonological awareness facilitate[s] decoding skill, which in turn determines word recognition ability, which in conjunction with listening comprehension determines reading comprehension" (Stanovich, 2000, p. 61).

The Case for Phonics

Perhaps the most influential arguments for teaching phonics are based on studies comparing the relative effectiveness of different approaches to teaching beginning reading. Collectively these studies suggest, with impressive consistency, that programs including systematic instruction on letter-to-sound correspondences lead to higher achievement in both word recognition and spelling, at least in the early

grades and especially for slower or economically disadvantaged
students. (Adams, 1990, p. 31)

The most conspicuous difference between good and poor readers is found in the swift and accurate recognition of individual
words, in decoding, and the mastery of this skill is at the heart
of reading acquisition. (Juel, 1991, p. 777)

The ability to decipher print offers clear advantages. (Ehri,
1987, p. 21)

Chall (1983) and other reading researchers have developed classifi-
cation systems to describe the strategies employed in teaching reading.
According to these scholars, there are two major approaches in play in
the quest for literacy acquisition. Brown and Felton (1990) and Chall
(1983) contrast these two pathways as follows:

In principle, meaning-emphasis approaches attempt to enable
the beginning reader to emulate skilled reading by processing
words and sentences for meaning. In code-emphasis, the task
of the beginning reader is to learn the relationships between
letters and sounds in our written language system. In practice,
these methodologies differ primarily in the emphasis each
places on the type of clues that are given to facilitate word
recognition. For example, in meaning-emphasis approaches,
context and picture clues are emphasized, while code-emphasis approaches stress the use of information within the word
(i.e., sound-symbol relationships) as the primary tool for word
identification. (Brown & Felton, 1990, p. 229)

Code-emphasis: teaches decoding skills at the beginning of
reading instruction as a means to word recognition and comprehension; tends to give early attention to letters and
sounds. . . . Meaning-emphasis: emphasizes comprehension,
"bringing meaning to print," right from the beginning.
Advocates sight words, experience charts, use of contextual
clues, and/or meaning-emphasis basal series. Begins with
"meaningful language units" or "wholes," such as words,
phrases, and sentences. Considers phonics only one of many
useful skills, to be introduced later, after the child is reading,
when he or she needs to learn how to recognize unfamiliar
words. (Chall, 1983, p. 33)

The question at hand is this: Why "feature" phonics or the code-based approach to reading inside a comprehensive program designed to help students master literacy skills? The answer is fairly straightforward: Wherever one looks on the literacy landscape, the terrain is covered with evidence that phonics is both a necessary element in the process of literacy acquisition and an especially effective method of enhancing reading achievement.

On the first front—phonics as a necessary factor in learning to read well—research has consistently shown that the "spelling-to-speech transitions" (Adams, 1998, p. 74) that are at the heart of decoding words are of "critical importance to the reading process" (p. 74), and that "good readers give priority to phonological, letter- and word-chunk cues in word recognition" (Pressley, 1998b, p. 277). Or conversely, that "phonological factors, especially difficulties in converting spellings to sounds, [is] the primary area that differentiates skilled from less-skilled readers" (Beck, 1998, pp. 19-20).

Investigators have also amassed a portfolio of support for the position "that difficulty in learning to read is rarely the result of visual-spatial or perceptual-motor deficits" (Klenk & Kibby, 2000, p. 671; see also Adams, 1990; Shankweiler, 1991) but rather is "cognitive" in nature (Shankweiler, 1991, p. xv). Collectively, the evidence "point[s] to a phonological processing deficit as the core cause of poor reading" (Foorman et al., 1998, p. 37). That is, the "initial obstacle in learning to read [is] a difficulty in becoming aware that words can be analyzed as sequences of phonemes" (Shankweiler, 1991, p. xvi), from "problems in breaking apart words and syllables into phonemes" (Fletcher & Lyon, 1998, p. 61). In short, from "poorly developed word recognition skills" (Adams, 1998, p. 74) arising from "weaknesses in basic decoding skills" (Adams, 1994, p. 5). These investigators have confirmed that "the spelling-sound stage" (Juel, 1991, p. 774) of reading acquisition is "the critical hurdle for the child" (p. 774) in learning to read.

Concomitantly, in ascertaining "the centrality of phonology (phonics, decoding, word analysis) in reading" (Chall, 1991, p. 23), analysts have also uncovered the costs of the inability to connect sounds and letters and to unpack words. They have documented that "poor decoding skill can limit what the child reads" (Juel, 1991, p. 775) and that truncated "phonological factors may interfere with the use of language and reasoning in reading development" (Chall, 1991, p. 23). The narrative of "a deficiency in phonological processing" (Liberman et al., 1989, p. 20) has been nicely laid out by Williams (1991):

Consider what it means for a child not to have mastered phonics: he or she is stuck with a very small reading vocabulary, and one that has no way to grow with further reading practice, as oral vocabulary increases. He or she must be content with guessing at words, which good readers do not do.

The child who has not mastered phonics also makes very slow progress in achieving the stage of reading fluency and automaticity. If one reads slowly and haltingly, one cannot process the incoming information effectively with respect to its meaning, so comprehension is impaired, and certainly one's motivation to read declines. (p. 17)

Support on the second point—phonics linked to higher student achievement—is found in the importance given to phonics instruction in effective schools (Samuels, 1981; Weber, 1971) and effective reading programs (Anderson, 1998; Chall, 1991; Stein et al., 1999). As I describe in detail in Chapter 9, evidence is also discernable in studies that examine the ability of educators to intervene successfully to prevent reading disabilities from derailing students placed at risk of reading failure (Blachman et al., 1999). Adams (1998) provides a précis of the work on this topic as follows:

Reading disability can be prevented through well-designed, early instruction. However, such instruction must include attention to phonics, and it is most effective when it includes explicit, systematic instruction on the alphabetic principle, including phonemic awareness and on the spelling-sound patterns and conventions of English. (p. 86)

Research on reading instruction also reveals "ample evidence that those approaches to beginning reading that fall in the code-emphasis/ linguistic/phonics domain produce advantages in word recognition" (Beck, 1998, p. 21). Indeed, the body of scholarship both "favors the major theoretical premises on which code-emphasis approaches to reading instruction are based" (Vellutino, 1991, p. 437) and reveals "a strong relationship between phonological processing ability . . . and the acquisition of beginning reading skill" (Brown & Felton, 1990, p. 224). Or, as the National Reading Panel recently concluded, "systematic phonics instruction produce[s] a significant impact on children's growth as readers" (NICHHD, 2000b, 2:114): "development of letter-sound associations and explicit decoding instruction focusing on the sounds of words is definitely associated with later reading success" (Pressley et al., 1996).

The positive connection between phonics and reading achievement in the early grades has been drawn by a variety of reading researchers (see Adams, 1990; Chall, 1983; Pressley, 1998b; and Stanovich, 2000 for reviews). These analysts show that "phonics knowledge and the skills that come from decoding and encoding practice will make children better readers sooner" (Williams, 1991, p. 17). An emphasis on code in the reading program has been shown to be particularly efficacious for young readers (NICHHD, 2000b), and as I explore in Chapter 9, for children who "begin schooling at risk for reading failure" (Brown & Felton, 1990, p. 237), and for "low-income children and those with reading or learning disabilities" (Chall et al., 1990, p. 6; see also Adams, 1990; Pressley et al., 1996; Stanovich, 2000).

A focus on phonics is correlated with the ability of children to read both words and nonwords (Blachman et al., 1999). In addition to "facilitat[ing] word identification" (Anderson et al., 1985, p. 37), a code emphasis also "produce[s] better results for spelling and vocabulary development (Adams, 1994; Foorman, 1995; Williams, 1991) and for the development of "wider reading habits both in and out of school" (Beck, 1998, p. 15). And there is "substantial evidence that reading comprehension in later grades is correlated with the ability to decode in grades 1 and 2" (Blachman et al., 1999, p. 268). Or stated in an alternative manner, "the capacity to read with fluency and reflective comprehension depends on . . . a deep and ready knowledge of spellings and spelling-sound correspondence" (Adams, 1991, p. 42).

There is also an expanding body of research that exposes the limited capacity of non code-based strategies to support the acquisition of literacy skills and to enhance reading achievement. That is, not only does the research consistently "support beginning programs that are code-oriented as compared to those that are meaning-oriented" (Chall, 1983, p. 43), especially "holistic programs that deemphasize phonological analysis and letter-sound training" (Stanovich, 2000, p. 367), but the power of "meaning-emphasis approaches, such as forms of whole language that play down the need for explicit decoding instruction" (Pressley, 1998b, p. 115) is empirically suspect (Chall, 1983; Stanovich, 2000). As Williams (1991) notes, "there is no real data on the other [meaning-emphasis] side" (p. 13). In short, the evidence to date is "at variance with the major theoretical premises on which whole-language approaches are based" (Vellutino, 1991, p. 437).

The crux of the problem is that the cueing systems that are featured in meaning-based instruction have been shown to be considerably less effective than the phonological cueing system highlighted in code-oriented instruction (Juel, 1991). In particular, research has called into question the robustness of "semantic-contextual information and syntactical information" (Pressley, 1998b, p. 129), what Richardson (1991) refers to as "configuration" strategies (p. 2), as vehicles to facilitate the mastery of literacy skills. That is, "with regard to the role accorded context by whole-language advocates, the contradictory evidence is definitive" (Vellutino, 1991, p. 438). The notion that "reading is a context-driven process and that skilled readers use semantic and syntactic constraints in full measure to generate predictions as to the words that are likely to appear in a given context" (Vellutino, 1991, p. 437) that is at the foundation of whole-language instruction has been "greatly overestimated" (p. 438) and lacks credible support (Brown & Felton, 1990). Or cast in more direct form, "context is an insufficient and unreliable strategy" (Stein et al., 1999, p. 277).

> In contrast to the substantial data base in favor of synthetic phonics instruction and the growing data base in support of decoding by analogy, there is very little support for teaching students to decode by orienting primarily to semantic- and syntactic-contextual cues as opposed to graphemic-phonemic cues. (Pressley, 1998b, p. 147)

Anderson (1998) sums up the narrative here quite effectively when he asserts that "anyone who thinks that a child can achieve a high level of reading proficiency relying on other 'cueing systems' without mastering the letter-sound patterns of the language is simply uninformed" (p. 4).

Some Caveats

> Even while the studies collectively affirm that phonics instruction is, on average, a positive component of early reading development, they also demonstrate that there are enormous differences in the outcomes of any program depending on the particular schools, teachers, children, and implementation vagaries involved. (Adams, 1994, p. 4)

> Obviously, not all phonics-oriented reading programs are well planned and well implemented. If the program offers no justification to the child concerning its purpose or ultimate utility; if the program starts with sound/letter correspondences without adequate attention to phonological skills; if

there is only decoding and no encoding instruction; if it is all drill and no fun, that is, no games, no interesting reading materials, no opportunity for a sense of achievement; if little attention is given to reading real text, so that there is only limited practice in actually using the skills for the purpose for which they are ultimately intended; if the instructional sequence is unsystematic; if the instruction continues for too short a period of time; or if the teacher is unprepared or unwilling, or if he or she puts his or her own needs ahead of the needs of the children, then the program will not be very effective. (Williams, 1991, p. 17)

It is helpful to hold a few cautions in mind as I construct the case for keeping the "development of word recognition skills . . . paramount in beginning reading instruction" (Pressley, 1998b, p. 143). First of all, the proposition that phonics is the indispensable method in learning to read must be held concomitantly with the knowledge that "phonics is by no means all there is to learning to read" (Adams, 1994, p. 5): "letter-sound training may be a necessary component of the instructional program, it is not a sufficient one" (Vellutino, 1991, p. 441). At the macro level, phonics instruction works best when it is part of a balanced reading program: "approaches in which systematic code instruction is included alongside meaning emphasis, language instruction, and connected reading are found to result in superior reading achievement overall" (Adams, 1990, p. 49). At the micro level, phonics is one element, albeit a critical one, in the skill toolbox that youngsters need to gather on the journey to literacy mastery. Phonics needs to be "integrated into a total reading program" (Stahl, 1992, p. 622). It should not dominate reading instruction (Stahl et al., 1998). As Dieterich (cited in Chall, 1983, p. 81) cautions, we need to be "on guard against the fallacy that, if a moderate amount of phonics from the start is advantageous, a large amount will be better." Stahl (1992) recommends that "no more than 25% of reading time be spent on phonics instruction and practice" (p. 622).

Acknowledging the critical nature of phonics provides little guidance for addressing the question of how letter-sound relations should be taught. There are, as Adams (1994) observes,

literally hundreds of "phonic" programs and thousands of "phonic" techniques, and the differences among them are substantial. Across instructional programs, for example, the phonic strands differ in starting point as well as stopping point. They differ in the methods, materials, procedures, and progression for everything taught in between. And they differ in fundamental strictures and assumptions about what to and what not to teach, about when to and when not to teach, and about how to and how not to teach. Moreover, whereas some of the differences between programs are just differences, others stand as genuine conflicts and incompatibilities. (p. 5)

It is also important to note that phonics is not an "outcome" (Pearson, 1996, p. 270). It is not the goal of reading, it is "a means to an end" (NICHHD, 2000a, p. 10). The aim of "phonics instruction is to get children to notice orthographic patterns in words and to use these patterns to recognize words" (Stahl, 1992, p. 623)—"to help children read words automatically" (Stahl et al., 1998, p. 343). The goal of reading, in turn, is "to understand the messages conveyed in text" (Pressley, 1998b, p. 143), that is, "reading is always directed toward meaning" (Anderson et al., 1985, p. 44). As described earlier, phonics is the key to word recognition, which makes such understanding possible. Phonics is the starting point, automatic word recognition is the "intermediate stage" (Richardson, 1991, p. 5), and comprehension is the end point (Dole et al., 1991; Pearson, 1996; Pressley, 1998a).

Other cautions apply to phonics instruction as well. There appears to be an optimal time for phonics, primarily in the early grades before youngsters have mastered a range of reading skills (NICHHD, 2000b, Stahl, 1992). As Anderson and his colleagues (1985) remind us in *Becoming a Nation of Readers*, "phonics instruction should [be] completed by the end of the second grade" (p. 43).

Also, while it is appropriate to teach phonics and its component elements of phonemic awareness and the alphabetic principle in isolation, such training does not lead directly to reading development (Hatcher et al., 1994; Kameenui, 1998). The largest payoff comes when phonics is "combined with direct instruction in reading" (Kameenui et al., 1998, p. 61). Since a key in making a difference "is not just teaching children phonics . . . but persuading them to use it" (Adams, 1994, p. 18), students need "to apply these skills . . . in their daily reading and writing" (NICHHD, 2000a, p. 10). Or as Richardson (1991) captures it, "even the most systematic phonics approaches work better as children get increased opportunities to read children's literature" (p. 5). All of this is consistent with Cunningham's (1990) and Pressley's (1998b) findings that "phonics inside metacognitively rich instruction" (Pressley, 1998b, p. 100) is more effective than skill and drill alone. In short, the type of instruction received matters a good deal.

It is also instructive to remember that not all phonics instruction is equally valuable. As I discuss below, explicit phonics holds the high pedagogical ground. Also, because children differ in the amount of decoding skills they possess (NICHHD, 2000b,), there is not a single pattern of good teaching. Rather, in "light of this [understanding] teachers need to be flexible in their phonics instruction in order to adjust it to individual student needs" (NICHHD, 2000a, p. 11).

Finally, phonics need not be dull. As the National Reading Panel authors report, "it is critical for teachers to understand that systematic phonics instruction can be provided in an entertaining, vibrant, and creative manner" (p. 11). Nor does it need to be, nor should it be, the same for all students. Phonics instruction should "accommodate individual differences in students rather than being one-size-fits-all instruction" (Pressley, 1998b, p. 143).

Phonics Instruction

The integration of training in phonological skills with letter-sound training (or more broadly with phonically based reading instruction) may be particularly effective as a way of improving reading skills. (Hatcher et al., 1994, p. 42)

These facts and findings provide converging evidence that explicit, systematic phonics instruction is a valuable and essential part of a successful classroom reading program. (NICHHD, 2000a, p. 10)

What is important is that phonics instruction is done well. (Stahl et al., 1998, p. 339)

In this final section of the chapter, I offer some insights from the empirical literature on phonics that should inform the work of school leaders. My starting point is that because "phonics instruction is one of the essential ingredients" (Anderson et al., 1985, p. 36) in helping children learn to read, "teachers of beginning reading should present well-designed phonics instruction" (Anderson et al., 1985, p. 118): "the research quite strongly endorses the practice of incorporating activities that foster the development of both alphabetic coding and phoneme awareness as part of the instructional program" (Vellutino, 1991, p. 439). My voyage is also directed by the research that shows that "phonics can be taught" (Copeland et al., 1994, p. 30), "that

children can acquire phonemic awareness through direct instruction"
(Cunningham, 1990, p. 442), and that the alphabetic principle can be
nurtured by skilled teachers.

Need and Benefits

> Research suggests that children without phonemic awareness
> tend to be poor readers and that training in phonemic aware-
> ness can improve reading achievement. (Snider, 1995, p. 446)

> In sum, these findings led the Panel to conclude with much
> confidence that phonemic awareness training is more effective
> than alternative forms of training or no training in helping
> children acquire phonemic awareness and in facilitating
> transfer of PA skills to reading and spelling. PA training
> improves children's reading performance in various types of
> tasks, including word reading, pseudoword reading, and read-
> ing comprehension. Benefits are evident on standardized tests
> as well as experimenter-designed tests of reading and spelling.
> Improvement in reading and spelling is not short-lived but lasts
> beyond the immediate training period. (NICHHD, 2000b, 2:19)

Calls for instruction in phonics are based on four needs. First of all,
as I have explained in considerable detail earlier, phonemic awareness
is "truly critical for learning to read and write an alphabetic script"
(Adams, 1994, p. 16)—"it is clearly a domain that begs for instructional
support" (Adams, 1994, p. 16). Second, many youngsters possess very
limited decoding skills. Third, phonemic awareness and alphabetic
understanding "have not yet been incorporated on a wide scale into
reading programs" (Williams, 1991, p. 15; Blachman, 1991). Indeed,
attention to these critical foundations of literacy is often "incidental
or lacking overall" (Copeland et al., 1994, p. 40). Particularly discouraging here is research over the last thirty years that concludes that
many teachers are not sufficiently knowledgeable to teach phonics. As
Liberman, Shankweiler, and Liberman (1989) assert,

> Many teachers are being trained to teach reading without
> themselves ever having learned how an alphabetic orthogra-
> phy represents the language, why it is important for beginners
> to understand how the internal phonological structure of
> words relates to the orthography, or why it is hard for children
> to achieve this understanding. (p. 23)

Finally, it is quite clear from research over the last three decades that "developing awareness of the phonological structure of oral language that is the basis for scaffolding written language onto oral language" (Fletcher & Lyon, 1998, p. 59) is neither automatic nor does it come naturally or emerge spontaneously: "awareness of phoneme segmentation does not develop spontaneously even by adulthood but arises as a concomitant of reading instruction and experience" (Liberman et al., 1989, p. 16). And it "requires experiences above and beyond those provided by the reading of connected text" (Treiman, 1998, p. 290). Or, as Pressley (1998b) asserts, "for the most advanced levels of phoneme awareness to develop, formal instruction in reading seems essential" (p. 97).

> Useful knowledge of the spelling-to-speech correspondences of English does not come naturally. For all children, it requires a great deal of practice and for many children, it is not easy. The acquisition of this knowledge depends on developing a reflective appreciation of the phonemic structure of the spoken language; on learning about letter-sound correspondences and spelling conventions of the orthography; and on consolidating and extending this knowledge by using it in the course of one's own reading and writing. Each of these accomplishments depends, in turn, on certain insights and observations that for many if not most children are simply not forthcoming without special instructional guidance and support. (Adams, 1998, p. 74)

In summary, effective instruction in beginning reading "requires explicit instruction that informs children about phonemic awareness and the alphabetic principle and careful attention to the order in which activities are presented" (Snider, 1995, p. 446).

Evidence also converges on the benefits of providing phonics instruction (Cunningham, 1990; NICHHD, 2000a), that is, "that early and systematic instruction in decoding leads to better achievement" (Stahl et al., 1994, p. 181). Researchers consistently document the practical utility of providing explicit instruction in the area of phonemic awareness. "Phonemic awareness instruction helps children learn to read" (NICHHD, 2000b, 2:5) and does so more effectively "than alternative forms of training or no training" (2:19). It is deemed to be clearly effective in fostering (1) the "ability to manipulate phonemes" (NICHHD, 2000b, 2:40); (2) "decoding skill" (NICHHD, 2000b, 2:20) and "decoding achievement" (Chall, 1983, p. 15); (3) "the subsequent acquisition of reading skills" (Pressley, 1998b, p. 104), especially word identification; (4) the "acquisition of writing skills" (NICHHD, 2000b, 2:7); (5) "reader knowledge of orthographs and their utility in word recognition" (Pressley, 1998b, p. 267); and (6) "children's reading and spelling performance" (NICHHD, 2000b, 2:34) "in both the short and long term" (2:28). Likewise, these same analysts report that "children who develop strong letter-sound knowledge . . . perform better on all tests" (Chall, 1983, p. 17). It is important to note that these instructional benefits are robust for all groups of students but are strongest for younger children and at-risk youth (NICHHD, 2000b).

A Systematic and Explicit Platform

Intensive, explicit phonic instruction is a valuable component of beginning reading programs. (Adams, 1990, p. 53)

Systematic phonics instruction makes a more significant contribution to children's growth in reading than do alternative programs providing unsystematic or no phonics instruction. (NICHHD, 2000b, 2:132)

A Framework

Once the case is made for the importance of phonics, or for a code-based emphasis in beginning reading programs, the question of what types of phonics instruction might be most beneficial for young learners still needs to be answered. Instruction in phonics is generally "described in terms of the methods used to teach children about letter-sound relations and how to use letter-sounds to read or spell" (NICHHD, 2000b, 2:123). Stahl, Duffy-Hester, and Stahl (1998) list five instructional strategies in phonics: analytic, synthetic, spelling-based, analogy-based, and embedded. The NICHHD National Reading Panel (2000b) defines these core methods as follows:

Analogy Phonics—Teaching students unfamiliar words by analogy to known words (e.g., recognizing that the rime segment of an unfamiliar word is identical to that of a familiar word, and then blending the known rime with the new word onset, such as reading *brick* by recognizing that *–ick* is contained in the known word *kick*, or reading *stump* by analogy to *jump*).

Analytic Phonics—Teaching students to analyze letter-sound relations in previously learned words to avoid pronouncing sounds in isolation.

Embedded Phonics—Teaching students phonics skills by embedding phonics instruction in text reading, a more implicit approach that relies to some extent on incidental learning.

Phonics through Spelling—Teaching students to segment words into phonemes and to select letters for those phonemes (i.e., teaching students to spell words phonetically).

Synthetic Phonics—Teaching students explicitly to convert letters into sounds (phonemes) and then blend the sounds to form recognizable words. (p. 8)

At the risk of blurring some finer points, the central distinction in the methods is between "direct-synthetic" (Chall, 1983, p. 42) forms of instruction in which "students are systematically taught letter-sound associations and how to blend the sounds made by letters to pronounce and recognize words" (Pressley, 1998b, p. 125) and alternative methods that hold that "sounds are not to be isolated and thus letter sounds are rarely taught as such" (Chall, 1983, p. 22) and in which instruction in blending is eschewed. In general, in these alternative approaches, "sounds are . . . to be inferred from words" (p. 22).

A point of interest to school leaders is that instructional strategies in phonics can be defined with reference to a handful of central characteristics—systematicity, explicitness, intensity, and directness— that are best arranged on continua. To begin with, approaches vary in the degree of "systematicity of instruction" (Kameenui et al., 1998, p. 52). The NICHHD National Reading Panel (2000b) asserts that "the hallmark of a systematic phonics approach or program is that a sequential set of phonics elements is delineated and these elements are taught along a dimension of explicitness depending on the type of phonics method employed" (p. 8). In systematic phonics instruction, "a full array of letter-sound correspondences to be taught are identified" (NICHHD, 2000b, 2:99). On the other end of this first continuum, one finds "less systematic instruction of phonics" (Pressley, 1998b, p. 147). Here, phonics instruction is provided "on an as-needed basis" (p. 147). It is a type of "incidental phonics instruction" (NICHHD, 2000a, p. 8) in which "the teacher does not follow a planned sequence of phonics elements to guide instruction but highlights particular elements opportunistically when they appear in text" (p. 8): "phonics lessons are conducted opportunistically in the context of meaningful reading and writing" (Snow et al., 1998, p. 199).

In addition, phonics instruction "can be identified by examining both how letter-sound correspondences are taught and how students are taught to read unfamiliar words" (Stein et al., 1999, p. 276). That is, these various methods of phonics instruction are also characterized by their degree of explicitness. In more explicit phonemes instruction, "the sounds associated with letters are identified in isolation and then 'blended' together to form words" (Anderson et al., 1985, p. 39). Explicit phonics programs "provide extensive instruction to develop children's knowledge of the alphabetic system and how to use this knowledge to read words in and out of text" (NICHHD, 2000b, 2:114). There is a definitive focus on "systematic instruction of skills" (Pressley, 1998b, p. 278). Thus "in an explicit phonics approach, the predominant word identification strategy is phonologically based" (Stein et al., 1999, p. 276): "letter-sound correspondences and spelling connections are explicitly taught and interactively practiced and extended" (Snow et al., 1998, p. 204). In explicit instruction, "teaching may be *connected* to what students are reading and writing, but not necessarily be *integrated* into those authentic experiences" (Duffy-Hester, 1999, p. 488). In less explicit or more implicit phonics instruction, "the sound associated with a letter is never supposed to be pronounced in isolation" (Anderson et al., 1985, p. 39). In "an implicit phonics approach . . . students are asked to identify the sounds associated with individual letters in the context of whole words" (Stein et al., 1999, p. 276).

The level of intensity is the third characteristic of phonics instruction. An intensive approach "means spending a lot of time and making good use of that time" (Anderson, 1998, p. 5). Intensity implies a heavier concentration of phonics instruction and an abundance of "opportunities to learn letter-sound patterns" (Anderson, 1998, p. 5). It means that basic phonics skills are thoroughly taught.

Directness, in turn, comprises two ingredients. It includes the extent to which "carefully designed sequences of instruction" (Kameenui et al., 1998, p. 52) are prevalent in the reading program, sequencing that moves the reader from easier to harder concepts (Snider, 1995). It also refers to the degree of teacher centeredness and the amount of "direct teacher instruction" (Stahl et al., 1998, p. 342) or "direct phonic[s] teaching" (Hatcher et al., 1994, p. 55).

The Evidence

The central message for school leaders here is that "not all [phonics] interventions are equal" (Snow et al., 1998, p. 200). While the question has not been completely answered (Stahl et al., 1998), the preponderance of evidence and all the trend lines suggest that "the ability to read requires a number of skills that must be developed via direct and informed instruction" (Fletcher & Lyon, 1998, p. 81). Indeed, Stanovich (2000) maintains "that direct instruction in alphabetic coding facilitates early reading acquisition is one of the most well established conclusions in all of behavioral science" (p. 399). In short, employing the framework I just introduced, the evidence argues for a reading program that features a synthetic approach to word identification and that addresses phonics in a systematic, explicit, and direct manner and with a high degree of intensity.

On the topic of method, there is considerable evidence that "direct-synthetic phonics instruction works best" (Adams, 1990, p. 49), that "direct- [synthetic] phonics seems . . . to be more effective than indirect-analytic phonics" (Chall, 1983, p. 21). Adams (1990) sums up the story line here quite nicely as follows:

> There was but one single class of instructional methods that resulted in gains significantly larger than any of the others. This class of methods consisted in teaching students about letters and letter sounds, first separately and then blended together. It consisted, in short, of explicit, systematic phonics. (p. 48)

Turning to the defining "characteristics" I delineated above, there is a fair amount of support for the claim that a program that highlights explicitness and systematicity will be more productive in terms of student learning than a program that is more indirect, more implicit, and less structured. Indeed, nearly all of the available evidence finds that "explicit, systematic phonics is a singularly successful mode of teaching young or slow learners to read" (Adams, 1990, p. 56), and that "an introductory method that provides them with direct instruction in what they need to know is critical" (Liberman et al., 1989, p. 24).

To begin with, reading research holds "that specially designed instruction generally tends to produce more learning than less systematic instruction" (Pflaum, Walberg, Karegianes, & Rasher, 1980, p. 17), and that "early and systematic instruction in decoding leads to better reading achievement than later and less systematic instruction" (Stahl et al., 1994, p. 181). Indeed, the power of systematic instruction and "organized exposure" (Stahl, 1998, p. 42) vis-à-vis "unsystematic exposure" (p. 42) in phonics is widely acknowledged in the reading research community (NICHHD, 2000a).

In a similar vein, "the amount of improvement in word-reading skill appears to be associated with the degree of explicitness in the instructional method" (Snow et al., 1998, p. 206). Every major research review on the issue over the last three decades "supports a prominent role for explicit instruction in phonics and phonological skills" (Fletcher & Lyon, 1998, p. 50), especially "for enhancing the achievement of disadvantaged students" (Snow et al., 1998, p. 177) and "students who may be at risk of reading failure" (Stein et al., 1999, p. 276). In addition, explicit phonics instruction is an important characteristic of high-performing teachers (Wharton-McDonald et al., 1998) and a defining element of effective reading programs (Stein et al., 1999; Wilder, 1977). Implicit or "incidental instruction" (Foorman, 1995, p. 385) in phonics, on the other hand, is less effective in helping students master essential literacy skills (Foorman, 1995; NICHHD, 2000b).

Concomitantly, data are accumulating to support the claim that "greater intensity . . . of early phonological training" (Snow et al., 1998, p. 250) is connected to enhanced reading performance, that "stronger phonics" (Chall, 1983, p. 42) instruction is more effective, and that "intensive training in phonics produce[s] superior word reading skills" (NICHHD, 2000b, 2:126). Nicholson (1999) provides the conclusion from the research as follows: "intensive early instruction in the skills of phonemic awareness and letter-sound relationships will enable children from all social backgrounds to get off to a better start in learning to read and spell" (p. 18).

Finally, scholars reviewing the reading literature from a number of perspectives have touted the "lasting effects of direct instruction" (Snow et al., 1998, p. 176) in decoding. They affirm "the critical importance of direct, explicit teaching in the development of phonemic awareness" (Lundberg, 1991, p. 52), especially in comparison to "indirect, intrinsic approaches" (Pressley, 1998b, p. 127) and whole-language and embedded-phonics instruction (Snow et al., 1998): "We do know that methods that emphasize direct instruction in alphabetic reading skills produce better growth in these skills than methods that do not" (Torgesen, 1997, p. 39).

A Caveat

To make the case that systematic, explicit phonics instruction should be featured in beginning reading programs—that "the sound-symbol system of print needs to be systematically and explicitly taught to beginning readers and writers in school" (Purcell-Gates, 1998, p. 68)—is not the same as building the case for a single method or approach. As Anderson (1998) reminds us, affirming that "explicit or direct phonics instruction . . . is the proven way" (p. 4) is not the same as arguing that it is "the only way" (p. 4). Indeed, there is evidence that other phonics methods (e.g., the analogy-based strategy) can be effective when used in conjunction with more explicit phonics instruction (Pressley, 1998b; Stahl et al., 1998). More implicit and more incidental approaches can also prove effective if "used along with, but not in place of, explicit activities" (Snider, 1995, p. 449; Purcell-Gates, 1998). The central conclusion here is that explicit, systematic, direct phonics instruction for beginning readers is essential, not that it represents all that can or should be done to help youngsters learn to read words. "Employing only one approach to the exclusion of the other[s]" (Pressley, 1998b, p. 149) is not a productive way to attack phonics instruction (Anderson et al., 1985; Fletcher & Lyon, 1998). My caveat also extends to ensuring the deployment of decoding instruction that is "flexible enough to permit students to use the approach or approaches that work for them" (Pressley, 1998b, p. 147). Or, as Purcell-Gates (1998) so nicely phrases it: "At all times, the teachers of beginning readers and writers need to keep in mind the variant ways that their learners' speech dialects will map onto print and to allow for this in their instruction" (p. 68).

Multiple Opportunities to Practice

Children learn to read by reading words, in stories or in lists. (Stahl, 1992, p. 622)

Practice given in reading words is extremely important. (Stahl et al., 1998, p. 342)

Analysts who have forged the knowledge base in beginning reading offer a number of other important instructional insights that should direct the work of school leaders as they help build effective reading programs for young children. A critical conclusion is that, because training that helps youngsters apply phonics skills in reading words produces "much larger . . . reading outcomes" (NICHHD, 2000b, 2:33), phonics instruction should provide ample opportunities to read words, in addition to blending, segmenting, and sound-to-letter work (Stahl et al., 1998). Or, as the NICHHD National Reading Panel Subgroups (2000b) authors capture it, "in addition to teaching PA skills with letters, it is important for teachers to help children make the connection between the PA skills taught and their application to reading and writing tasks" (2:33). "Phonics is much more likely to be useful when children hear the sounds associated with most letters both in isolation and in words" (Anderson et al., 1985, p. 118).

According to Stahl, Duffy-Hester, and Stahl (1998), three types of practice in reading words can be emphasized in a phonics program: "reading words in isolation, reading words in stories (i.e., expository and narrative texts), and writing words" (p. 342). Research suggests that a balanced portfolio of all three forms of practice can be helpful. On the first issue, it is instructive to remember that reading words in isolation is not problematic. Rather, it is important "for children to look at words in isolation at times so that they can examine patterns in words without the distraction of context" (Stahl et al., 1998, p. 342). Thus "good phonics instruction might contain a moderate amount of word practice in isolation" (p. 342).

Although it is generally necessary for phonics to be taught directly, and although it is quite appropriate for these skills to be honed in reading isolated words, phonics instruction is "most effective when it is integrated with the teaching of reading" (Snider, 1995, p. 446), when instruction "provides opportunities to use what has been learned in reading words in sentences and stories" (Anderson et al., 1985, p. 42). Of special relevance to the issue of practice in conjunction with reading text is the need to employ texts "emphasizing graphemic-phonemic elements that the child knows at some level already (i.e., through instruction)" (Pressley, 1998b, p. 128). In other words, the need to keep the spotlight focused on decodable text, that is, "connected text containing a high percentage of words conforming to the letter-sound correspondences that have previously been introduced" (Stein et al., 1999, p. 277).

It is by employing texts featuring "a high percentage of words that contain letter-sound correspondences that were taught" (Stahl et al., 1998, p. 342), students have "the opportunity to apply their newly acquired phonics skills" (Stein et al., 1999, p. 277), "to practice, extend, and refine their knowledge of letter-sound relationships" (Anderson et al., 1985, p. 47). This is an especially important guideline for school leaders to orient around for two reasons: (1) because "the type of text selection students read influences the development of phonologically based word identification strategies" (Stein et al., 1999, p. 277), and (2) because studies over time have consistently shown that basal readers, which are the backbone of most early reading programs, "typically contain a low percentage of decodable text" (p. 277), that is, "many texts do not match what is being taught" (Stahl et al., 1998, p. 343).

Turning to the third leg of the practice stool—practice in writing—
"a great deal of evidence indicates that giving children the opportunity to use invented spelling is a prime way to help them develop
phonemic awareness and the alphabetic principle" (Copeland et al.,
1994, p. 29), which are the heart and soul of phonics work. In addition
to invented spelling—"the practice of encouraging children to spell
words as they sound" (Snow et al., 1998, p. 187)—"writing words
from dictation . . . [is a] valuable way of practicing letter-sound correspondence" (Stahl et al., 1998, p. 343). Both forms of writing practice
"promote growth in word recognition" (Copeland et al., 1994, p. 29),
in "the acquisition of conventional spelling" (Snow et al., 1998, p. 187),
and in "help[ing] children learn to read" (NICHHD, 2000b, 2:34).

Related Instruction Insights

> However, the findings suggest that when multiple PA skills
> are the objective, it is prudent to teach one at a time until
> each is mastered before moving on to the next. (NICHHD,
> 2000b, 2:31)

Scholars in the area of beginning reading leave us with a few final
insights about productive phonics instruction. They help us understand that while it is often useful to teach phonics skills directly, it is
generally desirable to provide students "with an appreciation of task
requirements and an awareness of the utility of their actions"
(Cunningham, 1990, p. 435). Meaning can and should be brought
to skills-based instruction, for, as Cunningham (1990) maintains, "in
general, instructional programs which emphasize conceptual or met-
alevel rather than simply procedural knowledge appear to provide a
stronger base for the retention and transfer of information across
situations" (p. 431). In particular, for early reading instruction understanding "of what reading is all about, how print functions, what
stories are, and so on" (Stahl, 1992, p. 620) provides context or "met-
alevel knowledge" (Cunningham, 1990, p. 435) that facilitates reading
acquisition.

The National Reading Panel (NICHHD, 2000b) also provides
some concrete research-anchored advice for teaching phonics. These
authors report that small-group instruction is an especially efficacious
format for developing phonics skills. They suggest 30 minutes as the
outside limit on individual phonics training sessions. Their review of
the literature confirms that focused attention on one or two skills is
more productive "than when a multitude of skills are taught" (2:21).

Summary

In the next chapter, I unpack the significance of developing a balanced literacy curriculum. In this chapter, I provided evidence why phonics should be featured in the curriculum program in the early grades. I began by dissecting phonics into its essential elements. I reviewed the evidence linking phonics with reading acquisition. I closed the chapter by presenting some information on the teaching of phonics and reviewing important caveats to keep in mind as phonics instruction unfolds in schools.

8

Deepening
the Curriculum

In terms of practical application, the issue of method preference
is an important one. (Pflaum et al., 1980, p. 12)

The materials and activities used in developing reading skill
are of critical importance. (Adams, 1990, p. 5)

There is considerable evidence that methods and materials do
make a difference in students' reading achievement. (Chall,
1991, p. 24)

My analysis of curriculum in Chapters 7 through 10 is built on
seven findings from the literacy research. First, as the introductory
quotes to this chapter attest, method matters. Cast in alternative
fashion, "if the method is limited, students' learning will be limited
no matter how talented the teacher" (Stigler & Hiebert, 1999, p. 175).
Second, "curricula can be seen as vehicles for specifying and promoting valued forms of expertise" (McNaughton, 1999, p. 8). Third,
"there is more than one route to successful, or at least adequate, reading performance" (Konold et al., 1999, p. 13). Fourth, while "literacy
acquisition is a complex process" (NICHHD, 2000b, 2:43), and while
there has been considerable debate among scholars about whether
"one particular method or approach to beginning reading is better
than another" (Chall, 1983, p. 3), the last two decades have

furnished us with some robust information about productive approaches to ensuring early reading success (Adams, 1990; NICHHD, 2000b). Fifth, whatever methods are agreed upon need to hold for all youngsters: "the same types of materials and activities [should be] experienced by all students regardless of ability" (Pressley, 1998b, p. 160), and these common approaches should grow from a common set of learning objectives (Hall & Moats, 1999; Hallinger & Murphy, 1985). Sixth, as I discussed in Chapter 7, method must be adjudicated on the basis of connection to "the main task[s] of reading in the early grades" (Chall et al., 1990, p. 44), that is, "promot[ing] facility in word identification" (Vellutino, 1991, p. 442) or "teach[ing] the children to recognize words they already know" (Chall et al., 1990, p. 44) and "foster[ing] the disposition as well as the ability to read" (Adams, 1994, p. 3). Finally, curriculum does not occur in a vacuum. It is mediated by instruction. That is, "reading curricula do not, by themselves, determine the success or failure of a school's reading program" (Armor et al., 1976, p. 32). The power of the curriculum is intricately fastened to the quality of implementation.

There are a variety of organizational arrangements that can be employed to expose the elements of productive curricular programs. The framework that I use for the core program features two central dimensions. I tuck issues that often appear in the foreground of this discussion, for example, specificity of objectives, relevance of materials, flexibility and individualization, and so forth within these larger domains. In Chapter 7, I began by exploring the importance of explicit instruction in phonics, an emphasis on core-oriented curriculum in helping young children learn to read well. In the current chapter, I discuss the importance of deepening the curricular program. I begin by examining the significance of creating a balanced reading program, one that blends together central elements from the literacy palette into an integrated and coherent picture. I also describe the critical role literate classroom and school environments serve in ensuring youngsters master literacy skills.

Creating a Balanced Program

> Through implementing balanced reading instruction programs, we are more likely to support the reading and overall literacy growth of the children we teach, particularly children who struggle with reading. (Duffy-Hester, 1999, p. 488)

Low-income children benefit most from programs that work best for most children—a strong reading program that provides for learning skills as well as wide reading in the primary grades. (Chall et al., 1990, p. 167)

Outstanding primary-level literacy teachers (defined by their positive effects on the literacy achievement of their students) balance elements of whole language (e.g., immersion in authentic literature and writing experiences) and systematic skills instruction. (Pressley, 1998b, p. 186)

Over the last twenty years, research has taught us that, in addition to keeping one eye focused on phonological awareness, "balance is critical" (Raphael, 1998, p. 167); an "either/or mentality in thinking about beginning reading programs" (Manning, 1995, p. 653) has not served us well. An explicit focus on phonics is a "necessary but not sufficient condition" (Foorman et al., 1997, p. 255). Investigators have shown that "strong administrators promote balanced reading programs" (Sherman, 2001, p. 7). While the "jury is still out on the exact nature of balancing that works" (Pressley, 1998b, p. 182), a variety of scholars have identified the elements of the balancing equation. For example, according to Au, Carroll, and Scheu (2000), a balanced literacy curriculum attends thoughtfully to six dimensions: ownership, voluntary reading, reading comprehension, the writing process, language and vocabulary knowledge, and word reading and spelling strategies identification (p. 38). For Hall and Moats (1999), a comprehensive and balanced literacy program requires that the following "components . . . be taught in combination [and] in a logical sequence" (p. 14):

- Speech sound, or phonological awareness
- Letter recognition
- Sound-symbol connections (sound-letter correspondence)
- Advanced word attack
- Sight vocabulary
- Fluent reading of text
- Spelling
- Understanding the language in books (words, sentences, paragraphs)
- Written composition
- Listening and speaking (pp. 14-15)

Pressley's (1998b) research suggests that the following factors are carefully weighed in balanced literacy programs:

- Extensive reading at the heart of language arts instruction
- Diverse grouping patterns (e.g., whole group instruction, small-group instruction, cooperative learning experiences, individual reading)
- Teaching of both word-level and higher-order (e.g., comprehension, critical thinking) skills and processes
- Development of student background knowledge
- Regular instruction in writing, including lower-order mechanical skills and higher-order composition skills (e.g., planning, drafting, revising as a process)
- Extensive evaluation of literacy competencies using diverse assessments
- Integration of literacy and content-area instruction
- Efforts to promote student motivation for reading and writing (pp. 193-194)

I employ these and other designs to explore balanced literacy instruction in this section. Before I turn to that assignment, some points about "balance" need clarification.

First of all, it is important to establish that balance is neither a fixed idea nor a set mixture of practices. For example, research helps us see that the components vary across age and grade level (Stahl et al., 1994).

> Thus, learning to recognize words may involve radically different instruction as children go through the grades. In the awareness stage, children may benefit from exposure to materials, in an activity-based classroom congruous with whole language principles, as long as adequate attention is paid to phonological awareness. In the accuracy phase, children need more direct instruction, but this instruction can be provided in a variety of classroom approaches. In the fluency stage, children need practice reading texts at an appropriate level, often using rereading. (Stahl, 1998, p. 43)

Likewise, the elements needed to create balance are expressed differently depending on the literacy backgrounds students bring to school.

Children who have already developed phonics skills and can apply them appropriately in the reading process do not require the same level and intensity of phonics instruction provided to children at the initial phases of reading acquisition. (NICHHD, 2000a, p. 11)

Children who enter first grade with a limited literacy background may need more direct instruction to develop concepts that should have been learned through rich home experiences with literacy. Children with stronger literacy backgrounds may benefit from more time to choose their reading, with teacher support to read more and more complex materials. (Stahl, 1998, p. 55)

Also, although it is appropriate to characterize a balanced literacy program as employing "a wide curriculum," that is, "one that provide[s] a range of multifaceted activities that enable teaching and learning to take place on a number of dimensions and in a number of different activity contexts" (McNaughton, 1999, p. 9), it is important to note that the elements are "deliberately integrated" (Wharton-McDonald et al., 1998, p. 114). Balance eschews raw eclecticism, with its accompanying fragmentation and inefficiency (Fountas & Pinnell, 1999). Balance is not simply a layer cake of all types of elements outlined above (Stahl et al., 1998). Neither is it simply "adding phonics instruction to literature-based instruction" (Stahl, 1998, p. 32), a process in which "the various components from the various philosophical stances [are] stitched together with the loosest sutures" (Stahl, 1998, p. 32). It is not just "a little of this and a little of that" (Fountas & Pinnell, 1999, p. 177), nor is it the result of teachers' "failure to firmly commit to a particular philosophy" (Stahl, 1997, p. 25). Rather, balance represents a type of "principled eclecticism" (p. 25), "a well planned . . . and highly structured" (Weber, 1971, p. 16) pattern of connecting best practices across an array of instructional designs and philosophies (Stahl, 1997), grounded in theory and practice (Duffy-Hester, 1999). As such, balanced literacy programs combine elements in ways that "create instruction that is more than the sum of its parts" (Pressley, 1998b, p. 1).

Underscoring Skills and Literacy

The point is that phonics knowledge and decoding skill are the heart of reading, and that good phonics instruction is well integrated with the rest of reading instruction, which, most importantly, includes the provision of sufficient and appropriate text for students to read. (Williams, 1991, p. 17)

The overarching conclusion is that balanced elementary instruction—that is, a balancing of whole language and skills components—seems more defensible than instruction that is only immersion in reading and writing, on the one hand, or predominantly skills driven, on the other. (Pressley, 1998b, p. 265)

Developing balance in the literacy curriculum for the early years is first and foremost about acknowledging that "neither extreme of the current great debate in beginning reading is likely to lead to maximum student achievement in literacy" (Wharton-McDonald et al., 1998, p. 122; Turner, 1989). While it is clear from the analyses in the last chapter that an explicit focus on phonics is critical to success in the early grades, balance rests upon a rejection of the "reductionistic dichotomy [of] only phonics *or* only whole language" (Pressley, 1998b, p. 134). It encompasses a willingness to confront the fact "that both sides in the current great debate are wrong, that excellent elementary instruction is much more than the beginning reading instruction that either of the extreme groups holds dear" (p. 181). It is a recognition that "research supports a balanced approach" (Vellutino, 1991, p. 442) or a "balanced perspective for literacy instruction" (Morrow et al., 1999, p. 474) and that "teachers whose students [are] the highest achievers offer primary-level literacy instruction that include[s] a balance of whole-language practices and skills instruction" (Wharton-McDonald et al., 1998, p. 122).

The classrooms where reading and writing seem to be going best are ones in which there is a lot of coverage of skills, and a great deal of teacher support as children apply the skills they are learning to the reading of excellent literature and to writing. (Pressley, 1998b, p. 270)

It is an explicit acceptance that the calculus of early reading instruction is a "balancing of skills and whole language" (Pressley, 1998b, p. 134). Balance affirms "the importance of teaching children explicitly about the code of English orthography and in noting that good readers must have access to many experiences with literacy that go beyond the specifics of phonics instruction" (Snow et al., 1998, p. 174).

A balanced reading curriculum is based on the knowledge that both the skills-based model and language model are insufficient (Anderson et al., 1985; NICHHD, 2000a; Stanovich, 2000), that neither "constitute[s] a complete reading program" (NICHHD, 2000b, 2:6). Such a curriculum operates from a platform that each dimension has its own place in a reading program (Stahl, 1997) and "that whole language and explicit decoding approaches produce complementary advantages" (Pressley et al., 1996, p. 252): "authentic reading and writing are important in the development of literacy, but systematic instruction in skills is also very important" (Pressley, 1998b, p. 21). Balance privileges research that shows that "explicit decoding instruction and whole language make unique contributions to the development of competence in literacy" (Pressley et al., 1996, p. 251), and that "practice drawn from both are needed to meet the different needs of children" (Stahl et al., 1994, p. 182).

A number of reading scholars help us see more clearly what we mean when we observe that "combination approaches work better than any single approach" (Hall & Cunningham, 1996, p. 196). They explore more deeply what balance is not. Thus "this new approach is much more than an unsatisfactory compromise between two schools of thought. The more sophisticated approach emphasizes the importance of specific skills for specific children at specific times, in the context of a literature-rich program. No pieces are left out" (Hall & Moats, 1999, pp. 26-27). It is not about "provid[ing] mixed instructional messages" but about "meld[ing] these different approaches so they can be used to achieve different goals in the same classroom" (Stahl, 1997, p. 25).

> Balanced instruction means much more systematic instruction of skills than does any version of whole language, with its emphasis on teaching only when there is demonstrated need. Balance also means much more involvement with literature and writing than occurs in many skills emphasis classrooms. (Pressley, 1998b, p. 282)

It is a mixture of "reading instruction between direct instruction of skills and whole language, using the strengths of each" (Stahl, 1998, p. 53). Balance holds that it is "necessary for literacy development to proceed at once from the parts to the whole (consistent with a skills-based, hierarchical model of instruction) and from the whole to the parts (consistent with the whole-language approach to instruction)" (Wharton-McDonald et al., 1998, pp. 122-123). It recognizes "that children learning to read require concepts about the broader purposes of printed language, as well as the specific skills required to recognize letters and words and match letters and sounds" (Anderson et al., 1985, p. 31). The story line for schools is that "in addition to—and often as part of explicit skills instruction . . . teachers [should] provide many opportunities for students to engage in reading and writing activities" (Wharton-McDonald et al., 1988, p. 114).

In conclusion, on the first level the call for a balanced program is an appeal "to develop primary-level instruction that is rich in skills instruction and whole language immersion" (Pressley, 1998b, p. 183), a curriculum that "incorporate[s] much from whole language but include[s] more teacher-directed instruction, especially in terms of decoding and comprehension strategies" (Stahl et al., 1994, p. 182). Thus, "the most sensible beginning-reading curriculum should be a balance of skills development and authentic reading and writing" (Pressley, 1998b, p. 181). It is the curriculum that "is the best bet for maintaining and even enhancing student motivation to do literate things, providing students with the skills they need to be successful in reading and writing and having them practice those skills by reading interesting books and writing about topics that are important to them" (p. 284).

Ensuring a Variety of Learning Experiences

A balanced approach to literacy instruction calls for a curriculum framework that gives reading and writing equal status. Such a framework recognizes the importance of both the cognitive and affective dimensions of literacy. It acknowledges the meaning-making involved in the full process of reading and writing, while recognizing the importance of the strategies and skills used by proficient readers and writers. (Au et al., 2000, p. 35)

Thus, the "return" to balanced reading instruction is in fact a return to a circumstance that has never occurred before— a concurrent emphasis on decoding, comprehension, and motivation. (Stahl, 1998, p. 35)

While balance is, to a great extent, about "instruction in skills integrated with literature" (Hall & Moats, 1999, p. 21), it is also more than this. It is a product of the thoughtful "drawing on multiple theoretical perspectives" (Duffy-Hester, 1999, p. 487). As implied in the discussion above, balance also means accepting that "attention to basic reading skills [is] the essence" (Samuels, 1981, p. 264) of good beginning reading programs, while acknowledging that "this does not deny or diminish the fact that constructing meaning from textual material is the most important goal of reading" (Kameenui et al., 1998, p. 47; Brown & Felton, 1990). That is, it necessitates "a concurrent emphasis on decoding, comprehension, and motivation" (Stahl, 1998, p. 35). Or, as Fletcher and Lyon (1998) maintain, a literacy "balanced diet" (Sherman, 2001, p. 15) argues for "an emphasis on developing word recognition skills as part of a complete approach to reading instruction" (Fletcher & Lyon, 1998, p. 80).

> Systematic phonics instruction is only one component—albeit a necessary component—of a total reading program; systematic phonics instruction should be integrated with other reading instruction in phonemic awareness, fluency, and comprehension strategies to create a complete reading program. (NICHHD, 2000a, p. 11)

Stated in an alternative fashion, balance suggests stressing both "basic and more cognitively challenging material" (Puma et al., 1997, p. 4). In short, a balanced reading curriculum highlights several important goals as well as varied approaches to instruction.

Balance also speaks to the issue of materials. On one hand, it means not permitting any particular materials to overwhelm the curriculum—or what Chall and her colleagues (1990) label "the exclusive use of one focus" (p. 152), a situation often found in American classrooms in which "reading from basal reading series accounts for 75% to 90% of classroom reading instruction time" (NICHHD, 2000b, 4:48). On the flip side, it conveys the marshaling of a "breadth of materials" (Wilder, 1977, p. 275) and the conscious use of an assortment of "meaningful and interesting" (Samuels, 1981, p. 268), relevant, and structured literacy materials. Balance denotes student "access to an array of appropriate texts" (Allington, 1997b, p. 9), including "predictable texts" (Pikulski, 1994, p. 38) and challenging materials, with careful matching to students' instructional levels (Fountas & Pinnell, 1999; Snow et al., 1991; Stahl et al., 1994). The literacy curriculum should include all types of books, newspapers, magazines, documents, basal readers, and so forth, although workbook pages and worksheets should be de-emphasized (Anderson et al., 1985; Stahl, 1997; Walmsley & Allington, 1995). Students "should sample the full range of fiction and nonfiction genres" (Walmsley & Allington, 1995, p. 31). On a macro level, balance refers to the "use of multiple reading programs in every classroom" (Fisher & Adler, 1999, p. 21; Weber, 1971).

Also integral to the dynamic of proportion in literacy programs is the focus on "diverse learning tasks" (Duffy-Hester, 1999, p. 490) and "different kinds of literate activity" (Fountas & Pinnell, 1999, p. 166), with a variety of reading formats. That is, "students are provided with varied opportunities to engage in reading in the classroom program" (Duffy-Hester, 1999, p. 490). Students "experience literacy in a variety of forms" (Morrow et al., 1999, p. 474), "including students reading along with teacher, echo and choral reading, shared reading, students reading aloud with others, daily silent reading, student rereading of books and stories, and reading homework" (Pressley, 1998b, p. 158). Provisions are made for "whole group, small group, paired, and one-to-one instruction" (Morrow et al., 1999, p. 474). Many different components of the reading program are visible, including "developmental, recreational, functional and diagnostic reading" (Patty et al., 1996, p. 73). "Voluntary reading" (Au et al., 2000, p. 38) mixes with teacher-determined activities. As noted above, familiar texts and familiar materials blend in with more challenging reading material. Many types of reading are stressed. Independent reading, guided reading, and shared reading are all emphasized (Duffy-Hester, 1999; Fountas & Pinnell, 1999). Repeated reading and frequent opportunities to read aloud are provided in balanced early literacy programs (Dowhower, 1987; Eldredge, 1990). So too are social and cooperative forms of literacy (Jonson, 1998). In short, in a balanced program students are "afforded opportunities to read diverse texts in a variety of ways" (Duffy-Hester, 1999, p. 489) and "for a variety of purposes—for pleasure and enjoyment, for information, [and] for intellectual growth" (Walmsley & Allington, 1995, p. 31).

A balanced approach to literacy necessitates a curriculum design that "prominently include[s] writing activities" (Pikulski, 1994, p. 36). Phonics emphasis is not seen as "an excuse for not having the time to give students real writing experiences" (Copeland et al., 1994, p. 41). As Anderson and his colleagues (1985) aver, "to learn to read, children's environment must be rich in experiences with written language" (p. 31). Or alternatively, since "children's early writing experiences can play an invaluable role in the development of phonemic awareness" (Copeland et al., 1994, p. 34) and since writing "contributes substantially to children's learning to read words" (Williams et al., 2000, p. 6), that is, "writing [is] a positive component of beginning reading instruction" (Adams, 1990, p. 42), "effective teachers encourage frequent writing of prose to enable deeper understanding of what is read" (American Federation of Teachers, 1999, p. 22).

In a comprehensive literacy program, the focus on writing is itself balanced, stressing a variety of types of writing (Pressley et al., 2000; Snow et al., 1991), including writing stories, developing written responses to stories, journal writing, dictation of stories to be penned by others, shared writing, and writing at home (Morrow et al., 1999). Children should be

> given regular opportunities to communicate their ideas in written form on a variety of topics (ranging from their own experiences and imagination to subject area topics), for a variety of purposes (ranging from expressing their own feelings to informing teachers or others what they know, exploring new topics, or persuading others to their point of view), and to a variety of audiences (ranging from the student himself to the teacher to peers). (Walmsley & Allington, 1995, p. 31)

And writing should be integrated into reading activities and "into the content areas" (Morrow et al., 1999, p. 466); that is, "writing across the curriculum is a significant component of the literacy program" (Patty et al., 1996, p. 7).

Because "learning to be a writer is accomplished through thousands of varied experiences in producing writing" (Fountas & Pinnell, 1999, p. 176), in a balanced program writing should be a daily classroom activity (Pikulski, 1994). As with reading, writing should reinforce the development of skills and promote the construction of meaning (Au et al., 2000; Knapp & Needels, 1991). It must allow children to "communicate their own ideas" (Snow et al., 1991, p. 168) to "real audiences" (Anderson et al., 1985, p. 80).

Creating a Literate Environment

> Analyses of schools that have been successful in promoting independent reading suggest that one of the keys is ready access to books. (Anderson et al., 1985, p. 78)

> A convergence of evidence also exists on the need for children to have access to a rich and varied supply of books and stories that are of appropriate difficulty and engaging. In other words, attractive and well-stocked schools and classroom libraries are important factors in developing early reading. (Allington, 1997a, p. 32)

Schools (and homes) that promote mastery of reading and writing "immerse children in the world of literacy" (Mattson, 1994, p. 60; Postlethwaite & Ross, 1992). They are places with "print-rich environments" (Patty et al., 1996, p. 7). They are forums "rich with accessible materials" (Morrow et al., 1999, p. 469) that actively involve children with books and other literacy materials (Fountas & Pinnell, 1999; Huck, 1999). They recognize that a focus on systematic phonics "does not need to diminish the development of a language rich environment" (Beck, 1998, p. 28).

The Importance of a Print-Rich Environment

The classroom must be alive with materials that attract students' attention and support their learning. (Fountas & Pinnell, 1999, p. 180)

In a print-rich environment, students are drawn to reading (Neuman, 1999): "placing young children in environments that invite and support literacy stimulates them to do things that are literature" (Pressley et al., 2000, p. 27). As a starting point, we know that "when classroom life is rich in literature and authentic reading, students are more motivated" (Pressley, 1998b, p. 249). In addition to promoting early literacy development, these cultures foster in children a "love of reading" (Sherman, 2001, p. 6) and they plant seeds "to support the lifetime reading habit" (Sanacore, 1997, p. 67). Not surprisingly, they produce "a significant increase in the amount of reading" (Moore, Jones, & Miller, 1980, p. 446). Specifically, print-rich literacy environments are associated with positive attitudes toward reading (Moore et al., 1980); increases in "children's concepts of print, writing [and] letter name knowledge" (Neuman, 1999, p. 308); positive effects on students' autonomous use of literature (Pressley et al., 2000); and improvements in reading comprehension, vocabulary, and language usage (Moore et al., 1980; Pressley et al., 2000).

The DNA of a print-rich or literate environment is access to books and a "wealthy base of materials" (Wilder, 1977, p. 272). This access "makes a big difference in children's early literacy development" (Ivey, 2000, p. 44). Or, in recast form, "the sheer availability of books" (Snow et al., 1998, p. 181) is a "key factor in reading development" (Gambrell & Morrow, 1996, p. 122). Efforts to connect youngsters with books, exposure to a wide variety of related print material (Snow et al., 1991), and engagement in language experiences in writing activities

(Hall & Cunningham, 1996) are also defining elements of a literate climate. Snow and her colleagues (1991) provide the following portrait of an enriched literacy environment, and juxtapose it with references to impoverished and average cultures.

> Impoverished: Lack of reading materials. Infrequent library visits. Teacher does not carry out reading activities appropriate to child's reading level. Physical environment bleak and lacking displays of student work.
> Average: Standard instruction, following basal text. Some variety in reading materials. Some library visits.
> Enriched: Variety of reading materials (trade books and basal readers). Frequent library visits. Stimulating activities, e.g., doing word meaning exercises, vocabulary, writing (creative and expository). Teacher asks many inferential questions of students. Physical environment includes displays of student work. (p. 159)

Assessments of schools provide a chilling picture of the literacy environment that many children confront, as these two reviews confirm:

> If we were to survey a random sample of elementary school classrooms in the United States on any one day of the school year, we would find too many classrooms that do not have even enough textbooks for each child. Classrooms often lack a small library of story and informational books, and few classrooms have enough encyclopedias and dictionaries for all students. Moreover, the greater the number of at-risk children in the school, the more limited is the print environment in the classrooms and in the school. (Chall et al., 1990, p. 117)

> Fully fifteen percent of the nation's schools do not have libraries. In most of the remaining schools, the collections are small, averaging just over 13 volumes per student. In 1978, schools that did have libraries were adding less than a book a year per student, which does not even keep up with loss and wear. According to a 1984 evaluation, "the collections of the school library . . . are in increasing jeopardy; inventories have been shrinking, and what remains is bordering on the obsolete." (Anderson et al., 1985, p. 78)

The overall message here for school leaders is quite clear: "if we want our children to become readers, books must be easily and readily available" (Huck, 1999, p. 117). And for this to occur, schools and their leaders must "allocate more resources for a wide range of reading materials" (Ivey, 2000, p. 44).

The Centrality of School and Classroom Libraries

> The more effective school has a library that is well stocked with books and in which the book stock constantly grows to meet the demands of the school enrollment. (Postlethwaite & Ross, 1992, p. 42)

More effective schools are facilities with good school libraries (Anderson et al., 1985; Briggs & Thomas, 1997). Schools where literacy success is the norm are communities with librarians—librarians "who encourage wide reading and help match books to children" (Anderson et al., 1985, p. 119). They are places where children use the library regularly (Hallinger & Murphy, 1985; Postlethwaite & Ross, 1992) and frequently check out books (Briggs & Thomas, 1997).

Schools where children excel at reading are communities with literate classroom environments (Anderson et al., 1985; Moll, 1991; Pressley et al., 2000). Classrooms are forums "in which a wide variety of materials and activities are used for literacy" (Snow et al., 1991, p. 164). Classrooms are characterized as "rich with stories being told, read, and reread. Learning centers dedicated to development of listening, reading, and writing [are] typical" (Pressley, 1998b, p. 158). They are defined by an assortment of materials on a variety of subjects at a range of levels of difficulty (Jonson, 1998; Sanacore, 1997; Snow et al., 1991).

Because "classroom libraries seem to be a critically important source of reading material for students" (Pressley, 1998b, p. 256), a well-developed library—one that floods the classroom with books—is at the heart of the literate environment. Classroom libraries are most effective when they are "well stocked" (Briggs & Thomas, 1997, p. 44)—that is, numbers matter—and when they provide a varied collection of materials (Honig, 1997; Jonson, 1998).

The Central Role of the Teacher

> Effective reading teachers specially introduce books and "sell" them with enthusiasm. (Johnson, 1998, p. 94)

In addition to classroom and school print environments that are rich and deep, "children need an excellent instructional environment as well" (Neuman, 1999, p. 306). As Snow, Burns, and Griffin (1998) discovered, "the impact of books on children's literacy development depends strongly on how teachers make use of them" (p. 181). The research is dotted with insights on actions teachers can take to create a powerful instructional environment and, as a consequence, areas on which leaders can work to strengthen literacy in the early grades.

Clustering books by themes is helpful (Huck, 1999). So too is scheduling time regularly to read to students (Pressley et al., 2000) and encouraging the rereading of stories (Huck, 1999). Teaching youngsters how to select books is a productive activity, as is providing children with opportunities to choose their own reading material (Pressley, 1998b). Enriching all the curricular areas with books is a powerful strategy for developing needed reading skills (Morrow et al., 1999). Teaching "phonics and decoding skills in a print-rich environment" (Snow et al., 1998, p. 199) is also productive.

Promoting "social interactions revolving around books" (Pressley, 1998b, p. 247) is an especially robust strategy for enhancing the inherent value of reading material. The goal here is to structure time for children to talk about and in other ways "respond to books" (Huck, 1999, p. 122) they are reading, including sharing stories they have written in conjunction with reading. Such processing and sharing can be done with the teacher or other adults or with classmates or cross-age peers (Labbo & Teale, 1990; State of New York, 1974). Finally, there is some evidence that teachers who involve children in creating and maintaining the literate environment can positively influence early literacy development (Adams, 1990).

Summary

In this chapter, I deepened our understanding of an effective curricular program for beginning reading, beyond what I reported about phonics in Chapter 7. I began with an examination of the importance of balance in the reading program. I closed with an analysis of the critical nature of a print-rich literacy environment for young readers.

9

Building Effective Prevention and Remediation Programs

It is clear from our review of the history of instructional support programs that in general these programs have not adequately met the needs of students assigned to them. (Walmsley & Allington, 1995, p. 25)

Successful interventions with the type of child with reading disabilities served in public schools will require major changes in public policy and intervention approaches. (Foorman et al., 1997, p. 274)

An important aspect of any early-grade curricular program is the weaving together of structures and strategies into a literacy safety net that protects slow and underperforming students from failure. Snow and her colleagues (1998) portray the issue as follows:

Many children learn to read with good instruction, but some do not. And many children have problems learning to read because of poor instruction. In all cases, the question is what kinds of additional instruction (usually called "interventions" because they are not part of the regular school reading instruction) are likely to help. (p. 247)

Investigators define the number of youngsters requiring additional reading instruction by employing a variety of approaches, all of which help define the landscape of needed supplemental services. For example, Adams and Bruck (1993) highlight surveys that "suggest between 7-15% of the school population suffers from specific reading disabilities, that is, from difficulties in learning to read and write that are not attributable to an identifiable deficiency, emotional disturbance, or other handicapping condition such as sensorial impairment or physical disability" (p. 127). Klenk and Kibby (2000) report that in 1996 "nearly 13.5% (3,618,859) of elementary school children and 4.5% (774,564) of secondary students received remedial reading services" (pp. 674-675). They also document that "nearly 80% of students identified as learning disabled—and thus eligible for special education services—have reading difficulties" (p. 679). Adams (1994), in turn, pegs the number of first graders experiencing difficulty in processing the phonological dimensions of language at 25% (p. 16).

For much of our educational history, no specific efforts were made to address the special needs of these learners. When they attended school, they were thrown into the mix with their peers and progressed as best they could. By 1920, however, new approaches to the challenges posed by poor readers began to materialize. In particular, ability grouping and curricular differentiation were woven into the instructional program. In the 1960s and 1970s, separate programs to help educate children who were not proficient readers were added to the intervention portfolio. In the pages that follow, I describe what I have learned about these efforts. I also outline the ingredients of effective prevention and remediation work in the early grades—the strands of robust literacy safety nets.

A Snapshot of the Current State of Affairs

Most remedial and special education support programs have not proven to be effective in accelerating the reading growth of struggling readers. (Duffy-Hester, 1999, p. 481)

Current approaches to compensatory education systematically underchallenge disadvantaged students. (Birman, 1988, p. 25)

Special learning opportunities for students experiencing problems in reading often occur in discrete programs (e.g., Title I, special education) that are only loosely hinged to the core curricular program and that regularly fail in their promise to bring youngsters back into the education mainstream through mastery of literacy skills. In Chapter 10, I dedicate considerable space to exposing the lack of congruence and absence of integration between the regular and special programs in elementary schools. The reality is that all too often, rather than being mutually supportive and expansive, regular and remedial programs are independent and competitive. For a more complete unfolding of this narrative, readers are directed to Chapter 10.

Concomitantly, researchers have also discovered that the conditions in these special programs generally disadvantage youngsters academically (Barr & Dreeben, 1991; Birman, 1988; Duffy-Hester, 1999; Garcia & Pearson, 1991; Haynes & Jenkins, 1986; Knapp & Needels, 1991; Spiegel, 1995). The scholarship of Allington and his colleagues is especially informative on this disheartening state of affairs. Their investigations reveal that the challenges poor readers bring to school are often exacerbated rather than alleviated or solved by the educational interventions they encounter there (Allington, 1980, 1983, 1984a, 1984b, 1991; Allington & McGill-Franzen, 1989b; Allington et al., 1986; Johnston & Allington, 1991; Walmsley & Allington, 1995). Most damaging, these analysts find that *neither* the quantity nor the quality of literacy experiences of poor readers is improved through participation in the various special and supplemental programs schools provide.

Poor readers, these reviewers assert, often confront "a learning environment that differs from that presented better readers" (Allington, 1984a, p. 93), differs in ways such that "students who need the most and the best get the least and worst" (Allington & McGill-Franzen, 1989b, p. 538). Thus the education received by struggling readers, rather than fostering growth, often "results in ever increasing deficits" (Allington, 1983, pp. 553-554). Not unexpectedly, Allington and his research team conclude that these instructional support programs do not sufficiently address the needs of non-proficient readers (Walmsley & Allington, 1995): "most children provided remedial reading never come fully up to grade level, that is, their reading problems are not cured" (Klenk & Kibby, 2000, p. 681).

In addition to the specific problems that I describe in detail below, interventions formulated to serve low-achieving readers and youngsters at risk of reading failure suffer from four broad-based design problems. To begin with, these programs are often judged to be producer-driven rather than being defined by student needs; that is, they are "designed to fit the teaching preferences of school staff" (Birman, 1988, p. 25). Second, the program calculus is more often labeling than teaching (Brown et al., 1986). Clay (1994) corrals this dynamic quite nicely as follows:

> Some children begin to lag behind their classmates in the new learning. Educators have explained this by pointing to individual differences—linguistic, cultural, intellectual, emotional, organic or psychological—labels which place children into categories which are supposed to "explain" why we find them hard to teach. Over time educators have paid more attention to the reliability of their categories than to devising ways to have such children learn by some alternative means. (p. 121)

Third, as I explained in the first part of the book, compensatory and supplemental blueprints often locate failure outside the school and the actions of its staff (Dudley-Marling & Murphy, 1997; Pressley, 1998b; Wagner, 1999). Rather than attributing variations to "differences in curriculum, opportunities, and instructional tasks" (Walmsley & Allington, 1995, p. 29), reading problems are situated in the socio-economic and home environment in which children are ensconced, or attributed to individual disability (Allington & McGill-Franzen, 1989a), "without examining the learning environment or reflecting on the teaching process itself as a possible source of difficulty" (McGill-Franzen, 1987, p. 488). "Environmental deficits" and "neurological dysfunctions" become the prime causal variables in the formula of poor reading performance.

Finally, in much of the safety net design, compliance issues are much too heavily illuminated. The spotlight is much less frequently directed on issues of learning and teaching. According to Walmsley and Allington (1995),

> Currently, the design of instructional support programs for children who have not found learning to read easy is more likely to reflect minimal compliance with federal and state program regulations than to reflect the best evidence on how best to accelerate reading and writing development. (p. 22)

Breaking the Cycle of Failure: Elements of Effective Safety Net Reading Programs

What can be concluded from this project is that reversing patterns of failure for poor children requires solutions that attend to a complex array of elements. (Hiebert et al., 1992, p. 565)

There is no simple solution in designing more effective reading instruction for poor readers. The interaction of variables such as time allocated, content covered, direct instruction, instructional emphasis, and so on is complex and simple mandates for singular changes will not automatically better meet the needs of the poor readers. (Allington, 1984a, p. 94)

As the number of students experiencing reading problems has increased over the last two decades, as schools' less-than-stellar performance record has become more visible, and as economic, political, and moral shifts in society have underscored the importance of literacy success for all, "interest has grown in identifying programs that will prevent this cycle of educational failure from occurring" (Ross et al., 1995, p. 774). And considerable progress has resulted, not only in the formulation of portraits of effective safety net programs but, perhaps even more importantly, in teasing out the central ingredients of preventative and remedial reading programs "that contribute to positive results" (Pinnell et al., 1994, p. 32). I describe these elements and guidelines—"guidelines that [can] be used as the basis for evaluating and improving any remedial program" (Spiegel, 1995, p. 89)—in the following pages. At the same time, I debunk some of the "questionable 'remedies'" (Klenk & Kibby, 2000, p. 668) that have been hardwired into the practice of remedial reading.

A note or two before describing these elements is in order. First, compensatory reading instruction refers to "any reading instruction provided for students [who are] reading below grade level" (Wilder, 1977, p. 259). Second, my measure of success is performance on achievement tests. I concur with Edmonds (1979) and Allington and Walmsley (1995) that "so long as traditional achievement tests are used as the primary means by which the public judges success, then ensuring that children meet these demands will always remain the critical goal for remediation" (p. 254). Third, while I acknowledge that "we are still far from providing [everything that] is needed" (Chall et al., 1990, p. 164), we do "have the knowledge to prevent the deceleration of literacy achievement" (p. 164). The work ahead is as much about implementation as it is about knowledge production. Finally, supporting all that follows is the knowledge that "the most critical elements of an effective program for the prevention of reading disability at the elementary level are (a) the right kind and quality of instruction delivered with the (b) right level of intensity and duration to (c) the right children at the (d) right time" (Torgesen, 1998, p. 34).

Act as if Failure Is Preventable

> A much more substantial portion of children in the bottom quartile can be taught to read than is the case in status quo instruction. (Hiebert & Taylor, 2000, p. 476)

> Even with modest funding, it is possible to increase the reading levels of at-risk children in the elementary years and thereby reduce the number of children who fail to meet literacy standards. (Allington & Walmsley, 1995, p. 253)

The first guideline states that, while we continue to struggle with effectively serving those pupils "with the most severe phonologically based reading disabilities" (Torgesen, 1997, p. 26), "reading failure is fundamentally preventable for nearly all children, regardless of home background. This includes most students currently categorized as learning disabled" (Slavin et al., 1991, p. 408). Studies from a variety of scholarly domains attest to "the long term value of early intervention" (Spiegel, 1995, p. 89) and the power of "curricula that are adapted specifically to the needs of reading disabled children" (Torgesen & Hecht, 1996, p. 133) and poor readers. Research also demonstrates that without this type of intervention at-risk readers are unlikely to master literacy. Indeed, researchers have discerned that well-planned and implemented efforts at preventing reading failure and immediate remediation of reading problems translate into increases in IQ, higher reading test scores, fewer retentions, reduced use of special education services, lower drop-out rates, quicker movement of youngsters from the lowest achievement quartile, higher high school graduation rates, and a larger probability of employment as adults (Allington & Walmsley, 1995; Hiebert & Taylor, 2000; Snow et al., 1998; Spiegel, 1995).

Identify and Intervene Early

> The best solution to the problem of reading failure is to allocate resources for early identification and prevention. (Torgesen, 1998, p. 32)

Reading difficulties should be addressed as soon as they occur. (Chall et al., 1990, p. 166)

Over the last quarter century, researchers have uncovered a good deal of information about the context of reading mastery for poor readers. One important insight is that "the likelihood that a child will succeed in the first grade depends most of all on how much she or he has already learned about reading before getting there" (Adams, 1990, p. 82). Youngsters most likely to have problems "learning to read in the primary grades are those who begin school with less prior knowledge and skill in certain domains, most notably letter knowledge, phonological sensitivity, familiarity with the basic purposes and mechanisms of reading, and language ability" (Snow et al., 1998, p. 137). There is also an abundance of evidence that "waiting for difficulties to correct themselves may lead to even greater problems" (Chall et al., 1990, p. 166). Unaddressed difficulties cause deficiencies to expand (Juel, 1988; Pressley, 1998b) as "children who have problems early develop more serious problems later" (Chall et al., 1990, p. 166). What begins "as clear but relatively small differences in achievement among children in kindergarten grow exponentially over the primary grades until it is not uncommon to see achievement differences of more than 5 years by the middle of third grade" (Purcell-Gates, 1998, p. 66).

This prelude carries us to my second guideline for ensuring literacy success for poor and disabled readers: safety net programs for at-risk pupils should "identify early [and] remediate early" (Stanovich, 2000, p. 21) because "it is essential that children be identified as early as possible and remediation begun before the adverse effects of failure can set in" (Castle, 1999, p. 58). The winning strategy here is "to help all students be successful in reading at the beginning, before they become remedial readers" (Slavin et al., 1991, p. 405), to focus on prevention, and if remediation is necessary, to provide the remedy as early as possible.

It is especially important that safety net programs counteract prevailing norms for assisting at-risk readers. The first of these norms holds that "if a child experiences difficulties in learning, simply wait and the child will learn to read when ready" (Pressley, 1998b, p. 277). The second maintains that the best way to determine who needs reading assistance is to employ a discrepancy standard, an approach that requires students to have a significant deficit, often two years, before special services are energized (Gaffney, 1998) and improvement activities begun. Both of these norms are toxic to the literacy mastery of poor readers. They result, according to Torgesen (1998), in "a tragedy of the first order" (p. 32). Since research confirms that it is "very hard to make up for years of lost experiences" (Juel, 1988, p. 446) and because remediation efforts beyond the elementary grades have a poor track record, waiting to intervene as a general strategy "makes no sense" (Pressley, 1998b) and even when it is possible makes remediation "more difficult and more costly" (Torgesen, 1998, p. 32).

The obvious corollary of rejecting prevailing norms is "that if the child is not to be left farther and farther behind" (Chall et al., 1990, p. 160), and the "adverse effects of failure" (Castle, 1999, p. 58) overcome, identification and intervention must occur as early as possible (Brown & Felton, 1990; Fletcher & Lyon, 1998; Gaffney, 1998; Hiebert & Taylor, 2000). Reading problems need to be identified before they calcify (Taylor et al., 1992); "teachers must be vigilant in their search for children who are losing out" (Leinhardt et al., 1981, p. 358), and "close monitoring of students' reading achievements" (Rowe, 1995) is essential. Interventions should also take place early, the earlier the better. Perhaps the most salient question for school leaders "then, is what can be done in kindergarten and first grade to close gaps before they grow wider" (Purcell-Gates, 1998, p. 66).

Emphasize Prevention and Underscore Acceleration

> Children who have fallen behind need a program that helps them make accelerated progress. (Spiegel, 1995, p. 94)

Embedded in the analysis so far are three related strategies for creating effective safety net programs. First, given the significant costs of not providing services to youngsters who might need them, it is better to oversample and overserve than to wait for reading problems and achievement deficits to affirm the need for intervention (Gaffney, 1998); "as a practical matter, if schools desire to maximize their chances for early intervention with the most impaired children, they should provide this intervention to as many children as possible" (Torgesen, 1998, p. 35). Second, energy and resources should be directed "away from remediation after failure" (Jones & Smith-Burke, 1999, p. 283) and toward the instruction of those youngsters "identified as being at risk (e.g., weak or deficient in phonological processing skills)" (Brown & Felton, 1990, p. 226). Third, when remediation is required, "accelerating reading development . . . to prevent failure" (Klenk & Kibby, 2000, p. 674) is the appropriate path to follow (Allington & McGill-Franzen, 1995). As Spiegel (1995) observes, "children who have fallen behind will never catch up with their age peers if they make normal progress" (p. 94). Indeed, "the children who have been learning the slowest must learn *faster* than the other children so that they can catch up" (Johnston & Allington, 1991, p. 1001).

Focus on Instruction, not the Location of Service Delivery

> The test of Chapter 1 programs should be whether children are learning to read, not where the instruction occurs. (Hiebert et al., 1992, p. 568)

Another element in the blueprint of effective safety net programs is to prevent becoming a hostage to the issue of service provision venue (Moats, 1996). Many advocates of children with special needs maintain that supplemental services should occur within the regular classroom. And while there is evidence that children in reading programs can benefit from receiving services with their classmates, mainstreaming itself is no guarantee of success (Ross et al., 1995). Neither is focusing on "diagnostic-prescriptive pullout programs" (Foorman et al., 1998, p. 38). Indeed as Gelzheiser, Meyers, and Pruzek (1992) remind us, the research on location of compensatory services confirms that neither the pull-in nor the pull-out approach "for remedial reading students [is] generally superior in its effect on student reading achievement" (p. 134). The account here is similar to that found elsewhere in education: organizational form in and of itself has not, does not, and never will predict school performance (Murphy, 1991). This, in turn, informs leaders that "rather than restricting considerations to the location of instruction . . . the specific type and quality of instruction provided need[s] to be considered" (Gelzheiser et al., 1992, p. 147).

Develop a Systematic Plan of Action

> In an effective intervention the interdependence demands a systematic plan. (Clay, 1994, p. 128)

While location of service delivery is not a critical element in the success algorithm for at-risk readers, the presence of a thoughtful, well-developed plan to address the needs of these children is (Hiebert & Pearson, 1999; Manning, 1995). School leaders "must recognize that such programs are necessary and . . . institute them" (Postlethwaite & Ross, 1992, p. 45). "Conspicuous strategies"

(Kameenui, 1998, p. 331) to achieve desired ends are needed. These pieces of the reading achievement puzzle should be woven into an integrated plan (Taylor et al., 1999; Walmsley & Allington, 1995). As I discuss in Chapter 10, this will entail integration of the regular and special programs as well as the knitting together of the various special programs themselves.

Make Regular Classroom Instruction the First Line of Defense

> Effective classroom instruction can prevent reading failure in many children. (Fletcher & Lyon, 1998, p. 80)

Staying with the last line of discussion above, a key principle of effective literacy prevention and remediation programs is that they should ensure that regular classroom teachers are integrally involved in serving poor and disabled readers. Unfortunately, safety net programs have been constructed in many places in ways that have greatly diminished the classroom teachers' sense of responsibility for struggling readers (Dudley-Marling & Murphy, 1997) as well as their "ability to properly serve at-risk children" (Walmsley & Allington, 1995, p. 30). The tragedy of this is that "exemplary classroom programs can dramatically reduce the number of children who are currently classified as reading disabled or remedial readers" (Duffy-Hester, 1999, p. 481). Since effective classroom instruction goes a long way in preventing literacy problems, the actions of regular classroom teachers provide an important part of the scaffolding for safety net reading programs. Or as Allington and McGill-Franzen (1989b) phrase it,

> Increasing access to instruction in the regular education class and improving the quality of that instruction must not be overlooked in attempts to resolve the problems of students who fail to learn to read on schedule. (p. 540)

Since "it is nothing short of foolhardy to make enormous investments in remedial instruction and then return children to classroom instruction that will not serve to maintain the gains they made in the remedial program" (Snow et al., 1998, p. 258), focus must be directed toward "dramatic improvements in the . . . general education programs to circumvent many of the difficulties encountered by children in their early experiences with literacy instruction" (Klenk & Kibby,

2000, p. 676). Rather than defaulting on their responsibility to teach reading to poor readers and to be accountable for consequences of that work, regular teachers must assume "a more equal responsibility for reading instruction" (Haynes & Jenkins, 1986, p. 178).

> To enhance the quantity and quality of instruction for low-achievement readers, attention must be directed to the core curriculum and instructional opportunities in the regular education program. Since failure in the core curriculum results in referrals to instructional support programs, effects must begin with strengthening instruction in regular education. Support instruction needs to focus on enhancing performance in the core curriculum; ideally, this would accelerate the mastery of core curricular goals, tasks, and activities. To do this, regular education and support teachers must work collaboratively on the design and delivery of instruction, ultimately developing the "shared knowledge" necessary to create coherent instructional opportunities across school settings. In these models, regular and support teachers would hold "shared responsibility" for the instruction and achievement of low-achieving children. (Allington & McGill-Franzen, 1989a, pp. 92-93)

Provide Continuing Support

> Poor readers . . . require continuing support to fully recover from their early reading problems. (Hatcher et al., 1994, p. 53)

> For students experiencing difficulties in school, sustained, long-term, excellent instruction is more likely to be successful than short-term instruction. (Pressley, 1998b, p. 277)

While there is evidence that some struggling readers can be returned to the mainstream and can then continue to hold their own, for many children continuous extra support is a necessity. As Juel (1996) discovered in her research, it is probably too much "to ask that a quick fix in first grade can solve all reading difficulties from then on. Children who are dependent upon schools to learn to read are also more likely to be dependent upon schools for continued advancement" (p. 281). Hiebert and Taylor (2000) take an even stronger position, asserting that the assumption that a "one-time intervention can solve the reading challenges faced by children in high-poverty schools is not supported by the current research or by any theoretical models of reading" (p. 480). Thus according to Pressley (1998b), "reading interventions are somewhat analogous to sustained medical treatments, because being at risk for intellectual difficulties is a chronic condition, not a temporary state. To date, there is no quick and easy inoculation to prevent academic disabilities" (p. 179).

Researchers who study struggling readers find that without ongoing support, the possibility of slippage as students move beyond the early years is quite real (Hiebert & Taylor, 2000; Pressley, 1998b). In addition, continuation is required to assist those youngsters, especially for "the core of disabled readers" (Torgesen, 1998, p. 34), who were unable to accelerate to the level of their classmates in kindergarten or first grade. The goal of safety net reading programs should be, therefore, to provide the abundance of targeted assistance needed to prevent reading problems, to move youngsters quickly up the ladder of success, and then to furnish the steady support required for continued achievement (Allington & Walmsley, 1995). Here the message is that school leaders must attend to the "support structures that sustain gains" (Hiebert & Taylor, 1994, p. 214), paying particular attention to "a series of differentiated interventions across the primary grades" (Hiebert & Taylor, 2000, p. 477).

Emphasize Excellence Factors, not Differences, in the Regular Program

> The literacy instruction given to low-income children [should] be the same as that used successfully with most children. (Chall et al., 1990, p. 148)

> It is generally accepted that most children who struggle to read do not require instruction that is substantially different from their more successful peers; rather, they require a greater intensity of "high-quality instruction." (Klenk & Kibby, 2000, p. 668)

For many years, experiences for children at risk of failure to read well were designed from different blueprints and constructed from different materials than those employed in the regular program. I discuss the research that exposes the dysfunctional nature of this approach to serving poor readers throughout the text. What is central to my account at this point is that recent studies document that "many children who fall behind in beginning reading are not qualitatively different from other readers" (Pressley, 1998b, p. 132) and that at-risk pupils are advantaged when the "same elements of reading and writing instruction [are employed] for good versus weak readers" (Pressley et al., 1996, p. 272). In short, "there is little evidence that children experiencing difficulties learning to read, even those with identifiable learning disabilities, need radically different sorts of supports than children at low risk, although they may need more intensive support" (Snow et al., 1998, p. 3). In the same vein, "the needs of low-income children are not really special needs, they are the same as for most children" (Chall et al., 1990, p. 149). Thus "children who are having difficulty learning to read do not as a rule require qualitatively different instruction from children who are 'getting' it" (Snow et al., 1998, p. 12), and quality instructional programs for nonproficient readers should be based on the same principles as nonstruggling readers (Duffy-Hester, 1999).

Increase the Intensity of Instruction

> In general, programs designed to identify students with learning problems and provide them with additional instruction are successful only when they are intensive. (Slavin & Madden, 1989, p. 11)

> The best remedial reading help I know is to take twice as long and teach half as much. (Manning, 1995, p. 654)

To observe that the tapestry of additional learning opportunities for poor readers is best woven with the same threads employed in the regular problem does not gainsay the fact that these children should have "intensive assistance" (Vadasy et al., 1997, p. 127), especially as I conveyed earlier, a "more intensive intervention prior to placement in long-term remedial or special education programs" (Gaffney, 1998, p. 106). According to scholars who focus on the needs of children at risk of reading failure, "meeting the needs of individuals is primarily a matter of providing some students with larger amounts of high quality instruction" (Allington & McGill-Franzen, 1989a, p. 92), both in terms of the overall package of services offered and the specific instructional interventions themselves (Pinnell et al., 1994; Torgesen, 1998). My focus here is on the first of these dimensions, that is, the bundle of services that includes two elements: expanding learning time and providing more contact with teachers.

While we know from the analysis in Chapter 6 that "extra time is not sufficient in itself" (Snow et al., 1998, p. 272), that is, learning depends on "what occurs during that additional time" (Allington, 1983, p. 554), research also informs us that "unless educators are willing to accept the notion of unequal time allocation, they are dooming poor readers to continued deficits in reading" (Allington, 1983, p. 549). This is the case because "equivalence is in itself inequitable, since poor readers cannot narrow their achievement deficit with only equivalent instructional time, even if they were to learn with equal efficiency. Simply offering equivalent time ensures that the poorer readers' achievement deficits will remain, that they will necessarily be at least as far behind when they complete an academic year as when they started" (Allington, 1983, p. 549).

Formulated as a guiding principle, it is important that poor readers be provided "more time in reading and writing than children not at risk" (Snow et al., 1998, p. 272), that "opportunity to learn to read" (Morris et al., 1990, p. 135) be expanded. Or as Fletcher and Lyon (1998) express the theme, "spending more time reading and writing is the key to enhancing literacy levels . . . in children who are disabled in reading" (p. 82). And there is much convergence of evidence that "providing the opportunity for increased experiences in reading" (Allington, 1980, p. 875), including expanding the variety and number of books (Chall et al., 1990; Hiebert & Pearson, 1999), impacts positively on the mastery of literacy skills by struggling readers (Barr & Dreeben, 1991; Fletcher & Lyon, 1998; Johnston & Allington, 1991).

Intensity is also a product of the amount of contact that students at risk of reading failure have with adults, especially highly qualified instructors. A guiding principle is that these youngsters require more assisted-reading time and less time alone, especially in unmonitored seatwork with workbooks and worksheets, than is the norm in most classrooms (Eldredge, 1990). The socially mediated dimension of learning, always important, is enhanced for students at risk of reading failure; consequently, it is imperative that instructional density be increased by employing learning formats and participatory structures that increase interactions between learners and instructors (Weber, 1971).

Concretely, this means that "programs that reduce reading failure in public school classrooms involve individual or small group instruction" (Moats, 1996, p. 88). While there continues to be some debate about the robustness of small-group instruction vis-à-vis one-to-one tutoring, the important message here is to increase the use of instructional strategies that feature assisted opportunities to learn and that maximize learner-to-teacher contact—preferably a teacher-student ratio of less than one to ten (Birman, 1988; Hiebert et al., 1992).

Given this general approach, it appears that one-to-one instruction or one-to-one tutoring provides the gold standard for intensification (Clay, 1994; Iverson & Tunmer, 1993; Slavin et al., 1991; Torgesen & Hecht, 1996), and "preventive tutoring is the best available possibility for providing a reliable means of abolishing illiteracy among children who are at risk of school failure" (Wasik & Slavin, 1994, p. 171).

I close this discussion on intensification with a caveat. As I discuss in the next section, "quality" is the key issue in the consideration of adult contact. Richness of exchange depends on the quality of the teacher (Haberman, 1995; Wasik & Slavin, 1994), and "academic progress depends on what and how teachers teach" (Moats, 1996, p. 89). Particularly worrisome for many analysts is the use of low-skilled paraprofessionals to deliver instruction to learners at risk of reading failure (Birman, 1988; Klenk & Kibby, 2000), an arrangement in which the benefits of dense instruction are unlikely to materialize (Wasik & Slavin, 1994).

Match Instruction to Student Needs

Instruction in special programs should be individualized. (Spiegel, 1995, p. 93)

A consistent theme throughout the literature on productive safety net programs is that "teacher expertise is at the heart of highly effective early remedial programs and classroom programs that prevent the need for remedial instruction" (Johnston & Allington, 1991, p. 1005), and that poor readers "can succeed in school when better teaching methods are used" (Becker, 1977, p. 529). One important guideline embedded in this larger theme is that instructional support programs should be individualized. Let me be clear what I mean when I reference individualization, however. I do not refer to ersatz experiences commonplace in many supplemental reading programs in which individualization is little more than having youngsters work alone (Allington, 1991), often on "worksheets without any instruction" (Spiegel, 1995, pp. 93-94). Rather, this important idea is best characterized as the provision of "individually appropriate instructional interactions" (Allington, 1991, p. 17). Specifically, it encompasses (1) fitting instructional interactions to needs of individual pupils (Pinnell et al., 1994) "for pacing, concept representation, corrective feedback, and reinforcement" (Moats, 1996, p. 89); (2) focusing on "differences in individual learning rates" (Allington & McGill-Franzen, 1989a, p. 92); (3) "accommodat[ing] the different language

and literacy experiences that students bring to the classroom"
(Garcia & Pearson, 1991, p. 52); (4) matching different instructional
strategies to learning problems (Slavin et al., 1991); and (5) tailoring
reading materials to appropriate instructional levels (Spiegel, 1995).
In total, it refers to allowing a pupil "to participate at the cutting edge
of his or her knowledge" (Pinnell et al., 1994, p. 35).

Focus on Letters and Sounds

> One of the most important results of research on the nature of
> reading disability over the last 20 years has been the discov-
> ery that the most common form of this disability is caused by
> weaknesses in the ability to process the phonological features
> of language. (Torgesen, 1997, p. 17)

> The conclusion drawn from these findings is that systematic
> phonics instruction is significantly more effective than non-
> phonics instruction in helping to prevent reading difficulties
> among at-risk students and in helping to remediate reading dif-
> ficulties in disabled readers. (NICHHD, 2000b, p. 2:133)

Over the last quarter century, research has disclosed that "measures of letter knowledge continue to be the best predictor of reading
difficulties, and measures of phonemic awareness contribute additional predictive accuracy" (Torgesen, 1997, p. 35). Research also sub-
stantiates that early reading problems "reside largely in phonological
processing ability" (Kameenui et al., 1998, p. 48; see also Foorman,
1995; Juel, 1988; Lundberg, 1991; Torgesen, 1997; Torgesen & Hecht,
1996), or as Torgesen (1998) describes it, "the most common cause of
difficulties acquiring early word reading skills is weakness in the ability to process the phonological features of language" (p. 33). At-risk
readers, roughly 25 percent of first graders (Adams, 1994; Liberman
et al., 1989) from "a range of social strata" (Nicholson, 1999, p. 13),
"show exceptional difficulty in figuring out the correspondence
between spelling and sounds" (Adams & Bruck, 1993, p. 128) in
building the "phonemic awareness bridge between spoken and written language" (Snider, 1995, p. 453). Or more directly, "children with
poor reading ability are also low in phonemic awareness" (Castle,
1999, p. 58). They "suffer from a phonological deficit" (Stanovich,
2000, p. 75). They "do not decode well" (Pressley, 1998b, p. 71).
    This failure to master decoding in turn, it is argued, becomes "*the*
bottleneck in the meaning getting process" (Pressley, 1998b, p. 199).

As Liberman and her colleagues (1989), Pressley (1998b), and Stanovich (2000) all conclude, "deficient phonological processing" (Liberman et al., 1989, p. 19) results in "effortful decoding [that] consumes capacity that might otherwise be used to understand text" (Pressley, 1998b, p. 199). The consequence is that "fewer cognitive resources are left to allocate to higher-level processes of text integration and comprehension" (Stanovich, 2000, p. 393). This dynamic "prevents poor readers from being able to read as much text as good readers" (Juel, 1988, p. 441), a situation that "leaves a shaky foundation for later reading comprehension" (p. 446) and that causes these youngsters to fall farther and farther behind (Stanovich, 2000).

If there is a positive theme in this chronicle about children at risk of reading failure, it is that "research findings also suggest that we have the tools to break the cycle of early failure" (Blachman, 1996, p. 67). We know that nonproficient readers, "especially children from low-income backgrounds [that] start school with significantly lower levels of phonemic awareness than do those from middle-class backgrounds" (Nicholson, 1999, p. 12), require "intensive, direct, and systematic training in phonological structure" (Liberman et al., 1989, p. 27) if they are to be successful readers. An especially impressive array of studies demonstrates that "systematic instruction that is designed to make children with reading problems aware of the inter-relatedness of the sounds and visual patterns shared with different words" (Iverson & Tunmer, 1993, p. 120)—"explicit instruction and practice in attending to and manipulating the sounds within spoken words" (Snow et al., 1998, p. 248)—leads to improvement "in both reading and spelling" (Blachman, 1996, p. 67). The payoff seems to be most significant "for youngsters at risk due to socioeconomic disadvantage and/or weak initial preparedness in reading-related skills" (Snow et al., 1998, p. 249).

The summary message for school leaders is that "there is now widespread agreement that early reading instruction, particularly for children at-risk for problems in learning to read, should contain elements explicitly designed to stimulate phonological awareness" (Torgesen, 1997, p. 13), "or the ability to notice, think about, and manipulate individual sounds in words" (Torgesen & Hecht, 1996, p. 136). When "intense decoding instruction" (Pressley, 1998b, p. 66) is provided, research shows that "it is a very small percentage of students who cannot learn to read" (p. 56): "it is clear that direct phonics instruction is a potent positive influence on the development of the very skills (i.e., word identification and decoding) that constitute the core of a reading disability" (Brown & Felton, 1990, p. 239).

Provide Explicit Instruction

In reading disability, the nature of the problem dictates the nature of intervention: Children who are not able to break the print code can usually learn it when word structure is taught to them explicitly and directly. This type of instruction should be available in every school for those who need it. (Moats, 1996, pp. 88-89)

Instruction [must] be more explicit and comprehensive since the evidence shows that children who fail to learn to read must be explicitly taught. (Fletcher & Lyon, 1998, p. 68)

At a macro level, the final strand of the literacy safety net is based on points raised by Allington and McGill-Franzen (1989b) and Gaffney (1998).

Programs that offer more instruction, especially more high-quality instruction, are most likely to ameliorate reading failure. (Allington & McGill-Franzen, 1989b, p. 540)

Well over a decade ago, I read with interest a list Lewis (1983) made of recommendations for the reading instruction of students with learning disabilities. Her first recommendation, encapsulated in one word, was seared into my memory: "Teach." (Gaffney, 1998, p. 100)

At the micro level, this guideline illuminates the need for students at risk of reading failure to experience more direct or more explicit reading instruction (Adams, 1990; Snow et al., 1998; Stein et al., 1999). While some children seem able to intuit many of the strategies needed to master literacy skills (e.g., the alphabetic principle) (Liberman et al., 1989), it is clear that this is not the case for children with reading problems (Adams, 1990; Torgesen, 1998). At-risk learners "seem less likely than other children to incidentally acquire the knowledges, conventions, and strategies of fluent reading and writing" (Allington, 1991, p. 18). Because these "learners have difficulty developing efficient and effective strategies for solving problems" (Kameenui, 1998, p. 332), "we cannot assume that these children will acquire any necessary skills for reading words unless they are directly taught" (Torgesen, 1998, p. 34).

Poor and disabled readers need more help, more "instruction in which they play an active role" (Knapp & Needels, 1991, p. 101), "more guided reading and writing instruction" (Pressley et al., 1996, p. 274), and "high[er] levels of support" (Kameenui, 1998, p. 332). In addition, it appears that explicit instruction, or the ability "to offer scaffolded support while children are acquiring reading skills, may have increasing importance as the severity of the child's disability increases" (Torgesen, 1997, p. 42). Scaffolded support features tailored assistance based on ongoing assessments of students' progress (Clay, 1994; Slavin & Madden, 1989). Thus "carefully planned assessments that closely monitor the response of each child to the intervention" (Snow et al., 1998, p. 273) constitute a central dimension of explicit teaching. Included here are direct efforts to help youngsters learn self-monitoring techniques (Adams, 1998; Rosenshine & Meister, 1994). Unfortunately, as shown by my earlier analyses, adherence to the principle of explicit teaching often is honored in the breach (Allington, 1991), since guided "instruction is often supplanted by assignment of worksheets and workbooks with little teacher input or direction" (Spiegel, 1995, p. 93) or is ignored altogether (Adams, 1991).

Since I have already established that phonological deficits constitute the core reading problem for most struggling readers, it should not come as a surprise to learn that explicit instruction should highlight students' capacity to manipulate letters and sounds (Pressley et al., 1996) and to employ those abilities in "reading continuous text" (Snow et al., 1998, p. 272). Pupils who lack age-appropriate phonological awareness skills must be taught such skills directly. Instruction should be systematic and explicit with no dimensions of the process left to intuition. Poor readers in particular need "direct instruction in language analysis, explicit teaching of the alphabetic code" (Fletcher & Lyon, 1998, p. 65), and "extensive teaching of word-level skills" (Pressley et al., 1996, p. 274).

> Some of the word-level skills and knowledge these children will require instruction on include: phonemic awareness, letter-sound correspondences, blending skills, a small number of pronunciation conventions, use of context to help specify a word once it is partially or completely phonemically decoded, strategies for multi-syllable words, and automatic recognition of high-frequency "irregular" words. (Torgesen, 1998, p. 34)

Studies also document the need for "explicit instruction in comprehension-enhancing activities" (Palincsar & Brown, 1984, p. 121) or an "explicit teaching of comprehension strategies" (Knapp & Needels, 1991, p. 101).

Because research confirms that reading skills are learned most effectively when "phonological skills and reading skills [are] integrated" (Hatcher et al., 1994, p. 51), it is necessary that instruction on sounds and letter skills and on comprehension strategies "be embedded within as many opportunities for meaningful reading and writing as possible" (Torgesen, 1998, p. 34), that "explicit instruction of decoding and other skills [unfold] in the context of rich authentic reading and writing" (Pressley et al., 1996, p. 264). As McBride-Chang, Manis, Seidenberg, Custodio, and Doi (1993) report, "exposure to print" (p. 236) is key and a "literature-based reading program" (Paul, 1992, p. 13) is essential. Thus limiting explicit instruction to skill-based activities—a not uncommon practice in many remedial programs (Spiegel, 1995)—is likely to be less than maximally successful, or, to borrow a line from Hatcher and his research team (1994), only "working on phonological skills in isolation is not an optimal method for improving literacy skills" (p. 54).

A good deal of the explicit teaching portfolio must be devoted to "direct reading activities" (Haynes & Jenkins, 1986, p. 171). Struggling readers must have "opportunities to apply their strategies through just reading" (Spiegel, 1995, p. 90). Consistent with my earlier discussion, it is important in undertaking this reading that (1) "strategies and skills be embedded within meaningful and interesting tasks" (Hiebert et al., 1992, p. 566); (2) students be "involved in rich literacy experiences" (Hiebert & Taylor, 2000, p. 477) inside a challenging curriculum (Chall et al., 1990) that employs materials that match well with the phonics skills being taught (Anderson et al., 1985; Stein et al., 1999); and (3) "there is a focus on using text that children find . . . engaging" (Snow et al., 1998, p. 273)—in short, that skills take root within "practice in reading and interpreting meaningful text" (Adams & Bruck, 1993, p. 132).

Summary

In this chapter, I undertook two assignments. I provided a snapshot of the current state of affairs in terms of the provision of supplemental services to at-risk readers. I concluded that there is room for substantial improvement. I also detailed an assortment of elements that when woven together provide a robust safety net to ensure that poor readers reach mastery of literacy skills.

10

Coordinating the Curricular and Instructional Programs

Extensively coordinated programs distinguished successful schools from unsuccessful ones. (Wellisch et al., 1978, p. 219)

The incoherent nature of the curriculum may be as much a cause of disadvantaged students' failure to learn as anything. (Knapp & Needels, 1991, p. 89)

Remedial instruction is most effective when it supports and extends learning in the core classroom curriculum. We are unclear how best to measure congruence, but found a distinct lack of congruent instruction regardless of how we attempted to define it. (Allington et al., 1986, p. 27)

Analysts during the early years of teacher effects and effective schools research uncovered a recurring theme in America's classrooms and schools—they were marked by considerable fragmentation (Murphy, Hallinger, & Mesa, 1985). Systems within the school (e.g., assessment, professional development, resource allocation) were not joined. Neither did these activities spring forth from a common vision about the school's educational program. Linkages across and between teachers were thin at best. Standardized assessments operated with little regard for curricular frameworks and district objectives. That is, students were often tested on a curriculum that was not taught. And instruction was only loosely related to curriculum and assessment (Cooley & Leinhardt, 1980; Freeman, Kuhs, Porter, Floden, Schmidt, & Schwille, 1983; Haertel, 1986; Harnisch, 1983).

Incoherence within the literacy programs was common. Little connective tissue ever formed among reading and other subjects, even those such as social studies and science where the associations are most obvious (Chall et al., 1990; Durkin, 1978–1979). Indeed, reading was taught as a "discrete subject so that reading skills in the content areas [were] neglected or never taught" (Austin & Morrison, 1963, p. 3). Reading was even partitioned off from the language arts, such as spelling, writing, punctuation, and so on. The result was "a set of disaggregated language skills that lack[ed] meaning and coherence" (Knapp & Needels, 1991, p. 96), an "incoherent array of literacy lessons" (Allington, 1991, p. 14). The curriculum and instruction rarely connected different skills. Infrequently, for instance, were "decoding or vocabulary activities during reading instruction related to word structure or word meaning activities during spelling. Rarely were reading and composing tasks related on topic, genre, or text structure. Rarely were grammar or transcription tasks related to reading, writing, or composing activities" (Allington & McGill-Franzen, 1989a, p. 83). Teaching methods were the purview of individuals rather than the product of the community. One teacher could be using direct instruction, a second a basal program, and a third a language-based approach. Literacy connections across grade and across levels of schooling (e.g., primary, intermediate, middle school) were often conspicuous by their absence.

And when special education and compensatory education programs were factored into the narrative, the story line became even more confusing, uncoordinated, and fragmented. What transpired in these programs under the label of literacy often bore only scant resemblance to the activities occurring in regular classes.

Creating a Coherent Core Program

> Unless we offer instruction that is clear, consistent, and coherent we have little reason to expect our poor readers to make sense of our efforts. (Allington & Broikou, 1988, p. 807)

Reading instruction is most effective when combined with writing instruction. (NICHHD, 2000a, p. 18)

Aligning the Program Diamond

One of the most prevalent findings from research on classrooms and schools that promote high levels of reading achievement is that they are more tightly coordinated and display greater coherence. Coherence is considered to be "present when the reading instruction offered on different days or by different teachers (e.g., classroom and remedial or special education teachers) is consistently and mutually supportive" (Allington & Broikou, 1988, p. 807). In these classes and schools, there is a considerable amount of consistency throughout the educational program (Levine, 1982; Levine & Eubanks, 1983; Wellisch et al., 1978). High-performing schools, especially ones serving "challenged readers" (Hiebert & Taylor, 2000, p. 456), employ a schoolwide reading program (Hiebert & Taylor, 2000; Venezky & Winfield, 1979) and a "schoolwide approach to support reading instruction" (Hallinger & Murphy, 1985, p. 42). While there is no single solution to reading improvement across schools, the ability of a school to agree on a common platform and then to coordinate all activities based on that perspective is associated with reading achievement (Walmsley & Allington, 1995).

At its core, integration is defined by efforts to bring four key elements of the reading program into alignment: objectives, curriculum, instruction, and assessment. Objectives need to be clearly specified, through either state or district frameworks. Once they are specified, curricular materials need to be selected based on their match to these learning outcomes. In turn, "assessments must be aligned with goals" (Stigler & Hiebert, 1999, p. 142). Finally, the coordination loop needs to be closed by instructors who teach based on the objectives and who ensure that "tests and instructional activities [are] congruent" (Berliner, 1981, p. 222).

Aligning the Components of the Language Arts Program

Fashioning an integrated reading program requires that systems at the school and classroom levels be joined and coupled to the reading goals of the organization. Budgets must reflect that reading is the central task of the school. So too must the schedules of children and adults. Rewards should convey the importance of literacy, and professional development should demonstrate that reading is the top priority of the institution (Murphy et al., 1985).

As chronicled above, in less effective schools the central elements of the literacy program (e.g., writing, reading, spelling) are only weakly fastened. Effective programs, on the other hand, are distinguished by "coherent blocks of literacy instruction, that is, settings in which reading/writing/spelling/language tasks cohere, or hang together as a set of interrelated activities" (Allington, 1991, p. 12)—"language arts and reading assignments [are] interwoven with reading activities" (Hallinger & Murphy, 1985, p. 41) and the reading program "emphasizes the integration of listening, speaking, reading, [and] writing" (Van Vleck et al., 1994, p. 234). Highly accomplished classrooms are especially adept at interweaving reading and writing (Adelman, 1995; Harris & Sipay, 1990; Wharton-McDonald et al., 1998) and reading and spelling (Adams & Bruck, 1993; Treiman, 1998), at setting them up as "reciprocal processes" (Spiegel, 1995, pp. 91-92).

In schools in which all students master important literacy skills, there is a great deal of coordination "not only at particular grade levels but also across grade levels" (Hallinger & Murphy, 1985, p. 40). "A systematic, developmental language arts program is articulated and implemented from kindergarten through Grade 6" (Van Vleck et al., 1994, p. 236); it is created through the use of carefully articulated structures and interpersonal connections (Brookover, Schweitzer, Schneider, Beady, Flood, & Wisenbaker, 1978; Cohen & Miller, 1980; Fisher & Adler, 1999).

High-achieving programs and their teachers are also active in "integrat[ing] reading, writing, and other subjects" (Wharton-McDonald et al., 1998, p. 119). Simply put, "literacy [is] a part of everything that goes on" (p. 119); reading is considered to be "an integral part of all content areas" (Mahler, 1995, p 414). In the most expert schools, teachers make "numerous efforts to integrate related reading activities into instruction in other subject areas such as science and social studies" (Hallinger & Murphy, 1985, p. 40). Studies of effective teachers produce congruent conclusions, with "literacy development occurring throughout the day, connected both to formal curriculum and less formal activities" (Pressley, 1998b, p. 159).

Coherence also appears to be the product of continuity, both of staff (Taylor & Taxis, n.d.; Williams et al., 2000) and programs (Hoffman, 1991). In addition, there is abundant evidence in the research that coherence is the result of partnerships between the home and the school in the literacy area (Henderson, 1987). Key aspects of the partnership include (1) "shared responsibility" for helping children learn to read (Baker, Allen, Shockley, Pellegrini, Galda, & Stahl, 1996, p. 28); (2) programs that "connect students' lives at home and in school" (p. 23); and (3) the willingness of the school and home to work from the same literacy playbook.

Integrating the Regular and Special Programs

> Yet in most schools, these children, most of whom are low achievers in reading, receive services that are administratively and fiscally separate and, at least in theory, instructionally distinct. (McGill-Franzen & Allington, 1990, p. 149)

> From the evidence available, we must conclude that the expectation that participation in remedial or special education will enhance access to larger amounts of higher quality instruction remains yet unfilled. (Walmsley & Allington, 1995, p. 41)

While the center of interest here is the integration of regular and special programs in the service of enhanced reading achievement, it is helpful to begin by revisiting two points made previously. First, the key issue in helping students learn to read, particularly youngsters who are experiencing difficulties, is "to improve regular classroom instruction no matter what" (Johnston & Allington, 1991, p. 1002). This is the first and most vital line of defense in helping all children read well. Second, as I discussed at length in my treatment of safety net programs for youngsters, quality remedial programs (a) start early, (b) grow from the seedbed of quality instruction that advantages the general population, and (c) guarantee additional learning opportunities. It is only against this backdrop that our understanding of integration takes on meaning.

Lack of Congruence on Three Fronts

> Remedial and regular programs are indeed fragmented. (Walp & Walmsley, 1989, p. 364)

> Most schools offer instruction support services for children through both Chapter 1 and special education, with little overlap in planning, personnel, or participating children. (Allington & McGill-Franzen, 1989a, p. 76)

My analysis in this section leads me first to a description of the normal state of affairs between the regular and the special programs in schools and among the various special programs themselves.

A number of scholars have investigated these issues over the last two decades, especially Allington and his colleagues. The overriding conclusion is that there is little congruence among and between these programs. Rather, fragmentation is the norm (Walp & Walmsley, 1989). To begin with, the evidence confirms the lack of integration between the regular program and the various special programs (e.g., bilingual education, Title I). As Allington (1995) thoroughly documents, over the last quarter century a variety of ideas coalesced to produce an "array of special programs and specialist teachers" (p. 9). By design, each emphasized distinct administrative, curricular, and instructional blueprints (Allington & McGill-Franzen, 1989a, 1989b) and separate philosophical foundations, each of which bore only a limited corre-spondence to the infrastructure of the regular program. Not surpris-ingly, therefore, the links between the special and regular programs vary from weak to nonexistent (Allington & McGill-Franzen, 1995; McGill-Franzen & Allington, 1990).

Most critically, connections are severely frayed around the roles and functions of teachers. For example, researchers have regularly observed "that remedial and special teachers tend to work outside the mainstream education process and often in relative isolation from the regular education staff" (Allington & Broikou, 1988, p. 806), and that regular classroom instructors take little notice of the work unfolding in their specialist colleagues' classes. This partitioning results in a near absence of collaborative work and communication and a star-tling lack of understanding of the learning programs that define each other's classrooms (Allington & Broikou, 1988; McGill-Franzen & Allington, 1990).

Threadbare linkages, or "frequent lack of connection between regular instruction and the supplementary services" (Knapp & Needels, 1991, p. 116), also result in quite separate and often "different and incompatible . . . curricula" (Allington, 1991, p. 16) for the various programs. From the youngsters' perspective, this leads at best to a literacy curriculum that lacks coherence and coordination and at worst to "a set of unrelated, and at times, chaotic curriculum experiences" (McGill-Franzen & Allington, 1990, p. 176).

Over and above this well-documented lack of integration between regular and special programs, analysts have revealed two other coordination problems. First there is the "separation of different support programs designed to achieve similar goals with similar students" (Allington & McGill-Franzen, 1989a, p. 94). That is, many schools offer separate strategies and plans for special, bilingual, and remedial education, frameworks that often do "not mesh into a clear, unified plan" (p. 89) and that encourage little overlap in personnel. Second, there is an expanding understanding that, as was the case in the regular education literacy program, there is a fragmentation and a lack of coherence within each of the various special programs. Or as Haynes and Jenkins (1986) disclose, close scrutiny of any individual special program quickly throws into question the commonly accepted viewpoint that it "represents a standardized, uniform reading intervention" (p. 176).

While it is beyond the scope of this book to examine in detail the causes of this program fragmentation, one note along these lines is instructive in the quest for crafting more integrated programs. At the heart of the issue, as Venezky and Winfield (1979) recounted in their study of high-achieving reading programs, is that supplemental and support opportunities were constructed on a foundation of "professional-centered delivery of services" (p. 25). That is, programs can be traced back to "program and school context variables" (Haynes & Jenkins, 1986, p. 176) rather than to student needs and characteristics. Such a blueprint encourages "professional segregation" (Johnston & Allington, 1991, p. 991) and helps explain "variation in reading instruction across programs" (Haynes & Jenkins, 1986, p. 174).

When we layer this knowledge onto a system that, as we have seen throughout these chapters, is dominated by loose connections between parts, it is easy to understand how program fragmentation has become the norm in the area of special services. Or, as Allington (1991) captures it, "the fragmentation is simply enhanced" (p. 15). Factor in the historical penchant for school administrators to focus on organizational structures rather than learning and teaching, and it is difficult to see how a "student-centered reading" (Venezky & Winfield, 1979, p. 25) perspective that might ensure coordination could ever develop.

Lack of Congruence in Three Domains

There [is] little congruence between reading instruction in the classroom or remedial settings. (Allington et al., 1986, p. 22)

Remedial and special education clients were more likely to have cognitive confusion fostered . . . as a result of . . . 'planned fragmentation' of the curriculum. (Allington, 1991, p. 14)

Walp and Walmsley (1989) describe three types of congruence: procedural, instructional, and philosophical. According to these analysts,

procedural congruence is mostly concerned with the mechanics
of coordinating remedial reading and regular programs....
Instructional congruence is concerned with the content and the
delivery of the classroom and remedial programs: it encompasses the materials, the teaching techniques, and the way in
which the classroom and remedial programs are to complement
one another. Philosophical congruence is concerned with the
underlying theoretical or philosophical assumptions that drive
the programs in both settings. (pp. 364-365)

Limited philosophical congruence is at the heart of the problem I
am describing in this part of the chapter. On one level, this means that
each program in the school (e.g., regular education, special education) is powered by "competing theories of reading" (Allington &
McGill-Franzen, 1989a, p. 85), including divergent views about why
children are experiencing difficulties in learning to read. On another
plane, it indicates that staff do not share a common "instructional
focus" (Allington et al., 1986, p. 24). Finally, and in most tangible
form, it signifies that instructional goals are only partially shared
across the regular and the various special programs.

Diverse philosophical foundations in turn nurture the formation
of organizational arrangements and procedures that harden programmatic differences and thereby promote incongruity. For example, the
traditional delivery system that developed to serve special students,
that is, pull-out program rooms and separate classrooms, reinforces
distinctiveness. So too does the use of different teachers who occupy
separate space in the education profession and often separate geograph-
ical space in their school buildings (Johnston & Allington, 1991). In
short, incongruence and fragmentation are actually planned and built
into school operations (Allington & McGill-Franzen, 1989a, 1989b).

A lack of congruence on the philosophical front results in programs
that are poorly integrated on the curricular plane as well, or as Birman
(1988) asserts, on this key dimension special programs are "rarely
linked to regular programs in ways that fit the needs of individual
students" (p. 24). There is an abundance of evidence that regular and
special programs do not build from common curricular material.
Rather, youngsters in special programs "work in several different
curricula, often with curricula that present philosophical and pedagogical conflicts" (Johnston & Allington, 1991, p. 991). Investigators
often disclose, for example, that material in special programs is "selected
with little regard to sequencing, current classroom program, or prior
learning" (Allington et al., 1986, p. 22). Nor is there much evidence

that remedial programs "review or extend instruction offered in classroom reading materials" (p. 23). In the study by Allington and his colleagues (1986), for example, similar materials were used in regular and special classes less than one quarter of the time. In the Haynes and Jenkins (1986) investigation, the match was only 15 percent.

Scholars in this area also conclude that remedial reading instruction is often "quite distinct from regular instruction" (Johnston & Allington, 1991, p. 991) and, unfortunately, "different in ways that are likely to cause the problems attributed to [the special] students" (p. 1000). According to McGill-Franzen and Allington (1990),

> Regardless of whether the expressed goal of the specialist instruction was to support or to supplant the classroom reading program, instruction within the specialist program focused on different responses and types of tasks than did the instruction in the regular education classroom. (p. 168)

And, most tellingly, "what seems to best describe effective educational practice does not describe remediation" (Johnston & Allington, 1991, p. 991). Particularly disheartening are the data that disclose that pupils in the special programs "get less instruction and less personal instruction: Thus one predictable characteristic of remediation seems to be that these efforts are more likely to reduce the quantity of reading instruction rather than increase it" (p. 992). Children in the special programs read less and spend less time on comprehension: "The picture of reading instruction that emerges from these resource rooms is of students working independently; receiving little feedback, few explanations, or demonstrations from their teacher; and actually reading letters, words, or text only 25% of the time" (Haynes & Jenkins, 1986, pp. 171-173). These disadvantages for students in special programs often carry over to the regular program, especially in those cases where teachers displace responsibility for remedial youngsters to instructors in special classes (Allington, 1995).

Because "this lack of congruence leads to confusion and further difficulties for students who are already struggling to learn to read" (Klenk & Kibby, 2000, p. 675), it often "undermines the good efforts from both learners and teachers" (Allington & McGill-Franzen, 1989a, p. 85). There is also evidence to suggest that this dynamic contributes to producing the characteristics of troubled readers in the first place. The overall effect is that remediation has enjoyed only "limited success . . . in resolving the difficulties of learners who have failed to learn to read on the school's schedule" (Johnston & Allington, 1991,

p. 998; see also Foorman et al., 1998). Limited achievement is the norm for youngsters in special programs (Allington et al., 1986). So too is the fact that "few of [these] participants ever attain reading proficiency" (Johnston & Allington, 1991, p. 998). The situation has been labeled by Manning (1995) as "professionally reprehensible" and "ethically questionable" (p. 654).

Moving Toward Greater Congruence

Restructuring efforts need to . . . connect interventions across classrooms and Chapter 1. (Hiebert et al., 1992, p. 567)

Efforts should be made to ensure that students receive quality classroom reading instruction that is carefully coordinated with the compensatory instruction. (Pikulski, 1994, p. 34)

Schools that have reading specialists as well as special educators need to coordinate the roles of these specialists (Snow et al., 1998, p. 12)

Developing a reading program with a high degree of integration requires using the Walp and Walmsley (1989) framework introduced previously—with its three domains of philosophy, organization, and instruction—to craft a coordinated approach to reading. Successful integration begins with the development of a common philosophical foundation. Or as Walp and Walmsley (1989) maintain, "congruence between regular and remedial programs will never be complete until the philosophies underlying both programs are brought in line with one another" (p. 367). It extends into the forging of a unitary, school-wide reading program focusing on common goals and objectives (Slavin et al., 1994). It demands that organizational forms grow not from best practices in the management domain but from well-understood aims and from our best understanding of learning. Any organizational form can advantage or disadvantage special students. The key issue is the motive that informs the structure. The school point-of-view regarding instruction should animate structure (Birman, 1988). At the same time, a common plan of action and well-developed opportunities for regular communication and collaboration among teachers in the regular and special programs can be vital paths to infuse a common philosophy into the reading system—to create a coherent reading program (Slavin et al., 1994; Taylor & Taxis, n.d.; Venezky & Winfield, 1979).

Building coherence also necessitates working on the three fronts detailed earlier. That is, it requires that there be congruence within each special program. Second, it obliges the various special programs to hang together, to create "consistency within the support program instruction" (Allington & McGill-Franzen, 1989a, p. 88). Finally, it compels coordination between the regular and special programs (Heibert et al., 1992; Torgesen, 1997), especially at the "instructional level so that intervention from specialists coordinates with and supports classroom instruction" (Snow et al., 1998, p. 12). This, in turn, "will require a redefinition of the roles played by specialists . . . and classroom teachers. This redefinition involves not just modifying instructional efforts but profound changes in the expectations for . . . these teachers and an acceptance of altered roles for them in our schools" (Allington & Broikou, 1988, p. 808). In particular, it calls for the development of "shared knowledge" (p. 809) between the regular and special teachers, as well as cooperative planning of classroom lessons. It is congruence that is important because "we know that when classroom specialist teachers emphasize the same literacy skills in their instruction, learner attainment of mastery of those skills is enhanced and we have evidence that when classroom and remedial programs emphasize congruent skills and strategies, achievement improves" (Allington, 1991, p. 15).

Summary

In this chapter, I explored the topic of coherence within literacy programs. I touched on a variety of elements that define coherence in the core school program. Significant attention was also given to the connections between the regular and special programs and among the various special programs themselves. I reviewed the evidence on the importance of coordination, especially for students placed at risk of failure in school. I examined the literature that shows that coherence is the exception rather than the norm, and I crafted a platform for strengthening coherence and building integration into the literacy program.

11

Promoting the Learning of Staff

Good first teaching is not a program you can buy, but is the result of an investment in professional development. (Fountas & Pinnell, 1999, p. 183)

We want to suggest that the consistencies between our findings for teachers in the most effective schools and those for the most accomplished teachers may provide encouraging news for those who regard professional development as the center of gravity in any reform movement. (Taylor et al., 1999, p. 47)

This chapter is devoted to exploring three issues in the education of teachers of reading. I begin with an analysis of the importance of professional development. In this section, I also review the evidence concerning the normal state of affairs in literacy education in teacher education programs. In section two, I throw the spotlight on the elements of productive professional development work. I close by investigating professional development in the context of creating communities of practice among teachers.

Importance of Professional Development

> Opportunities for teachers to learn are an essential part of
> any project where patterns of reading acquisition move more
> children to proficient reading levels. (Hiebert & Taylor, 2000,
> p. 478)

> All four of the most effective schools cited the importance of
> ongoing professional development when giving reasons for
> their success. (Taylor et al., 1999, p. 28)

Over the last two decades, the knowledge base about promoting
literacy mastery for all youngsters, especially children from low-income
homes, has increased substantially (Chall et al., 1990), as attested to
by the material in this book. Concomitantly, we have learned much
about what is and what is not likely to work to bring this practical
wisdom to life in America's classrooms and schools. Disparagement
is a particularly ineffectual reform strategy because, no matter how
rhetorically and politically appealing, without a "system in which
[teachers] might spend time and energy studying and improving
teaching" (Stigler & Hiebert, 1999, p. 174) it lacks the power to fuel
change. Reform "mandates without accompanying inservice [also]
rarely work" (Allington & Broikou, 1988, p. 809) for, as Stigler and
Hiebert (1999) remind us, it is "silly to expect teachers to simply execute
improved teaching methods without providing them opportunities
to develop these methods and learn how to use them" (p. 142). The
quest for teacher-proof reading programs has been and will continue
to be illusionary as well (Allington & Walmsley, 1995; Ivey, 2000).

The conclusion with the greatest saliency is that "in order to
transform teaching [we must] first enhance the knowledge and skills of
individual teachers" (McGill-Franzen, 2000, p. 897). Most critically, "it
is imperative that teachers at all grade levels understand the course of
literacy development and the role of instruction in optimizing literacy
development" (Snow et al., 1998, p. 10). This knowledge leads to two
deductions: First, "teachers need opportunities for sustained professional development" (p. 258). Second, "schools must be places where
teachers, as well as students, can learn" (Stigler & Hiebert, 1999, p. 144).

I arrive at these conclusions based on both logical and empirical
evidence. On the first front, "in the final analysis, teachers are the
ones who provide the literacy environment and the instruction that
make the difference between learning well and not learning well"
(Chall et al., 1990, pp. 160-161). Because, as Stigler and Hiebert (1999)

observe, "they are the only ones who can ensure that students' learning improves . . . they are, necessarily, the solution to the problem of improving teaching" (p. 136).

On the empirical front, there is a wealth of evidence to demonstrate that teachers enter the profession without the completed skill sets they need to help all youngsters achieve at high levels in reading: "many classroom and specialist teachers simply lack the expertise necessary to deliver high quality reading instruction to low-achieving children" (Allington & McGill-Franzen, 1989a, p. 90). Or as Hiebert and Taylor (2000) discovered in their work, "the performance of the status quo group indicates that opportunities for expanding teachers' learning about beginning reading instruction are needed to initiate changes in the profiles of struggling beginning readers" (p. 478).

At the macro level, the problem is twofold. First, most "elementary teachers receive only a basic introduction to reading" (Anderson et al., 1985, p. 106). Because many states have weak course requirements in the area of reading (Hall & Moats, 1999), the total package of course-work is simply inadequate to prepare new teachers to teach reading well. The typical teacher education program, for example, includes only "one course in the teaching of reading and a related course in the teaching of language arts" (Anderson et al., 1985, p. 106). For princi-pals, the numbers are even more discouraging (Chance, 1991). Second, many teachers have been on the job for a lengthy period of time. For a good number of these educators, their training is outdated (Allington & McGill-Franzen, 1989a).

At the micro level, analysts have ascertained that a significant proportion of teachers are "unfamiliar with how to explicitly teach sounds, letters, and spellings" (Hall & Moats, 1999, p. 17). Parti-cularly troubling, given the "evidence showing the effectiveness of phonics instruction" (NICHHD, 2000a, p. 10) that I explored in detail in Chapter 7, is the fact that many teachers lack information about teaching phonological awareness and the alphabetic code (Blachman et al., 1999; Moats, 1996; NICHHD, 2000b). As Pressley (1998b) sur-mises, "the reason that teachers do not concern themselves with developing phonemic awareness is because they do not know how to develop it in children" (p. 102); "many primary teachers do not understand enough about phonics or commonly encountered word chunks in order to implement either a synthetic program or a decoding-by-analogy approach" (p. 144).

These same analysts trace these problems back to teacher education programs, programs that "often fail to address the beginning reading skills that research has shown to be critical to reading success"

(Blachman et al., 1999, p. 269). Their conclusions are that "teachers require much more extensive, demanding, and content-driven training if discoveries from the reading sciences are to inform classroom practice" (American Federation of Teachers, 1999, p. 13), and that schools must do a better job of "provid[ing] for teachers' continual professional growth" (Chall et al., 1990, p. 161).

There is also plentiful evidence of the central place of professional development in the larger portfolio of improvement strategies. For example, Askew and colleagues (2000) reference a study indicating "that every additional dollar spent on raising teacher quality netted greater student gains than did any other use of school resources" (p. 286). Specifically, there is a robust empirical link between professional development and student reading achievement. Rowe's (1995) study, for example, reveals "that professional development . . . appears to be a powerful means of engendering positive outcomes for students" (p. 87). National Reading Panel (2000) analysts reinforce this finding, reporting in their comprehensive review "that inservice professional development produced significantly higher achievement" (p. 17). The story line here has been nicely laid out by Anders, Hoffman, & Duffy (2000):

> Studies have suggested that resources committed to changes in teacher thinking and practices do effect change. Positive effects have been shown across a variety of areas ranging from targeted interventions on teacher questioning to skills instruction, to comprehension instruction, to impact on general approaches and philosophies such as "whole language." The impact of inservice has been shown on the development of teacher knowledge, attitudes, beliefs, practices, and teacher satisfaction. The impact has even been demonstrated in terms of positive effects on student growth in decoding, comprehension and cooperation, and attitudes. The impact has been shown across classroom-based, school-based, and district-based efforts; short-term and long-term projects; and across research methodologies ranging from case studies to full experimental designs. (p. 729)

Finally, employing the frames that underlie this volume, professional development is a defining characteristic of effective schools,

> Successful schools . . . frequently utilize staff development or inservice training programs to realize their objectives. (Phi Delta Kappa, 1980, p. 205)

effective teaching and effective teachers,

Ongoing support from colleagues and specialists, as well as regular opportunities for self-examination and reflection, are critical components of the career-long development of excellent teachers. (Snow et al., 1998, p. 10)

and effective reading programs,

There seems to be strong support across investigations of exemplary reading programs for teacher training. (Samuels, 1981, p. 267)

What all of this information conveys is that the ongoing learning of teachers in the area of literacy is imperative. Also, that "continuous professional support" (Pikulski, 1994, p. 38), "abundant staff development" (Taylor & Taxis, n.d., p. 10), and self-renewing development initiatives are needed to operationalize that learning (Patty et al., 1996). As the authors of *Becoming a Nation of Readers* remind us: "Schools should provide for the continuing professional development of teachers. Schools should have programs to ease the transition of novice teachers into the profession and programs to keep veteran teachers abreast of advancing knowledge" (Anderson et al., 1985, p. 120). Since "most of the costs of restructuring and reforming American elementary schools will be people costs—renewing, refreshing, extending, and enhancing the professional expertise of the teachers . . . who carry out the daily work of educating children" (Allington & Walmsley, 1995, p. 263), district and school leaders and state policymakers will need to engage "major initiatives to train teachers already on the job" (Hall & Moats, 1999, p. 27).

Elements of Productive
Professional Development Work

Teacher development is effective when it is grounded in the practice of teaching children. As teacher developers work with children and with teachers, work in one area informs the other. Daily practice with children constantly builds the conceptual map that the teacher developer draws for powerful interactions with teachers. (Lyons & Pinnell, 1999, p. 210)

The theme of reflection has appeared time and again in this literature. It appears that an important part of inservice teacher education is to provide opportunities and tools for

teachers to reflect on their own practices systematically as
they move toward change. (Anders et al., 2000, p. 730)

Researchers who have examined the reasons why professional
development serves to enhance teacher performance and student
outcomes, and analysts who have traced the characteristics of professional development programs that are the most effective, have
amassed a fruitful body of wisdom for school teachers who are
engaged in strengthening early reading programs. To begin with,
professional development is most efficacious when it is highly
valued at the school by the teachers and especially by the principal
(Fisher & Adler, 1999). Adult learning also works best when educators at the site have a "positive attitude toward staff growth and
development" (Hoffman & Rutherford, 1984, p. 87) and a commitment
to improvement (Mattson, 1994).

Thinking about professional development from the perspective
of structure or organization, we know that most staff development
is free standing, short term, nonsystematic, and infrequent. We
also understand that these characteristics make implementation of
change problematic and do little to enhance reading performance
(Richardson, 1998). On the other hand, professional development is
most effective in garnering improvements in literacy when it is part
of a thoughtful plan, is long term in nature, and employs frequent
learning sessions for teachers (Hiebert & Pearson, 1999; Morris et al.,
1990; Samuels, 1981). Inservice tends to be most influential when the
"education programs involve teachers who choose to participate"
(Anders et al., 2000, p. 730). Furthermore, because "achieving and
sustaining . . . gains is often difficult when improvements are introduced on a classroom-by-classroom basis" (Snow et al., 1998, p. 11),
schoolwide professional development often leads to more favorable
results (Richardson, 1998; Taylor et al., 1999). Inservice in effective
reading programs is carefully joined to other aspects and dimensions
of the organization (Au & Asam, 1996; Phi Delta Kappa, 1980) and
"the aspects of school change" (Askew & Gaffney, 1999, p. 87). The
provision of sufficient time for learning is also a distinguishing
characteristic of quality professional development for enhanced
literacy (Anders et al., 2000; Taylor & Taxis, n.d.). Finally, professional
development in successful schools and effective reading programs
is defined by high levels of administrative support (Anderson et al.,
1985; Dungan, 1994; Hiebert & Pearson, 1999) and involvement,
especially "principal participation in training" (Samuels, 1981,
p. 268). Indeed, "staff development programs are most meaningful

when principals and other administrators participate directly in them at the classroom level" (Manning, 1995, p. 656).

Continuous and intensive support over time is an essential ingredient of inservice programs that promote high levels of student reading achievement (Askew & Gaffney, 1999; Hiebert et al., 1992). Another critical point is "that teacher change needs support in the context of practice" (Anders et al., 2000, p. 730). Effective professional development grows from "child-driven data gathering" (Askew & Gaffney, 1999, p. 85) and from student needs. It builds from student performance data and school results (Briggs & Thomas, 1997).

The programs that are successful are practice-anchored and job-embedded; that is, they are context sensitive. "Context specificity" (Hiebert & Pearson, 1999, p. 13) contains a number of key ideas, but primarily it means "building from analysis of [one's] own setting" (p. 13). Sensitivity to context implies that "teachers learn in the classrooms and schools in which they teach" (Stigler & Hiebert, 1999, p. 135). They "learn how to teach more effectively while teaching" (Lyons & Pinnell, 1999, p. 205) rather than in traditional out-of-class and school activities. Growth is "connected to and derived from teachers' work with children" (Askew & Gaffney, 1999, p. 87) and effectiveness comes to be defined in terms of "what works with the children [one is] teaching" (Duffy-Hester, 1999, p. 489; see also Pinnell et al., 1994). The center of gravity is real challenges in the classroom (Au & Asam, 1996), that is, "resolving instructional problems" (Manning, 1995, p. 656). "All theory building is then checked against practice" (Askew & Gaffney, 1999, p. 85) and "application is direct and obvious" (Stigler & Hiebert, 1999, p. 165).

Concomitantly, professional learning is not insular. Effective programs are adept at bringing outside help to bear on local issues as appropriate (Rowe, 1995). Schools with quality inservice programs are also likely to be part of a network of support of others engaged in learning efforts (Allington, 1997b; Hiebert et al., 1992; Pinnell et al., 1994) and to be part of "collaborative arrangements" (Fisher & Adler, 1999, p. 19) formed "among different role groups" (Anders et al., 2000, p. 730).

A trusting context for learning, especially the freedom to try out ideas in a safe environment, is also a key element of effective professional development (Lyons & Pinnell, 1999; Neuman, 1999). So too is the tendency to focus on growth rather than deficits. Finally, there is abundant support for the claim that reflection is a critical variable in the effective training equation (Askew & Gaffney, 1999; Duffy-Hester, 1999). Lyons and Pinnell (1999) phrase this idea nicely when they explain that "teacher development is effective when there is a balance between demonstration of specific teaching approaches and the reflection and analysis needed to build the process of thinking about teaching" (p. 210). The "teacher as inquirer" (Richardson, 1998, p. 307) and teacher as researcher metaphors hold center stage in effective professional development (Richardson, 1998).

Professional Development as Learning Community

> It seems that schools in which the reading programs are liveliest and most effective are schools in which ideas about reading are aired and shared among teachers. (Wilder, 1977, p. 276)

> Teachers in all four of the most effective schools reported collaboration within and across grades as a reason for their success. (Taylor et al., 1999, p. 26)

Over the past fifteen years, research on teaching, school improvement, and professional development has helped us deepen our understanding of teacher learning and its impact on students. Specifically, this work has shown us that "schools will benefit from becoming collaborative, learning communities" (Taylor & Taxis, n.d., p. 12), or communities of practice (Richardson, 1998). Studies in these areas indicate that "almost all successful attempts to improve reading involve teachers working together to improve students' learning" (Stigler & Hiebert, 1999, p. 135) and that "schools that are especially effective in teaching reading are characterized by . . . collegiality and a sense of community" (Anderson et al., 1985, p. 113). Explorations of "especially effective schools suggest that programs of professional development are most successful when several teachers from the same school . . . are involved" (p. 111). In other words, "effective teacher development depends in large part on building a community of learners" (Lyons & Pinnell, 1999, p. 216). Two concepts that are difficult to bring to life in many American schools, collaboration and cooperation, are woven into the center of the community-of-practice tapestry (Askew & Gaffney, 1999; Hiebert & Taylor, 2000).

Analysts have unearthed a number of elements of communities of practice as they relate to professional development. One is that staff development is cooperatively planned by teachers (Anderson et al., 1985; Patty et al., 1996). Teachers' views are represented and taken seriously (Rutter, 1983). According to Allington and Walmsley (1995), teachers are regarded as "coprofessionals" (p. 261) rather than simply as employees. A second ingredient is "shared conversations around the act of teaching" (Lyons & Pinnell, 1999, p. 215), what Askew and Gaffney (1999) label "a sharing of knowledge" (p. 87), and Samuels (1981) describes as the "cross-fertilization of ideas about reading" (p. 264). According to Johnston (1999), this "openness of discussion maximizes the possibility of distributed cognition—the system of collective thought in which the whole is more than the sum of the parts" (p. 40). So too is cooperative problem solving a characteristic of professional learning communities (Clay, 1994). Shared information and shared resolution of problems undergird the growth of other pieces of the collaborative landscape—shared language (Lyons & Pinnell, 1999), shared work (Hoffman & Rutherford, 1984), and a focus on making historically self-contained and isolated teacher work open and public (Jones & Smith-Burke, 1999). From all of this flow two significant outcomes, "shared ownership" (Askew & Gaffney, 1999, p. 91) and "collective responsibility" (Briggs & Thomas, 1997, p. 34), that are at the heart of literacy improvement in elementary schools.

Scholars have also documented tangible ways that communities of professional practice are energized and maintained. Some of the most referenced include: the use of regularly scheduled meetings between regular classroom teachers and special teachers (Fisher & Adler, 1999); the formation and the employment of grade-level teams as forums for discussion about reading instruction; the use of shared work time to attack literacy challenges (Stigler & Hiebert, 1999); the establishment of study groups (Taylor & Taxis, n.d.) and action research teams (Anders et al., 2000); creating interdependencies (Briggs & Thomas, 1997) and establishing forums for teachers and administrators to work together on "the journey of developing more effective instructional strategies" (Danridge et al., 2000, p. 657); having teachers who participate in reading-based learning experiences outside the school, including visiting other sites and sharing knowledge gained with colleagues (Taylor et al., 1999); creating opportunities for teachers to observe colleagues in the act of teaching reading (Briggs & Thomas, 1997); providing formal and informal strategies to engage teachers in leadership roles in the area of literacy (Briggs & Thomas, 1997); nurturing the development of "informal consultations" (Armor et al., 1976, p. 28) among teachers; and building formal mentoring strategies to "support mentors who have demonstrated records of success in teaching reading" (Snow et al., 1998, p. 10).

As I chronicled in the first part of this chapter, training that builds from the quality indicators outlined above and that nurtures the development of communities of professional practice advances a variety of important outcomes. Teachers become "good educational consumers" (Fisher & Adler, 1999, p. 24); that is, effective and "independent evaluators of knowledge claims" (Stanovich, 2000, p. 383). Teachers become better able to "think critically about the art of teaching" (Askew et al., 2000, p. 286). More vital literacy programs emerge and the quality of teacher instruction is enhanced (Taylor et al., 1999). And most importantly, there is a noticeable increase in student learning.

Summary

In this chapter, I examined the role of teacher professional development in enhancing student performance in reading and the related language arts. The two major sections of the chapter were devoted to an analysis of the elements of effective professional development work and an examination of the importance of thinking of professional development in terms of creating communities of literacy practice. Around that work, I depicted the normal state of affairs in the area of professional development and portrayed the connections between quality professional development and enhanced student achievement.

12

Collaborating With the Home to Strengthen Literacy Achievement

There is growing evidence that increasing literacy activities at home can make a difference in literacy acquisition. (Pressley, 1998b, p. 183)

The results provide strong empirical support for the benefits of Reading Activity at Home, regardless of family socio-economic status. (Rowe, 1995, p. 84)

I begin my analysis here with Juel's (1991) observation that "there are various routes a child might take to gain information necessary to advance as a reader. These routes will be shaped by both home and school experiences" (p. 779). According to Chall and her colleagues (1990) and Snow and her research team (1991), both the family and the school are important variables in the literacy equation, with students doing best "when both the home and the school provide optimal conditions for literacy development" (Chall et al., 1990, p. 166). Conversely, "risk of failure increases if either home or school provides a less than optimal environment for learning to read" (Snow et al., 1991, p. 158).

Other insights about this bi-directional relationship (Gadsden, 1998) have been formulated over the last twenty years. First, home endeavors that influence reading performance largely mirror school activities (Chall et al., 1990). Second, while weaknesses in one area can be overcome to some extent by strengths in the other domain, "deficits in either . . . the home or school contribution cannot be completely compensated for by strengths in the other" (Snow et al., 1991, p. 157). Third, because, as I sketched out in the second chapter, "the reading task goes through qualitative changes at different stages of development . . . home factors that facilitate reading development . . . differ by stage as well" (Chall et al., 1990, p. 141); that is, "certain aspects of the home environment [are] more important for early development while others [are] more important for later develop-ment" (p. 138). In accordance with my focus in this book, my gaze is directed toward the development of a literate home for the early years. I also attend to the reciprocal relationship between school and family and, in keeping with my central theme, I highlight the factors that school leaders can influence to create "home press" (Greaney & Hegarty, 1987, p. 6) for literacy.

Research findings pile on top of each other confirming the powerful influence of the home on student reading achievement. Coupled with data that disclose that youngsters (a) spend nearly 90 percent of their time outside of school (Fraser, 1989, p. 711), (b) devote a miniscule amount of time to reading, and (c) commit massive amounts of time to nonliteracy related activities such as watching television (Anderson et al., 1988), the potential for large gains in reading performance from home activity is quite evident.

Findings coalescing around the position that "parental provision of a strong literacy environment in the home [is] positively associated with children's literacy and language development, [is] strongly asso-ciated with language (word meanings), and also significantly associ-ated with reading" (Chall et al., 1990, p. 129) flow from half a dozen different research tributaries. Studies on the development of young children, for example, reveal that "parents play roles of inestimable importance in laying the foundation for learning to read" (Anderson et al., 1985, p. 27): "Among literacy researchers, it has become some-thing of a truism to assert that literacy development begins at birth, with many opportunities for events in the home life of preschoolers that have implications for literacy development" (Pressley, 1998b, p. 81). Other scholars have drawn fairly robust linkages between out-of-school reading and student achievement (Rowe, 1995) and between amount of school reading and home literacy environment.

Turning to the framework undergirding this volume, studies of low-income children and minority youngsters who excel in reading isolate parental involvement and support as key elements of the success algorithm (Chall et al., 1990; Snow et al., 1991). In a similar vein, investigators of skilled readers underscore a host of home-based explanatory factors, which when bundled together create "high levels of literacy in the home environment" (Snow et al., 1991, p. 60). Parental fingerprints are also found on effective early intervention programs in reading (Pikulski, 1994) and effective Title I programs (Taylor et al., 1990). Investigations of effective literacy teachers divulge that these educators "make a strong commitment to parental involvement" (Jonson, 1998, p. 95). Likewise, studies of effective schools generally disclose "close links between the school and the community with substantial efforts to involve as many parents as possible, mostly through the use of deliberate strategies" (Rowe, 1995, p. 89). Researchers who directly explore home-school connections also "find a positive link between some, but not all, parental involvement attempts and student success in school" (Baker et al., 1996, p. 24). They confirm that these more program-anchored linkages are "positively and statistically significantly related to the school effectiveness rating and to all measures of student growth" (Taylor et al., 1999, p. 23).

In the next two sections of this chapter, I extract the findings from these various lines of study to complete my portrait of leadership for literacy. Following the organizational design of others (e.g., Henderson, 1987), I cluster the results into two broad categories: (1) promoting the "educating family" (Snow et al., 1991, p. 68) or helping parents in their education role—what Auerbach (1995) describes as "helping parents help their children acquire literacy" (p. 12), and (2) fashioning linkages between home and school. Before I proceed, however, a couple of caveats are needed. First, as Beck (1998) alerts us, while a literate environment in the home can be helpful, it does not guarantee literacy. Nor can it, as Auerbach (1995) observes, triumph alone over the host of significant problems such as poverty, inadequate housing, lack of health care, and so forth, confronting many families. Second, "it is important to look at different aspects of the home environment separately because different experiences may predict different outcomes" (Baker, Scher, & Mackler, 1997, p. 78).

Promoting the Educating Family

Adults who live and interact regularly with children can profoundly influence the quality and quantity of their literacy experiences. (Snow et al., 1998, p. 138)

The resources and opportunities available to children in their home environments are significant influences on literacy development. (Baker et al., 1996, p. 21)

Students who reported more home support for literacy had higher average reading achievement. (Foertsch, 1992, p. 5)

Assisting family members to become successful literacy mentors entails four key tasks: establishing a literate environment in the home, teaching, providing a supportive context, and influencing children's "patterns of activities" (Anderson et al., 1988, p. 291).

Establishing a Literate Environment

High levels of literacy in the home environment are related to children's higher levels of school achievement. (Snow et al., 1991, p. 60)

Considerable evidence informs us that provision of literacy in the home is "related at impressive levels of significance to student achievement . . . in word recognition, vocabulary, and reading comprehension" (Snow et al., 1991, p. 206), and that "a more stimulating and organized home environment seems to result in an upward deflection in reading achievement between first and sixth grade" (Jimerson et al., 1999, p. 123). We are also aware that "the early home environment provides a foundation for early achievement [and] in addition continues to influence levels of achievement across time" (p. 124). Establishing a literate context is one way of forging "a press for reading in the home" (Greaney & Hegarty, 1987, p. 11). It entails first of all furnishing literacy opportunities to youngsters, or creating a print-rich culture in the home (Bush, 1995; Morrow, 1995). This, in turn, includes a wide range of age-appropriate activities to ensure accessibility (Allington, 1991; Baker et al., 1997), including buying youngsters books, taking them to the library, maintaining in the home a "generous provision of books and reading materials" (Snow et al., 1991, p. 162), and providing "access to chalkboards and pencils and paper" (Anderson et al., 1985, p. 24).

The literate home contains interesting pictures, shelves of books, magazines, newspapers, alphabet blocks, and children's books. This is a home that places high value on education. (Richardson, 1991, p. 6)

Children who are avid readers come from homes that have books, subscriptions to children's magazines, and in which both adults and children have library cards. Public and school libraries are especially important for children from poor homes. (Anderson et al., 1985, p. 78)

A second strand of home literacy culture is "parents' own literacy practices" (Snow et al., 1991, p. 61). Literate homes are settings in which adults "provide models of intellectual activity" (p. 63). A literate home context is one in which parents model good literacy behavior (Baker et al., 1997; Hallinger & Murphy, 1995), especially the reading habit (Greaney & Hegarty, 1987). Adults in these homes express an interest in reading. They tend to read and write more and they do so at "high discourse levels" (Purcell-Gates, 1998, p. 63). And in homes where adults read frequently, students come to value reading (Baker et al., 1997), have higher average reading achievement (Foertsch, 1992), and know more about writing as a system (Purcell-Gates, 1998).

Direct Teaching

Yet the most important activity for building the knowledge and skills eventually required for reading is that of reading aloud to children. (Adams, 1990, p. 86)

When young children learn to read well, it is often because adults at home "provide books, interest, attention, and teaching" (Chall et al., 1990, p. 16). While in the previous section our attention was devoted to the topic of "books," the agenda here is "teaching." The message is that while furnishing a print-rich environment is important, more important still is the ability of adults in the home to engage children in literacy experiences (Baker et al., 1997), to focus youngsters on print (Purcell-Gates, 1998), and to involve them in reading-related activities (Smith, 1997). A key point to bear in mind is that while reading is generally a solitary activity, "literacy is learned within a social context" (Neuman et al., 1998, p. 248)—"children's literacy develops in a social network of interested individuals who provide support, encouragement, and learning and teaching opportunities" (Baker et al., 1996, p. 37). When parents and others in the home are at the hub of that social network, children master literacy skills and become good readers.

One dimension of teaching involves providing support for homework (Anderson et al., 1985; Samuels, 1981). Homework extends engaged time, thus increasing opportunity to learn. And because opportunity to learn is a dominant variable in the student performance algorithm, "amount of homework [has] positive relationships to achievement" (Fraser, 1989, p. 715). Parent support for homework has other benefits as well. It allows parents "to support the kind of learning that goes on at school" (Snow et al., 1991, p. 117), it informs them "about the child's school experiences" (p. 117), and it conveys positive messages to school staff. Support for homework can be partitioned into a variety of components. One element, labeled by Wolf (cited in Greaney & Hegarty, 1987, p. 8) as "academic guidance," involves parents encouraging youngsters to complete assigned work. Another factor is the provision of a quiet space to work (Auerbach, 1995). A third piece of the support puzzle is allocating time for completing assignments. Also important is the supervision of homework, at least checking for completion (Chall et al., 1990; Fraser, 1989). Finally, staying connected to the school in terms of being familiar with homework policies and guidelines and understanding homework's relation to school goals are important ways that parents provide support (Creemers, 1994; Henderson, 1987).

Reading with children in the home is another component of teaching (Morrow, 1995; Pikulski, 1994). In fact, reading aloud to children is identified in *Becoming a Nation of Readers* as "the single most important activity for building the knowledge required for eventual success in reading" (Anderson et al., 1985, p. 10). This is the case because it is associated with (a) the development of "more positive views toward reading" (Rowe, 1995, p. 66); (b) deeper engagement in leisure reading (Baker et al., 1997); (c) "increased confidence and motivation to read" (Rowe, 1995, p. 66); (d) enhanced knowledge about the alphabetic principle and concepts of print (Adams, 1990; Purcell-Gates, 1998); and (e) "interest in independent reading" (Baker et al., 1997, p. 71)— the formation of a "predisposition to read frequently and broadly in subsequent years" (p. 69). Over and above this, reading aloud to children is correlated with "literacy acquisition" (Pressley, 1998b, p. 183) and higher levels of student achievement (Auerbach, 1995).

In dissecting the concept of reading aloud to children, two central ideas are exposed. First, it is best accomplished in informal ways rather than in a school-like atmosphere (Pressley, 1998b). Or, to borrow a phrase from *Becoming a Nation of Readers*, it should be done "with a light touch" (Anderson et al., 1985, p. 117). Second, the "reading to" activity is important, but it is only part of the story. Specifically, "the type of activity addressed in those interactions makes a difference" (Williams, 1991, p. 16): "Thus it is not only the act of reading that is important; also important are the kinds of conversations reader and children have with one another during the reading session, the affective quality of those interactions, and the print-related discussions that ensue" (Baker et al., 1997, p. 74). The advantages are "greatest when the child is an active participant, engaging in discussions about stories, learning to identify letters and words, and talking about the meaning of words" (Anderson et al., 1985, p. 10).

> It is not just reading to children that makes the difference, it is enjoying the books with them and reflecting on their form and content. It is developing and supporting the children's curiosity about text and the meanings it conveys. It is encouraging the children to examine the print. It is sometimes starting and always inviting discussions of the meanings of the words and the relationships of the text's ideas to the world beyond the book. And it is showing the children that we value and enjoy reading and that we hope they will too. (Adams, 1990, p. 87)

Thus at the core of the activity is the quality of the "conversation between adults and children about the content of books" (Snow et al., 1991, p. 162).

The final sphere of direct teaching broadens the concept beyond "school-like literacy activities within the family" (Auerbach, 1995, p. 26) to include adults "participating in a variety of activities with children" (Snow et al., 1991, p. 84)—to encompass the "wide range of experiences [that] contribute to literacy development" (Auerbach, 1995, p. 18). The focus is first and foremost on "the importance of everyday experiences in relation to literacy" (Gadsden, 1998, p. 39), the fitting of literacy into the ongoing activities of life (Neuman et al., 1998; Snow et al., 1998). It is also on the use of family outings to build literacy skills (Snow et al., 1991). As with the other dimensions of direct teaching—that is, support for homework and reading aloud to children—extended access to adults is the starting point. As was the case earlier, however, "wide experience alone is not enough" (Anderson et al., 1985, p. 22). The way "in which parents *talk* to their children about an experience" (p. 22) is critical.

Providing a Supportive Context

A supportive context provided by parents may be more important than any transfer of skills. (Auerbach, 1995, p. 17)

Research across all four dimensions of the framework that undergirds this book affirms that "it is important to understand . . . the extent to which home support is available for reading" (Foertsch, 1992, p. 21). Home support here is conceptualized along three fronts. The first is providing access to adults, "especially adults who engage in a variety of activities" (Chall et al., 1990, p. 159). Adult contact is a valuable resource, one that advantages youngsters in acquiring literacy skills and in learning to read.

The second front comprises a bundle of values that form the architecture "for structuring the environment" (Baker et al., 1997, p. 70)—"beliefs and attitudes . . . that influence literacy development" (Snow et al., 1998, p. 138). Especially important here is the extent to which reading either takes on an air of significance or is a "peripherally valued activity" (Adams, 1990, p. 87). Parental expectations for reading achievement and academic performance are also critical factors in the value framework (Greaney & Hegarty, 1987; Rowe, 1995).

The final front is composed of support functions that parents undertake to strengthen literacy acquisition. Encouraging reading is one such activity (Baker et al., 1997). Buying books and securing access to the library are indicators here. Ensuring student attendance at school is important. So too is staying abreast of and supporting school goals and programs in the literacy area. Keeping in touch with the school seems to be an especially productive support activity. Acting as an advocate for the child at school is productive "because it shapes teachers' perceptions, which in turn influence student achievement" (Auerbach, 1995, p. 20). Taking an interest in schoolwork is a type of support activity associated with literacy acquisition. So also is the monitoring of schoolwork (Anderson et al., 1985).

Influencing Activity Patterns

Increasing supervised homework and reducing television . . . have an outstanding record of success in promoting achievement. (Fraser, 1989, p. 711)

I have already catalogued an assortment of ways that parents influence the activities of their children in relation to literacy. Carving out structured time for completing reading homework is one method. Providing regular access to adults for conversations about books and other literacy topics is another. Scheduling opportunities to read to children is a third way to influence how youngsters spend their time. Encouraging independent reading is still another strategy. "Exercising control over leisure time" (Snow et al., 1991, p. 63), especially placing reasonable limits on activities such as television viewing and chores are especially productive strategies to enhance literacy achievement (Foertsch, 1992; Nicholson, 1999). For example, a number of studies have linked heavier television watching with low reading scores (Chall et al., 1990; Donahue et al., 1999). Buttressing the literacy-enhancing elements of the leisure time portfolio, such as providing time for regular family outings and meals, is also a useful design principle.

Creating Linkages Between Home and School

> Overall, parent-school collaboration relate[s] positively to . . . children's reading, writing, and vocabulary development. (Chall et al., 1990, p. 131)

Research studies of effective schools and quality reading programs substantiate that "parent cooperation is important and that all efforts should be made to foster it" (Postlethwaite & Ross, 1992, p. 32). More directly, there is an abundance of evidence that "students' literacy growth is enhanced when their parents are engaged in a partnership with the school" (Sanacore, 1997, p. 67) and that student performance in terms of achievement scores is increased (Armor et al., 1976; Henderson, 1987). Key strands in this cooperative narrative include promoting parental involvement in the school, developing contacts between teachers and parents, and encouraging the codevelopment of literacy in the home.

Promoting Parental Involvement

> Parent involvement improves student achievement. When parents are involved, children do better in school. (Henderson, 1987, p. 1)

When the school and home operate from the same literacy playbook and work together to enhance literacy skills, children are advantaged (Baker et al., 1996). Having "parents as partners with schools in helping their children learn to read" (Morrow, 1995, p. 5) is the cornerstone of the collaboration. Active parental involvement is associated with a variety of preferred outcomes, everything from fostering ties between the school and the community (Patty et al., 1996), to strengthening the community (Phi Delta Kappa, 1980), to better schools (Henderson, 1987), to enhanced academic success in reading (Hoffman & Rutherford, 1984; Jimerson et al., 1999). Parental involvement works because it focuses attention on the critical area of literacy. It conveys clear messages to youngsters about the value of reading and signals to children that "school achievement is important and worth working at" (Snow et al., 1991, p. 117). And it shapes the way school personnel think about children and the expectations they hold for those pupils (Snow et al., 1991).

Drawing a magnet through the studies in each of the four areas of my design permits us to extract key elements of the school-parent partnership for literacy. We learn that parents do not need to be well educated in a formal sense to make the partnership function. We also discover that there is no one best way to build partnerships. Rather, "what works is for parents to be involved in a variety of roles over a period of time" (Henderson, 1987, p. 2). "Mutual expectations" (Sanacore, 1997, p. 67) are important, as is the ability of school leaders to carefully and systematically integrate parental energy and effort into school activities (Armor et al., 1976). A system for involvement that is "comprehensive, long-lasting, and well planned" (Henderson, 1987, p. 9) and that involves parents in the design (Neuman et al., 1998) results in maximum impact for youngsters. A design that "involves as many parents as possible through use of deliberate strategies" (Rowe, 1995, p. 89), that ensures frequent contact between home and school (Hiebert & Pearson, 1999; Hoffman & Rutherford, 1984) and, most critically, keeps the focus on the literacy program (Anderson et al., 1985) will be most advantageous.

Developing Contacts Between Teachers and Parents

> Teacher-parent contacts [are] positively related to literacy. (Chall et al., 1990, p. 133)

Research informs us that there are two key elements of "positive home-school relations": a "parental partner role" (Snow et al., 1991, p. 117) in the education of children, and contact between home and school. We understand from a variety of well-crafted studies that "effective schools report more links with parents than moderately effective [or] least effective schools" (Taylor et al., 1999, p. 24). We also know that traffic on the linkage boulevard in effective schools flows in both directions—that "both teacher-initiated and parent-initiated contacts are helpful in improving children's progress" (Chall et al., 1990, p. 157). In schools where literacy achievement is the norm, parents regularly initiate exchanges with the school (Edmonds, 1979, 1986). Concomitantly, "personnel in the most effective schools [make] a more concerted effort than personnel in other schools to reach out to parents" (Taylor et al., 1999, p. 31). There are "open channels of communication between the staff and the community" (State of New York, 1974, p. 54).

A deep network of contacts has "beneficial effects that [are] separate from good teaching practices" (Snow et al., 1991, p. 170). At the macro level, interactions often flower into "support networks" (Auerbach, 1995, p. 25) for parents and furnish a platform for advocacy for youngsters (Auerbach, 1995). Or, alternatively, "the gap between parents and teachers" (Snow et al., 1991, p. 15) can be bridged by regular contacts (Haberman, 1995). At the core of the benefit model is "the relationship between parent contacts and gains in student achievement" (Snow et al., 1991, p. 126). This relationship, in turn, is mediated by the influence of exchanges on the values, knowledge, and expectations of the parties (Chall et al., 1990). For example, teachers often interpret an absence of parent-initiated interactions as a lack of family interest in the education of their youngsters. Conversely, teachers are likely to ratchet up expectations for children whose parents maintain contact with the school. They seem comfortable attributing student success to home support.

> Parent-initiated contacts seem to modify teacher assessments of a child's abilities and prospects, perhaps signaling to the teacher that someone value[s] the child's schooling and ha[s] high aspirations for the child's ultimate educational achievement. (Snow et al., 1991, p. 126)

In laying this foundation, it is important to observe that contacts between school and home are often conspicuous by their absence and that even when they do occur they tend to be the result of the initiative of a specific parent or teacher (Samuels, 1981) rather than the outcome of school policy and structure. What appears to be essential for leaders dedicated to enhancing literacy is to craft opportunities for regular communication and to create a variety of exchange alternatives—opportunities that undermine the status quo outlined above (Hiebert & Pearson, 1999; Pressley et al., 2000). For, as Snow and her colleagues (1991) remark, "schools which do not make parents feel welcome to visit the classroom or to speak to teachers and administrators are not doing their best to ensure educational progress for all children" (p. 174).

Ongoing communication with homes by teachers is a critical ingredient in the contact strategy. Because "teacher visits with parents either in the classroom or at the students' homes [have been] found to contribute to improved reading achievement" (Armor et al., 1976, p. 38), some of this contact should be face-to-face. A final item of significance relates to the content of these contacts. Reading researchers argue from their data that to secure maximum benefits, exchanges should focus on academic issues, not behavioral problems.

Encouraging Codevelopment of Literacy

Given the importance of either direct or indirect parental involvement in students' educational progress, it is imperative that the work of schools be supported by programs designed to assist parents to take an active role in the development of their child's reading skills. (Rowe, 1995, p. 91)

Nurturing the codevelopment of literacy encompasses four sets of activities, all of which are joined to enhanced literacy acquisition for young learners. One component of the portfolio, indeed "one of the most important elements of literacy development" (Morrow, 1995, p. 6), focuses on "improving the parenting and basic literacy skills of adults" (Neuman et al., 1998), what is widely known as "family literacy." A second set of activities highlights assisting parents in learning "to work with their children—to provide helpful information and skills, thereby reinforcing a positive cycle of development for both parents and students" (Henderson, 1987, p. 4).

A particularly efficacious strategy is teaching parents how to productively read to their children (Baker et al., 1996), especially helping "parents become more responsive and 'dialogic' during shared reading" (Snow et al., 1998, p. 139). A closely related codevelopment strategy involves assisting parents "in creating the best possible language environment in the home—to create a literate home" (Richardson, 1991, p. 6). Finally, school actions that inform and "enable families to access and utilize [literacy] resources effectively" (Gadsden, 1998, p. 39) promote reading achievement for youngsters. Studies of effective schools reveal that educators play an important codevelopment role here in a number of ways. They (a) "make connections between families and community resources" (Hiebert & Pearson, 1999, p. 9) that foster literacy development; (b) co-construct at-home reading programs (Briggs & Thomas, 1997; Taylor et al., 1999) in which parents are provided "with resources and opportunities for interacting with their children around books" (Baker et al., 1997, p. 79); (c) "make good literature" (p. 79) and "trade books available to children to take home" (Snow et al., 1991, p. 172); and (d) "provide . . . specific activities for parents and children to complete together with books" (Jonson, 1998, p. 95).

Summary

In this concluding chapter, I reported how leaders can act to improve literacy achievement by nurturing and fortifying connections between the home and school. I clustered evidence culled from my four-part conceptual design under two broad ideas, helping parents help their children become more literate and creating linkages between the home and the school. All of the analysis was built on an introduction that unpacked the power parents possess to influence the literacy achievement of their children.

References

Adams, M. J. (1990). *Beginning to read: Thinking and learning about print*. Cambridge, MA: MIT Press.

Adams, M. J. (1991). Why not phonics and whole language? In W. Ellis (Ed.), *All language and the creation of literacy: Proceedings of the Orton Dyslexic Society Symposia* (pp. 40-53). Baltimore, MD: The Orton Dyslexia Society.

Adams, M. J. (1994). Phonics and beginning reading instruction. In F. Lehr & J. Osborn (Eds.), *Reading, language, and literacy: Instruction for the twenty-first century* (pp. 3-24). Hillsdale, NJ: Lawrence Erlbaum.

Adams, M. J. (1998). The three-cueing system. In J. Osborn & F. Lehr (Eds.), *Literacy for all: issues in teaching and learning* (pp. 73-98). New York: Guilford Press.

Adams, M. J., & Bruck, M. (1993). Word recognition: the interface of educational policies and scientific research. *Reading and Writing: An Interdisciplinary Journal, 5(2),* 113-139.

Adelman, N. E. (1995). Aiming reading instruction at deeper understanding. In M. S. Knapp (Ed.), *Teaching for meaning in high-poverty classrooms* (pp. 64-83). New York: Teachers College Press.

Allen, R. (2000, Summer). Before it's too late: Giving reading a last chance. *ASCD Curriculum Update,* 1-4, 6-8.

Allington, R. L. (1980). Poor readers don't get to read much in reading groups. *Language Arts, 57(8),* 872-876.

Allington, R. L. (1983). The reading instruction provided readers of differing reading abilities. *Elementary School Journal, 83(5),* 548-559.

Allington, R. L. (1984a). Content coverage and contextual reading in reading groups. *Journal of Reading Behavior, 16(2),* 85-96.

Allington, R. L. (1984b). Oral reading. In P. D. Pearson (Ed.), *Handbook of reading research* (Vol. 1, pp. 829-864). New York: Longman.

Allington, R. L. (1991). Effective literacy instruction for at-risk children. In M. S. Knapp & P. M. Shields (Eds.), *Better schooling for the children of poverty: Alternatives to conventional wisdom* (pp. 9-30). Berkeley, CA: McCutchan.

Allington, R. L. (1995). Literacy lessons in the elementary schools: Yesterday, today, and tomorrow. In R. L. Allington & S. A. Walmsley (Eds.), *No quick fix: Rethinking literacy programs in America's elementary schools* (pp. 1-15). New York: Teachers College Press.

Allington, R. L. (1997a). Whose claims are valid? *School Administrator, 54,* 32-34.

Allington, R. L. (1997b). Why does literacy research so often ignore what really matters? In C. K. Kinzer, K. A. Hinchman, & D. J. Leu (Eds.), *Inquiries in literacy: Theory and practice* (pp. 1-12). Chicago: National Reading Conference.

Allington, R. L., & Broikou, K. A. (1988). Development of shared knowledge: A new role for classroom and specialist teachers. *The Reading Teacher, 41(8)*, 806-811.

Allington, R. L., & McGill-Franzen, A. (1989a). Different programs: Indifferent instruction. In D. K. Lipsky & A. Gartner (Eds.), *Beyond separate education: Quality education for all* (pp. 75-97). Baltimore, MD: Paul H. Brookes.

Allington, R. L., & McGill-Franzen, A. (1989b). School response to reading failure: Instruction for Chapter 1 and special education students in Grades two, four, and eight. *The Elementary School Journal, 89(5)*, 529-542.

Allington, R. L., & McGill-Franzen, A. (1995). Flunking: Throwing good money after bad. In R. L. Allington & S. A. Walmsley (Eds.), *No quick fix: Rethinking literacy programs in America's elementary schools* (pp. 45-57). New York: Teachers College Press.

Allington, R. L., Stuetzel, H., Shake, M., & Lamarche, S. (1986). What is remedial reading? A descriptive study. *Reading Research and Instruction, 26(1)*, 15-30.

Allington, R. L., & Walmsley, S. A. (1995). No quick fix: Where do we go from here? In R. L. Allington & S. A. Walmsley (Eds.), *No quick fix: Rethinking literacy programs in America's elementary schools* (pp. 253-264). New York: Teachers College Press.

American Federation of Teachers. (1999, June). *Teaching reading is rocket science: What expert teachers of reading should know and be able to do.* Washington, DC: Author.

Anders, P. L., Hoffman, J. V., & Duffy, G. G. (2000). Teaching teachers to teach reading: Paradigm shifts, persistent problems, and challenges. In M. L. Kamil, P. B. Mosenthal, P. D. Pearson, & R. Barr (Eds.), *Handbook of reading research* (Vol. 3, pp. 719-742). Mahwah, NJ: Lawrence Erlbaum.

Anderson, L. M., Evertson, C. M., & Brophy, J. E. (1979). An experimental study of effective teaching in first-grade reading groups. *Elementary School Journal, 79(4)*, 193-223.

Anderson, R. C. (1998). Introduction: Reflections on literacy education. In J. Osborn & F. Lehr (Eds.), *Literacy for all: Issues in teaching and learning* (pp. 1-8). New York: Guilford Press.

Anderson, R. C. (1999). Foreword: Theoretical foundations for literacy acquisition. In J. S. Gaffney & B. J. Askew (Eds.), *Stirring the waters: The influence of Marie Clay* (pp. vi-vii). Portsmouth, NH: Heinemann.

Anderson, R. C., Hiebert, E. H., Scott, J. A., & Wilkinson, I. A. G. (1985). *Becoming a nation of readers: The report of the Commission on Reading.* Washington, DC: The National Institute of Education, U.S. Department of Education.

Anderson, R. C., Wilson, P. T., & Fielding, L. C. (1988). Growth in reading and how children spend their time outside of school. *Reading Research Quarterly, 28(3)*, 285-303.

Armor, D., Conroy-Oseguera, P., Cox, M., King, N., McDonnell, L., Pascal, A., et al. (1976, August). *Analysis of the school preferred reading program in selected Los Angeles minority schools* (Report No. R-2007-LAUSD). Santa Monica, CA: RAND.

Askew, B. J., Fountas, I. C., Lyons, C. A., Pinnell, G. S., & Schmitt, M. C. (2000). A review of Reading Recovery. In R. D. Robinson, M. C. McKenna, & J. M. Wedman (Eds.), *Issues and trends in literacy education* (2nd ed., pp. 284-303). Needham Heights, MA: Allyn & Bacon.

Askew, B. J., & Gaffney, J. S. (1999). Reading Recovery: Waves of influence on literacy education. In J. S. Gaffney & B. J. Askew (Eds.), *Stirring the waters: The influence of Marie Clay* (pp. 75-98). Portsmouth, NH: Heinemann.

Au, K. H., & Asam, C. L. (1996). Improving the literacy achievement of low-income students of diverse backgrounds. In M. F. Graves, P. van den Broek, & B. M. Taylor (Eds.), *The first R: Every child's right to read* (pp. 199-223). New York: Teachers College Press.

Au, K., Carroll, J., & Scheu, J. (2000). The six aspects of literacy: A curriculum framework. In R. D. Robinson, M. C. McKenna, & J. M. Wedman (Eds.), *Issues and trends in literacy education* (2nd ed., pp. 35-39). Needham Heights, MA: Allyn & Bacon.

Au, K., & Mason, J. A. (1981). Social organizational factors in learning to read: The balance of rights hypothesis. *Reading Research Quarterly, 17(1)*, 115-152.

Auerbach, E. S. (1995). Which way for family literacy: Intervention or empowerment? In L. M. Morrow (Ed.), *Family literacy: Connections in schools and families* (pp. 11-29). Newark, DE: International Reading Association.

Austin, M. C., & Morrison, C. (1963). *The first R: The Harvard report on reading in elementary schools*. New York: Macmillan.

Baker, L., Allen, J., Shockley, B., Pellegrini, A. D., Galda, L., & Stahl, S. (1996). Connecting school and home: Constructing partnerships to foster reading achievement. In L. Baker, P. Afflerbach, & D. Reinking (Eds.), *Developing engaged readers in school and home communities* (pp. 21-41). Mahwah, NJ: Lawrence Erlbaum.

Baker, L., Scher, D., & Mackler, K. (1997). Home and family influences on motivations for reading. *Educational Psychologist, 32(2)*, 69-82.

Barr, R., & Dreeben, R. (1991). Grouping students for reading instruction. In R. Barr, M. L. Kamil, P. B. Mosenthal, & P. D. Pearson (Eds.), *Handbook of reading research* (Vol. 2, pp. 885-910). White Plains, NY: Longman.

Beck, I. L. (1998). Understanding beginning reading: A journey through teaching and research. In J. Osborn & F. Lehr (Eds.), *Literacy for all: Issues in teaching and learning* (pp. 11-31). New York: Guilford Press.

Becker, W. C. (1977). Teaching reading and language to the disadvantaged— what we have learned from field research. *Harvard Educational Review, 47(4)*, 518-543.

Berliner, D. C. (1981). Academic learning time and reading achievement. In J. T. Guthrie (Ed.), *Comprehension and teaching: Research reviews* (pp. 203-226). Newark, DE: International Reading Association.

Birman, B. F. (1988, Spring). How to improve a successful program. *American Educator*, 22-29.

Blachman, B. A. (1991). Phonological awareness: Implications for prereading and early reading instruction. In S. A. Brady & D. P. Shankweiler (Eds.),

Phonological processes in literacy: A tribute to Isabelle Y. Liberman (pp. 29-36). Hillsdale, NJ: Lawrence Erlbaum.

Blachman, B. A. (1996). Preventing early reading failure. In S. C. Cramer & W. Ellis (Eds.), *Learning disabilities: Lifelong issues* (pp. 65-70). Baltimore: Paul H. Brookes.

Blachman, B. A., Tangel, D. M., Ball, E. W., Black, R., & McGraw, C. K. (1999). Developing phonological awareness and word recognition skills: A two-year intervention with low-income, inner-city children. *Reading and Writing: An Interdisciplinary Journal, 11(3),* 239-273.

Briggs, K. L., & Thomas, K. (1997, June). *Patterns of success: Successful pathways to elementary literacy in Texas Spotlight Schools.* Austin: Texas Center for Educational Research.

Brookover, W., & Lezotte, L. W. (1979, May). *Changes in school characteristics coincident with changes in student achievement* (Occasional Paper No. 17). East Lansing: Michigan State University, Institute for Research on Teaching.

Brookover, W. B., Schweitzer, J. H., Schneider, J. M., Beady, C. H., Flood, P. K., & Wisenbaker, J. M. (1978). Elementary school social climate and school achievement. *American Educational Research Journal, 15(2),* 301-318.

Brown, A. L., Palincsar, A. S., & Purcell, L. (1986). Poor readers: Teach, don't label. In V. Neisser (Ed.), *The school achievement of minority children: New perspectives* (pp. 105-143). Hillsdale, N. J.: Lawrence Erlbaum.

Brown, I. S., & Felton, R. H. (1990). Effects of instructions on beginning reading skills in children at risk for reading disability. *Reading and Writing: An Interdisciplinary Journal, 2(3),* 223-241.

Bush, B. (1995). Foreword. In L. M. Morrow (Ed.), *Family literacy: Connections in school and families* (pp. ix-x). Newark, DE: International Reading Association.

California State Department of Education. (1984, January). *Time and learning in California public schools.* Sacramento: Author.

Carter, C. J. (1997). Why reciprocal teaching? *Educational Leadership, 54(6),* 64-68.

Castle, J. M. (1999). Learning and teaching phonological awareness. In G. B. Thompson & T. Nicholson (Eds.), *Learning to read: Beyond phonics and whole language* (pp. 55-73). New York: Teachers College Press.

Chall, J. S. (1983). *Learning to read: The great debate* (Updated ed.). New York: McGraw-Hill.

Chall, J. S. (1991). American reading instructions: Science, art, and ideology. In W. Ellis (Ed.), *All language and the creation of literacy: Proceedings of the Orton Dyslexia Society Symposia* (pp. 20-26). Baltimore, MD: The Orton Dyslexia Society.

Chall, J. S., Jacobs, V. A., & Baldwin, L. E. (1990). *The reading crisis: why poor children fall behind.* Cambridge, MA: Harvard University Press.

Chance, C. (1991). Principals' perceptions of their involvement in the elementary school reading program. *Reading Improvement, 28(1),* 26-34.

Clay, M. M. (1994). Reading Recovery: The wider implications of an educational innovation. *Literacy, Teaching and Learning, 1(1),* 121-141.

Cohen, E. G., & Miller, R. H. (1980). Coordination and control of instruction in schools. *Pacific Sociological Review, 23(4),* 446-473.

Collins, C. (1980). Sustained silent reading periods: Effect on teachers' behaviors and students' achievement. *Elementary School Journal, 81(2)*, 109-114.

Cooley, W. W., & Leinhardt, G. (1980). The instructional dimensions study. *Educational Evaluation and Policy Analysis, 2(1)*, 7-25.

Copeland, K., Winsor, P., & Osborn, J. (1994). Phonemic awareness: A consideration of research and practice. In F. Lehr & J. Osborn (Eds.), *Reading, language, and literacy: Instruction for the twenty-first century* (pp. 25-44). Hillsdale, NJ: Lawrence Erlbaum.

Creemers, B. P. M. (1994). *The effective classroom*. London: Cassell.

Cunningham, A. E. (1990). Explicit versus implicit instruction in phonemic awareness. *Journal of Experimental Child Psychology, 50*, 429-444.

D'Agostino, J. W. (2000). Instructional and school effects on students' longitudinal reading and mathematics achievements. *Journal of School Effectiveness and School Improvement, 11(2)*, 197-235.

Danridge, J. C., Edwards, P. A., & Pleasants, H. M. (2000). Making kids winners: New perspectives about literacy from urban elementary school principals. *Reading Teacher, 53(8)*, 654-662.

Denham, C., & Lieberman, A. (Eds.) (1980). *Time to learn*. Washington, DC: National Institute of Education.

Dole, J. A., Duffy, G. G., Roehler, L. R., & Pearson, P. D. (1991). Moving from the old to the new: Research on reading comprehension instruction. *Review of Educational Research, 61(2)*, 239-264.

Donahue, P. L., Voelkl, K. E., Campbell, J. R., & Mazzeo, J. (1999, March). *NAEP 1998 reading report card for the nation and the states: Executive summary*. Retrieved from http://nces.ed.gov/nationsreportcard/pubs/main1998/1999500.asp

Dowhower, S. L. (1987). Effects of repeated reading on second-grade transitional readers' fluency and comprehension. *Reading Research Quarterly, 22*, 389-406.

Dudley-Marling, C., & Murphy, S. (1997). A political critique of remedial reading programs: The example of Reading Recovery. *The Reading Teacher, 50(6)*, 460-468.

Duffy-Hester, A. M. (1999). Teaching struggling readers in elementary school classrooms: A review of classroom reading programs and principles for instruction. *The Reading Teacher, 52(5)*, 480-495.

Dungan, F. (1994). Teachers say administrators can make a difference in the school's reading program. *State of Reading, 1(1)*, 46-48.

Durkin, D. (1978–1979). What classroom observations reveal about reading comprehension instruction. *Reading Research Quarterly, 54(4)*, 481-533.

Edmonds, R. R. (1979). Some school work. *Social Policy, 9(5)*, 28-32.

Edmonds, R. R. (1986). Characteristics of effective schools. In V. Neisser (Ed.), *The school achievement of minority children: New perspectives* (pp. 93-104). Hillsdale, NJ: Lawrence Erlbaum.

Ehri, L. C. (1987). Learning to read and spell words. *Journal of Reading Behavior, 19(1)*, 5-31.

Ehri, L. C. (1995). Phases of development in learning to read words by sight. *Journal of Research in Reading, 18(2)*, 116-125.

Eldredge, J. L. (1990). Increasing the performance of poor readers in the third grade with a group-assisted strategy. *Journal of Educational Research, 84(2)*, 69-77.

Ellis, A. B. (1975, February). *Success and failure: A summary of findings and recommendations for improving elementary reading in Massachusetts city schools.* Watertown, MA: Educational Research Corporation.

Fisher, C., & Adler, M. A. (1999, December). *Early reading programs in high-poverty schools: Emerald Elementary beats the odds.* Ann Arbor: University of Michigan, Center for the Improvement of Early Reading Achievement.

Fisher, C. W., & Berliner, D. C. (Eds.). (1983). *Perspectives on instructional time.* New York: Longman.

Fletcher, J. M., & Lyon, G. R. (1998). Reading: A research-based approach. In W. M. Evers (Ed.), *What's gone wrong in America's classrooms* (pp. 50-90). Stanford, CA: Hoover Institution Press.

Foertsch, M. A. (1992, May). *Reading in and out of school: Factors influencing the literacy achievement of American students in Grades 4, 8, and 12 in 1988 and 1990.* Washington, DC: U.S. Department of Education.

Foorman, B. R. (1995). Research on "The Great Debate": Code-oriented versus whole language approaches to reading instruction. *School Psychology Review, 24(3),* 376-392.

Foorman, B. R., Fletcher, J. M., Francis, D. J., & Schatschneider, C. (1998). The role of instruction in learning to read: Preventing reading failure in at-risk children. *Journal of Educational Psychology, 90(1),* 37-55.

Foorman, B. R., Francis, D. J., Winikates, D., Mehta, P., Schatschneider, C., & Fletcher, J. M. (1997). Early interventions for children with reading disabilities. *Scientific Studies of Reading, 1(3),* 255-276.

Fountas, I. C., & Pinnell, G. S. (1999). What does good first teaching mean? In J. S. Gaffney & B. J. Askew (Eds.), *Stirring the waters: The influence of Marie Clay* (pp. 165-185). Portsmouth, NH: Heinemann.

Fraser, B. J. (1989). Research syntheses on school and instructional effectiveness. *International Journal of Educational Research, 13(7),* 707-717.

Frederiksen, J., & Edmonds, R. (n.d.). *The identification of instructionally effective and ineffective schools.* Unpublished manuscript, Harvard University, Cambridge, MA.

Freeman, D. J., Kuhs, T. M., Porter, A. C., Floden, R. E., Schmidt, W. H., & Schwille, J. R. (1983). Do textbooks and tests define a national curriculum in elementary school mathematics? *Elementary School Journal, 83(5),* 501-503.

Gadsden, V. L. (1998). Family cultures and literacy learning. In J. Osborn & F. Lehr (Eds.), *Literacy for all: Issues in teaching and learning* (pp 32-50). New York: Guilford Press.

Gaffney, J. S. (1998). The prevention of reading failure: Teach reading and writing. In J. Osborn & F. Lehr (Eds.), *Literacy for all: Issues in teaching and learning* (pp. 100-110). New York: Guilford Press.

Gaffney, J. S., & Paynter, S. Y. (1994). The role of early literacy intervention in the transformation of educational systems. *Literacy Teaching and Learning, 1(1),* 23-29.

Gambrell, L., & Morrow, L. M. (1996). Creating motivating contexts for literacy learning. In L. Baker, P. Afflerbach, & D. Reinking (Eds.), *Developing engaged readers in school and home communities* (pp. 115-136). Mahwah, NJ: Lawrence Erlbaum.

Garcia, G. E, & Pearson, P. D. (1991). Modifying reading instruction to maximize its effectiveness for all students. In M. S. Knapp & P. M. Shields

(Eds.), *Better schooling for the children of poverty: Alternatives to conventional wisdom* (pp. 31-59). Berkeley, CA: McCutcheon.

Gelzheiser, L. M., Meyers, J., & Pruzek, R. M. (1992). Effects of pull-in and pull-out approaches to reading instruction for special education and remedial reading students. *Journal of Educational and Psychological Consultation, 3(2)*, 133-149.

Graff, H. J. (1979). *The literacy myth: Literacy and social structure in the nineteenth-century city.* New York: Academic Press.

Graff, H. J. (1995). *The labyrinths of literacy: Reflections on literacy past and present.* Pittsburgh: University of Pittsburgh Press.

Greaney, V., & Hegarty, M. (1987). Correlates of leisure-time reading. *Journal of Research in Reading, 10(1)*, 3-20.

Guthrie, J. T., Martuza, V., & Seifert, M. (1979). Impacts of instructional time in reading. In L. B. Resnick & P. A. Weaver (Eds.), *Theory and practice of early reading* (pp. 153-178). Hillsdale, NJ: Lawrence Erlbaum.

Guthrie, J. T., McGough, K., Bennett, L., & Rice, M. E. (1996). Concept-oriented reading instruction: An integrated curriculum to develop motivations and strategies for reading. In L. Baker, P. Afflerbach, & D. Reinking (Eds.), *Developing engaged readers in school and home communities* (pp. 165-190). Mahwah, NJ: Lawrence Erlbaum.

Haberman, M. (1995). *Star teachers of children in poverty.* West Lafayette, IN: Kappa Delta Pi.

Haertel, E. (1986). The valid use of student performance measures for teacher evaluation. *Educational Evaluation and Policy Analysis, 8(1)*, 45-60.

Hall, D. P., & Cunningham, P. M. (1996). Becoming literate in first and second grades: Six years of multimethod, multilevel instruction. In D. J. Leu, C. K. Kinzer, & K. A. Hinchman (Eds.), *Literacies for the 21st century: Research and practice* (pp. 195-204). Chicago: National Reading Conference.

Hall, S. L. & Moats, L. C. (1999). *Straight talk about reading: How parents can make a difference during the early years.* Chicago: Contemporary Books.

Haller, E. P., Child, D. A., & Walberg, H. J. (1988). Can comprehension be taught? A quantitative synthesis of "metacognitive" studies. *Educational Researcher, 17(9)*, 5-8.

Hallinger, P., Bickman, L., & Davis, K. (1996). Social context, principal leadership, and student reading achievement. *The Elementary School Journal, 96(5)*, 527-549.

Hallinger, P., & Murphy, J. (1985). Characteristics of highly effective elementary school reading programs. *Educational Leadership, 42(5)*, 39-42.

Harnisch, D. L. (1983). Item response patterns: Applications for educational practice. *Journal of Educational Measurement, 20(2)*, 191-206.

Harris, A. J., & Serwer, B. L. (1966). The CRAFT Project: Instructional time in reading research. *Reading Research Quarterly, 2(1)*, 27-56.

Harris, A. J., & Sipay, E. R. (1990). *How to increase reading ability: A guide to developmental & remedial methods* (9th ed.). New York: Longman.

Hart, B., & Risley, T. R. (1995). *Meaningful differences in the everyday experiences of young American children.* Baltimore, MD: Paul H. Brookes.

Hatcher, P. J., Hulme, C., & Ellis, A. W. (1994). Ameliorating early reading failure by integrating the teaching of reading and phonological skills: The phonological linkage hypothesis. *Child Development, 65(1)*, 41-57.

Haynes, M. C., & Jenkins, J. R. (1986). Reading instruction in special education resource rooms. *American Educational Research Journal, 23(2),* 161-190.

Henderson, A. T. (Ed.). (1987). *The evidence continues to grow: Parent involvement improves student achievement.* Columbia, MD: National Committee for Citizens in Education.

Hiebert, E. H. (1983). An examination of ability grouping for reading instructors. *Reading Research Quarterly, 18(2),* 231-255.

Hiebert, E. H., Colt, J. M., Catto, S. L., & Gury, E. C. (1992). Reading and writing of first grade students in a restructured Chapter 1 program. *American Educational Research Journal, 29(3),* 545-572.

Hiebert, E. H., & Pearson, P. D. (1999). *Building on the past, bridging to the future: A research agenda for the Center for the Improvement of Early Reading Achievement.* Ann Arbor: University of Michigan, Center for the Improvement of Early Reading Achievement.

Hiebert, E. H., & Taylor, B. M. (1994). Interventions and the restructuring of American literacy instruction. In E. H. Hiebert & B. M. Taylor (Eds.), *Getting reading right from the start: Effective early literacy interventions* (pp. 201-217). Boston: Allyn and Bacon.

Hiebert, E. H., & Taylor, B. M. (2000). Beginning reading instruction: Research on early intervention. In M. L. Kamil, P. B. Mosenthal, P. D. Pearson, & R. Barr (Eds.), *Handbook of Reading Research* (Vol. 3, pp. 455-482). Mahwah, NJ: Lawrence Erlbaum.

Hoffman, J. V. (1987). Rethinking the role of oral reading in basal instruction. *The Elementary School Journal, 87(3),* 367-373.

Hoffman, J. V. (1991). Teacher and school effects in learning to read. In R. Barr, M. L. Kamil, P. B. Mosenthal, & P. D. Pearson (Eds.), *Handbook of reading research* (Vol. 2, pp. 911-950). New York: Longman.

Hoffman, J. V., & Rutherford, W. L. (1984). Effective reading programs: A critical review of outlier studies. *Reading Research Quarterly, 20(1),* 79-92.

Honig, B. (1997). Reading the right way. *School Administrator, 54,* 6-9, 13-15.

Huck, C. S. (1999). The gift of story. In J. S. Gaffney & B. J. Askew (Eds.), *Stirring the waters: The influence of Marie Clay* (pp. 113-123). Portsmouth, NH: Heinemann.

Hymes, D. A. (1999). Foreword. In D. A. Wagner (Ed.), *The future of literacy in a changing world* (pp. xiii-xxiv). Cresskill, NJ: Hampton Press.

Iverson, S., & Tunmer, W. E. (1993). Phonological processing skills and the Reading Recovery program. *Journal of Educational Psychology, 85(1),* 112-126.

Ivey, G. (2000). Redesigning reading instruction. *Educational Leadership, 58(1),* 42-45.

Jimerson, S., Egeland, B., & Teao, A. (1999). A longitudinal study of achievement trajectories: Factors associated with change. *Journal of Educational Psychology, 19(1),* 116-126.

Johnston, P. (1999). Unpacking literate achievement. In J. S. Gaffney & B. J. Askew (Eds.), *Stirring the waters: The influence of Marie Clay* (pp. 27-46). Portsmouth, NH: Heinemann.

Johnston, P., & Allington, R. (1991). Remediation. In R. Barr, M. L. Kamil, P. B. Mosenthal, & P. D. Pearson (Eds.), *Handbook of reading research* (Vol. 2, pp. 984-1012). New York: Longman.

Jones, N. K., & Smith-Burke, T. (1999). Forging an interactive relationship among research, theory, and practice: Clay's research design and methodology. In J. S. Gaffney & B. J. Askew (Eds.), *Stirring the waters: The influence of Marie Clay* (pp. 261-285). Portsmouth, NH: Heinemann.

Jonson, K. F. (1998). The role of independent reading in a "balanced" reading program: Rethinking California's reading initiative. *Reading Improvement, 35(2),* 90-96.

Juel, C. (1988). Learning to read and write: A longitudinal study of 54 children from first through fourth grades. *Journal of Educational Psychology, 80(4),* 437-447.

Juel, C. (1991). Beginning reading. In R. Barr, M. L. Kamil, P. B. Mosenthal, & P. D. Pearson (Eds.), *Handbook of reading research* (Vol. 2, pp. 759-788). New York: Longman.

Juel, C. (1996). What makes literacy tutoring effective? *Reading Research Quarterly, 31(3),* 268-289.

Kaestle, C. F., Damon-Moore, H., Stedman, L. C., Tinsley, K., & Trollinger, W. V. (1991). *Literacy in the United States: Readers and reading since 1880.* New Haven, CT: Yale University Press.

Kameenui, E. J. (1998). The rhetoric of all the reality of some, and the unmistakable smell of mortality. In J. Osborn & F. Lehr (Eds.), *Literacy for all: Issues in teaching and learning* (pp. 319-338). New York: Guilford Press.

Kameenui, E. J., Simmons, D. C., Baker, S., Chard, D. J., Dickson, S. V., Gunn, B., et al. (1998). Effective strategies for teaching beginning reading. In E. J. Kameenui & D. W. Carnine (Eds.), *Effective teaching strategies that accommodate diverse learners* (pp. 45-70). Upper Saddle River, NJ: Merrill.

Klenk, L., & Kibby, M. W. (2000). Re-mediating reading difficulties: Appraising the past, reconciling the present, constructing the future. In M. L. Kamil, P. B. Mosenthal, P. D. Pearson, & R. Barr (Eds.), *Handbook of reading research* (Vol. 3, pp. 667-690). Mahwah, NJ: Lawrence Erlbaum.

Knapp, M. S., & Needels, M. (1991). Review of research on curriculum and instruction in literacy. In M. S. Knapp & P. M. Shields (Eds.), *Better schooling for the children of poverty: alternatives to conventional wisdom* (pp. 85-121). Berkeley, CA: McCutchan.

Konold, T. R., Juel, C., & McKinnon, M. (1999, June). *Building an integrated model of early reading acquisition.* Ann Arbor: University of Michigan, Center for the Improvement of Early Reading Achievement.

Koskinen, P. S., & Blum, I. H. (1984). Repeated oral reading and the acquisition of fluency. In J. A. Niles & L. A. Harris (Eds.), *Changing perspectives on research in reading/language processing and instruction* (pp. 183-187). Rochester, NY: National Reading Conference.

Kuhn, M. R., & Stahl, S. A. (2000, March). *Fluency: A review of developmental and remedial practices.* Ann Arbor: University of Michigan, Center for the Improvement of Early Reading Achievement.

Labbo, L. D., & Teale, W. L. (1990). Cross-age reading: A strategy for helping poor readers. *The Reading Teacher, 43,* 362-369.

Leinhardt, G., Zigmond, N., & Cooley, W. W. (1981). Reading instruction and its effects. *American Educational Research Journal, 18(3),* 343-361.

Leithwood, K. A., & Montgomery, D. J. (1984, April). *Patterns of growth in principal effectiveness.* Paper presented at the annual meeting of the American Educational Research Association, New Orleans, LA.

Levine, D. U. (1982). Successful approaches for improving academic achievement in inner-city elementary schools. *Phi Delta Kappan, 63(8),* 523-526.

Levine, D. U., & Eubanks, E. E. (1983). *Instructional and organizational characteristics of unusually effective inner city intermediate schools.* Unpublished manuscript, University of Missouri–Kansas City.

Lezotte, L., Hathaway, D. V., Miller, S. K., Passalacqua, J., & Brookover, W. B. (1980). *School learning climate and student achievement: A social system approach to increased student learning.* Tallahassee: Florida State University Foundation, The Site Specific Technical Assistance Center.

Liberman, I. Y., Shankweiler, D., & Liberman, A. M. (1989). The alphabetic principal and learning to read. In D. Shankweiler & I. Y. Liberman (Eds.), *Phonology and reading disability: Solving the reading puzzle* (pp. 1-33). Ann Arbor: University of Michigan Press.

Licktieg, M., Parnell, M. K., & Ellis, S. D. (1995). Ways elementary administrators support literacy education. *Reading Horizons, 35(4),* 299-309.

Lundberg, I. (1991). Phonemic awareness can be developed without reading instruction. In S. A. Brady & D. P. Shankweiler (Eds.), *Phonological processes in literacy: A tribute to Isabell Y. Liberman* (pp. 47-53). Hillsdale, NJ: Lawrence Erlbaum.

Lyons, C. A., & Pinnell, G. S. (1999). Teacher development: The best investment in literacy education. In J. S. Gaffney & B. J. Askew (Eds.), *Stirring the waters: The influence of Marie Clay* (197-220). Portsmouth, NH: Heinemann.

Mahler, W. R. (1995). Practice what you preach. *The Reading Teacher, 18(5),* 414-415.

Manning, J. C., (1995). "Ariston metron." *The Reading Teacher, 48(8),* 650-659.

Mattson, P. A. (1994). Baltimore Highlands Elementary School. *The Reading Teacher, 48(1),* 60-61.

McBride-Chang, C., Manis, F. R., Seidenberg, M. S., Custodio, R. G., & Doi, L. M. (1993). Print exposure as a predictor of word reading and reading comprehension in disabled and non-disabled readers. *Journal of Educational Psychology, 85(2),* 230-238.

McGill-Franzen, A. (1987). Failure to learn to read: Formulating a policy problem. *Reading Research Quarterly, 22(4),* 475-490.

McGill-Franzen, A. (2000). Policy and instruction: What is the relationship? In M. L. Kamil, P. B. Mosenthal, P. D. Pearson, & R. Barr (Eds.), *Handbook of reading research* (Vol. 3, pp. 889-908). Mahwah, NJ: Lawrence Erlbaum.

McGill-Franzen, A., & Allington, R. L. (1990). Comprehension and coherence: Neglected elements of literacy instruction in remedial and resource room services. *Reading, Writing, and Learning Disabilities, 6,* 149-182.

McNaughton, S. (1999). Developing diversity and beginning literacy instruction at school. In J. S. Gaffney & B. J. Askew (Eds.), *Stirring the waters: The influence of Marie Clay* (pp. 3-16). Portsmouth, NH: Heinemann.

Mintzberg, H. (1973). *The nature of managerial work.* New York: Harper & Row.

Moats, L. C. (1996). Implementing effective instruction. In S. C. Cramer & W. Ellis (Eds.), *Learning disabilities: Lifelong issues* (pp. 87-94). Baltimore, MD: Paul H. Brookes.

Moll, L. (1991). Social and instructional issues in literacy instruction for "disadvantaged" students. In M. S. Knapp & P. M. Shields (Eds.), *Better schooling for children of poverty: Alternatives to conventional wisdom* (pp. 61-84). Berkeley, CA: McCutcheon.

Moore, J. C., Jones, C. J., & Miller, D. C. (1980). What we know after a decade of sustained silent reading. *The Reading Teacher, 33(4),* 445-450.

Morris, D., Shaw, B., & Perney, J. (1990). Helping low readers in Grades 2 and 3: An after-school volunteer tutoring program. *The Elementary School Journal, 91(2),* 133-150.

Morrow, L. M. (1995). Family literacy: New perspectives, new practices. In L. M. Morrow (Ed.), *Family literacy: Connections in schools and families* (pp. 5-10). Newark, DE: International Reading Association.

Morrow, L. M., Tracey, D. H., Woo, D. G., & Pressley, M. (1999). Characteristics of exemplary first-grade literacy instruction. *The Reading Teacher, 52(5),* 462-476.

Murphy, J. (1990). Principal instructional leadership. In L. S. Lotto & P. W. Thurston (Eds.), *Advances in educational administration: Changing perspectives on the school* (Vol. 1, Pt. B, pp. 163-200). Greenwich, CT: JAI Press.

Murphy, J. (1991). *Restructuring schools: Capturing and assessing the phenomena.* New York: Teachers College Press.

Murphy, J. (1992). School effectiveness and school restructuring: Contributions to educational improvement. *School Effectiveness and School Improvement, 3(2),* 90-109.

Murphy, J. (2001, October) *Leadership for literacy: Policy leverage points.* Princeton, NJ: Educational Testing Service.

Murphy, J., & Hallinger P. (1986). The superintendent as instructional leader: Findings from effective school districts. *Journal of Educational Administration, 24(2),* 213-236.

Murphy, J., & Hallinger, P. (1989). Equity as access to learning: Curricular and instructional treatment differences. *Journal of Curriculum Studies, 21(2),* 129-149.

Murphy, J., Hallinger, P., & Mesa, R. P. (1985). School effectiveness: Checking progress and assumptions and developing a role for state and federal government. *Teachers College Record, 86(4),* 615-641.

Murphy, J., Weil, M., Hallinger, P., & Mitman, A. (1982). Academic press: Translating high expectations into school policies and classroom practices. *Educational Leadership, 40(3),* 22-26.

Murphy, J., Weil, M., Hallinger, P., & Mitman, A. (1985). School effectiveness: A conceptual framework. *The Educational Forum, 49(3),* 361-374.

Murphy, J., Weil, M., & McGreal, T. (1986). The basic practice model of instruction. *The Elementary School Journal, 87(1),* 83-95.

National Center for Educational Statistics. (1999). *The NAEP reading report card for the nation and the states.* Washington, DC: U.S. Department of Education.

National Center for Educational Statistics. (2000). *NAEP 1999: Trends in academic progress, three decades of student performance.* Washington, DC: U.S. Department of Education.

National Institute of Child Health and Human Development. (2000a). *Report of the National Reading Panel. Teaching children to read: An evidence-based assessment of the scientific research literature on reading and its implications for reading instruction* (NIH Publication No.00-4769). Washington, DC: Government Printing Office.

National Institute of Child Health and Human Development. (2000b). *Report of the National Reading Panel. Teaching children to read: An evidence-based assessment of the scientific research literature on reading and its implications for reading instruction: Reports of the subgroups* (NIH Publication No. 00-4754). Washington, DC: Government Printing Office.

Nespor, J. (1987). The role of beliefs in the practice of teaching. *Journal of Curriculum Studies, 19(4),* 317-328.

Neuman, S. B. (1999). Books make a difference: A study of access to literacy. *Reading Research Quarterly, 34(3),* 286-311.

Neuman, S. B., Caperelli, B. J., & Kee, C. (1998). Literacy learning, a family matter. *The Reading Teacher, 52(3),* 244-252.

Nicholson, T (1999). Literacy in the family and society. In G. B. Thompson & T. Nicholson (Eds.), *Learning to read: Beyond phonics and whole language* (pp. 1-24). New York: Teachers College Press.

Otto, W., Wolf, A., & Eldridge, R. G. (1984). Managing instruction. In P. D. Pearson (Ed.), *Handbook of reading research* (pp. 799-828). New York: Longman.

Palincsar, A. S., & Brown, A. L. (1984). Reciprocal teaching of comprehension-fostering and comprehension-monitoring activities. *Cognition and Instruction, 1(2),* 117-175.

Patty, D., Maschoff, J. D., Ranson, P. E. (1996). *The reading resource handbook for school leaders.* Norwood, MA: Christopher-Gordon.

Paul, T. (1992). *The national reading study and theory of reading practice.* Wisconsin Rapids, WI: Advantage Learning Systems.

Pearson, P. D. (1996). Reclaiming the center. In M. Graves & P. D. Pearson (Eds.), *The first R: Every child's right to read* (pp. 259-274). New York: Teachers College Press.

Pflaum, S. W., Walberg, H. J., Karegianes, M. L., & Rasher, S. P. (1980, July-August). Reading instruction: A quantitative analysis. *Educational Researcher, 9(4),* 12-18.

Phi Delta Kappa. (1980). *Why do some urban schools succeed? The Phi Delta Kappa study of exceptional urban elementary schools.* Bloomington, Indiana: Author.

Pikulski, J. J. (1994). Preventing reading failure: A review of five effective programs. *The Reading Teacher, 48(1),* 30-39.

Pinnell, G. S., Lyons, C. A., DeFord, D. E., Bryk, A. S., & Seltzer, M. (1994). Comparing instructional models for the literacy education of high-risk first graders. *Reading Research Quarterly, 29(1),* 9-39.

Postlethwaite, T. N., & Ross, K. N. (1992). *Effective schools in reading: Implications for educational planners.* The Hague, The Netherlands: International Association for the Evaluation of Educational Achievement.

Powell, A. G., Farrar, E., & Cohen, D. K. (1985). *The shopping mall high school: Winners and losers in the educational marketplace.* Boston: Houghton Mifflin.

Pressley, M. (1998a). Comprehension strategies instruction. In J. Osborn & F. Lehr (Eds.), *Literacy for all: Issues in teaching and learning* (pp. 113-133). New York: Guilford Press.

Pressley, M. (1998b). *Reading instruction that works: The case for balanced teaching.* New York: Guilford Press.

Pressley, M., Ranking, J., & Yokoi, L. (2000). A survey of instructional practices of primary teachers nominated as effective in promoting literacy. In R. D. Robinson, M. C. McKenna, & J. M. Wedman (Eds.), *Issues and trends in literacy education* (2nd ed., pp. 10-34). Needham Heights, MA: Allyn & Bacon.

Pressley, M., Wharton-McDonald, R., Ranking, J., Mistretta, J., Yokoi, L., & Ettenberger, S. (1996). The nature of outstanding primary-grades literacy instruction. In E. McIntyre & M. Pressley (Eds.), *Balanced instruction: Strategies and skills in whole language* (pp. 251-276). Norwood, MA: Christopher-Gordon.

Puma, M., Karweit, N., Price, C., Ricciuti, A., Thompson, A., & Vaden-Kiernan, M. (1997, April). *Prospects: Final report on student outcomes.* Cambridge, MA: Abt Associates.

Purcell-Gates, V. (1998). Growing successful readers: Homes, communities, and schools. In J. Osborn & F. Lehr (Eds.), *Literacy for all: Issues in teaching and learning* (pp. 51-72). New York: Guilford Press.

Raphael, T. E. (1998). Balanced instruction and the role of classroom discourse. In J. Osborn & F. Lehr (Eds.), *Literacy for all: Issues in teaching and learning* (pp. 134-169). New York: Guilford Press.

Resnick, D. P., & Resnick, L. B. (1977). The nature of literacy: An historical exploration. *Harvard Educational Review, 47(3),* 370-385.

Reutzel, D. R., & Hollingsworth, P. M. (1993). Effects of fluency training on second graders' reading comprehension. *Journal of Educational Research, 86,* 325-331.

Reutzel, D. R., Hollingsworth, P. M., & Eldredge, J. L. (1994). Oral reading instruction: The impact on student reading development. *Reading Research Quarterly, 29(2),* 41-62.

Richardson, S. O. (1991). Evolution of approaches to beginning reading and the need for diversification in education. In W. Ellis (Ed.), *All language and the creation of literacy: Proceedings of the Orton Dyslexia Society Symposia* (pp. 1-8). Baltimore, MD: The Orton Dyslexia Society.

Richardson, V. (1998). Professional development in the instruction of reading. In J. Osborn & F. Lehr (Eds.), *Literacy for all: Issues in teaching and learning* (pp. 303-318). New York: Guilford Press.

Roehler, L. R., & Duffy, G. G. (1991). Teachers' instructional actions. In R. Barr, M. L. Kamil, P. B. Mosenthal, & P. D. Pearson (Eds.), *Handbook of reading research* (Vol. 2, pp. 861-883). New York: Longman.

Rosenshine, B., & Meister, C. (1994). Reciprocal teaching: A review of the research. *Review of Educational Research, 64(4),* 479-530.

Ross, S. M., Smith, L. J., Casey, J., & Slavin, R. E. (1995). Increasing the academic success of disadvantaged children: An examination of alternative early intervention programs. *American Educational Research Journal, 32(4),* 773-800.

Rowe, K. J. (1995). Factors affecting students' progress in reading: Key findings from a longitudinal study. *Literacy, Teaching and Learning, 1(2),* 57-110.

Ruddell, R. B. (1997). Researching the influential literacy teacher: Characteristics, beliefs, strategies, and new research directions. In

C. K. Kinzer, K. A. Hinchman, & D. J. Leu (Eds.), *Inquiries in literacy: Theory and practice* (pp. 37-53). Chicago: National Reading Conference.

Rutter, M. (1983). School effects on pupil progress: Research findings and policy implications. *Child Development, 54(1),* 1-29.

Rutter, M., Maughan, B., Mortimore, P., & Ouston, J. (1979). *Fifteen thousand hours: Secondary schools and their effects on children.* Cambridge, MA: Harvard University Press.

Samuels, S. J. (1981). Characteristics of exemplary reading programs. In J. T. Guthrie (Ed.), *Comprehension and teaching: Research review* (pp. 255-273). Newark, DE: International Reading Association.

Sanacore, J. (1997). Guidelines for successful reading leaders. *Journal of Adolescent & Adult Literacy, 41(1),* 64-68.

Schneider, B. (1985). Further evidence of school effects. *Journal of Educational Research, 78(6),* 351-356.

Seifert, E. H., & Beck, J. J. (1984). Relationships between task time and learning gains in secondary schools. *Journal of Educational Research, 78(1),* 5-10.

Shankweiler, D. P. (1991). The contribution of Isabelle Y. Liberman. In S. A. Brady & D. P. Shankweiler (Eds.), *Phonological processes in literacy: A tribute to Isabelle Y. Liberman* (pp. xii-xvii). Hillsdale, NJ: Lawrence Erlbaum.

Shannon, P. (1996). Poverty, literacy, and politics: Living in the USA. *Journal of Literacy Research, 28,* 430-449.

Sherman, W. H. (2001, November). *Administrators facilitating successful reading instruction in elementary schools.* Paper presented at the annual meeting of the University Council for Educational Administration, Cincinnati, OH.

Singer, H., & Balow, I. H. (1981). Overcoming educational disadvantages. In J. T. Guthrie (Ed.), *Comprehension and teaching: Research review* (pp. 274-312). Newark, DE: International Reading Association.

Slavin, R. E. (1994). School and classroom organization in beginning reading: Class size, aides, and instructional grouping. In R. E. Slavin, N. L. Karweit, & B. A. Wasik (Eds.), *Preventing early school failure* (pp. 122-142). Needham Heights, MA: Allyn & Bacon.

Slavin, R. E., & Madden, N. A. (1989). What works for students at risk: A research synthesis. *Educational Leadership, 46(5),* 4-13.

Slavin, R. E., Madden, N. A., Karweit, N. L., Dolan, L. J., & Wasik, B. A. (1991). Research directions: Success for All: Ending reading failure from the beginning. *Language Arts, 68(1),* 404-409.

Slavin, R. E., Madden, N. A., Karweit, N. L., Dolan, L. J., & Wasik, B. A. (1994). Success for All: A comprehensive approach to prevention and early intervention. In R. E. Slavin, N. L. Karweit, & B. A. Wasik (Eds.), *Preventing early school failure* (pp. 175-205). Needham Heights, MA: Allyn & Bacon.

Smith, B. A. (2000). Quantity matters: Annual instructional time in an urban school system. *Educational Administration Quarterly, 36(5),* 652-682.

Smith, M. L. (1980). Teacher expectations. *Evaluation in Education, 4,* 53-55.

Smith, S. S. (1997). A longitudinal study: The literacy development of 57 children. In C. K. Kinzer, K. A. Hinchman, & D. J. Leu (Eds.), *Inquiries in literacy theory and practice.* Chicago: The National Reading Conference.

Snider, V. E. (1995). A primer on phonemic awareness: What it is, why it's important, and how to teach it. *School Psychology Review, 24(3),* 443-455.

Snow, C. E., Barnes, W. S., Chandler, J., Goodman, I. F., & Hemphill, L. (1991). *Unfulfilled expectations: Home and school influences on literacy.* Cambridge, MA: Harvard University Press.

Snow, C. E., Burns, M. S., & Griffin, P. (Eds.). (1998). *Preventing reading difficulties in young children.* Washington, DC: National Academy Press.

Soar, R. S., & Soar, R. M. (1979). Emotional climate and management. In P. Peterson & H. Walberg (Eds.), *Research on teaching: Concepts, findings and implications* (pp. 97-119). Berkeley, CA: McCutchan.

Spiegel, D. L. (1995). A comparison of traditional remedial programs and Reading Recovery: Guidelines for the success of all programs. *The Reading Teacher, 49(2),* 86-96.

Stahl, S. A. (1992). Saying the "p" word: Nine guidelines for exemplary phonics instruction. *The Reading Teacher, 45(8),* 618-625.

Stahl, S. A. (1997). Instructional models in reading: An introduction. In S. A. Stahl & D. A. Hayes (Eds.), *Instructional models in reading* (pp. 1-29). Mahwah, NJ: Lawrence Erlbaum.

Stahl, S. A. (1998). Understanding shifts in reading and its instructions. *Peabody Journal of Education, 73(3&4),* 31-67.

Stahl, S. A., Duffy-Hester, A. M., & Stahl, K. A. (1998). Everything you wanted to know about phonics (but were afraid to ask). *Reading Research Quarterly, 33(3),* 338-355.

Stahl, S. A., McKenna, M. C., & Pagnucco, J. R. (1994). The effects of whole-language instruction: An update and a reappraisal. *Educational Psychologist, 29(4),* 175-185.

Stanovich, K. E. (2000). *Progress in understanding reading: Scientific foundations and new frontiers.* New York: Guilford Press.

State of New York, Office of Education Performance Review. (1974, March). *School factors influencing reading achievement: A case study of two inner city schools.* Albany: Author.

Stein, M., Johnson, B., & Gutlohn, L. (1999). Analyzing beginning reading programs. *Remedial and Special Education, 20(5),* 275-287.

Stigler, J. W., & Hiebert, J. (1999). *The teaching gap: Best ideas from the world's teachers for improving education in the classroom.* New York: Free Press.

Taylor, B. M., Frye, B. J., & Maruyama, G. M. (1990). Time spent reading and reading growth. *American Educational Research Journal, 27(2),* 351-362.

Taylor, B. M., Hanson, B. E., Justice-Swanson, K., & Watts, S. M. (2000). Helping struggling readers: Linking small-group intervention with cross-age tutoring. In R. D. Robinson, M. C. McKenna, & J. M. Wedman (Eds.), *Issues and trends in literacy education* (2nd ed., pp. 267-283). Needham Heights, MA: Allyn & Bacon.

Taylor, B. M., Pearson, P. D., Clark, K. F., & Walpole, S. (1999, September). *Beating the odds in teaching all children to read.* Ann Arbor: University of Michigan, Center for the Improvement of Early Reading Achievement.

Taylor, B. M., Short, R. A., Frye, B. J., & Shearer, B. A. (1992). Classroom teachers prevent reading failure among low-achieving first grade students. *The Reading Teacher, 45(8),* 592-597.

Taylor, B. M., & Taxis, H. (n.d.). *Translating characteristics of effective school reading programs into practice.* Handout.

Teddlie, C., & Reynolds, D. (2000). *The international handbook of school effectiveness research.* London: Falmer.

Thompson, G. B. (1999). The process of learning to identify words. In G. B. Thompson & T. Nicholson (Eds.), *Learning to read: Beyond phonics and whole language* (pp. 25-54). New York: Teachers College Press.

Topping, K. J., & Sanders, W. L. (2000). Teacher effectiveness and computer assessment of reading: Relating value added learning information system data. *School Effectiveness and School Improvement, 11(3),* 305-337.

Torgesen, J. K. (1997). The prevention and remediation of reading disabilities: Evaluating what we know from research. *Journal for Academic Language Therapy, 1,* 11-47.

Torgesen, J. K. (1998). Catch them before they fall: Identification and assessment to prevent reading failure in young children. *American Educator, 22,* 32-39.

Torgesen, J. K., & Hecht, S. A. (1996). Preventing and remediating reading disabilities: Instructional variables that make a difference for special students. In M. F. Graves, P. van den Broek, & B. M. Taylor (Eds.), *The first R: Every child's right to read* (pp. 133-159). New York: Teachers College Press.

Treiman, R. (1998). Why spelling? The benefits of incorporating spelling into beginning reading instruction. In J. L. Metsala & L. C. Ehri (Eds.), *Word recognition in beginning literacy* (pp. 289-313). Mahwah, NJ: Lawrence Erlbaum.

Turner, R. L. (1989). The "great" debate—can both Carbo and Chall be right? *Phi Delta Kappan, 71(4),* 276-283.

Vadasy, P. F., Jenkins, J. R., Antil, L. R., Wayne, S. K., & O'Connor, R. E. (1997). The effectiveness of one-to-one tutoring by community tutors for at-risk beginning readers. *Learning Disability Quarterly, 20(2),* 126-139.

Van den Broek, P. (1996). On becoming literate: The many sources of success and failure in reading. In M. F. Graves, P. van den Broek, & B. M. Taylor (Eds.), *The first R: Every child's right to read* (pp. 189-196). New York: Teachers College Press.

Van Vleck, C., Fritzsche, E., Joiners, S., Lorvig, L., & Lentz, L. (1994). South Bay Elementary School. *The Reading Teacher, 48(3),* 234-236.

Vellutino, F. R. (1991). Introduction to three studies on reading acquisition: Convergent findings on theoretical foundations of code-oriented versus whole-language approaches to reading instruction. *Journal of Educational Psychology, 83(4),* 437-443.

Venezky, R. L., & Winfield, L. F. (1979, August). *Schools that succeed beyond expectations in teaching reading.* Newark: University of Delaware, Department of Educational Studies.

Wagner, D. A. (1999). Introduction. In D. A. Wagner (Ed.), *The future of literacy in a changing world* (pp. 3-19). Cresskill, NJ: Hampton Press.

Walmsley, S. A., & Allington, R. A. (1995). Redefining and reforming instructional support programs for at-risk students. In R. L. Allington & S. A. Walmsley (Eds.), *No quick fix: Rethinking literacy programs in America's elementary schools* (pp. 19-44). New York: Teachers College Press.

Walp, T. P., & Walmsley, S. A. (1989). Instructional and philosophical congruence: Neglected aspects of coordination. *The Reading Teacher, 42(6),* 364-368.

Wasik, B. A., & Slavin, R. E. (1994). Preventing early reading failure with one-to-one tutoring: A review of five programs. In R. E. Slavin, N. L. Karweit, & B. A. Wasik (Eds.), *Preventing early school failure* (pp. 143-174). Needham Heights, MA: Allyn & Bacon.

Weber, G. (1971, October). *Inner-city children can be taught to read: Four successful schools.* Washington, DC: Council for Basic Education.

Weick, K. E. (1976). Educational administration as a loosely coupled system. *Administrative Science Quarterly, 21(1)*, 1-26.

Wellisch, J. B., MacQueen, A. H., Carriere, R. A., & Duck, G. A. (1978). School management and organization in successful schools. *Sociology of Education, 51*, 211-226.

Wharton-McDonald, R., Pressley, M., & Hampston, J. M. (1998). Literacy instruction in nine first-grade classrooms: Teacher characteristics and student achievement. *The Elementary School Journal, 99(2)*, 101-128.

Wilder, G. (1977). Five exemplary reading programs. In J. T Guthrie (Ed.), *Cognition, curriculum, and comprehension* (pp. 257-278). Newark, DE: International Reading Association.

Wilkinson, I., Wardrop, J. L., & Anderson, R. C. (1988). Silent reading reconsidered: Reinterpreting reading instruction and its effects. *American Educational Research Journal, 25(1)*, 127-144.

Williams, E. J., Scharer, P. L., & Pinnell, G. S. (2000). *Literacy collaborative: 2000 research report.* Columbus: Literacy Collaborative at The Ohio State University.

Williams, J. P. (1991). The meaning of a phonics base for reading instruction. In W. Ellis (Ed.), *All language and the creation of literacy: Proceedings of the Orton Dyslexia Society Symposia* (pp. 9-19). Baltimore, MD: The Orton Dyslexia Society.

Wimpelberg, R. K. (1986, April). *Bureaucratic and cultural images in the management of more and less effective schools.* Paper presented at the annual meeting of the American Educational Research Association, San Francisco, CA.

Yair, G. (2000). Not just about time: Instructional practices and productive time in school. *Educational Administration Quarterly, 36(4)*, 485-512.

Young, J. R., & Beach, S. A. (1999). Young children's sense of being literate: What's it all about? In C. K. Kinzer, K. A. Hinchman, & D. J. Leu (Eds.), *Inquiries in literacy theory and practice* (pp. 297-307). Chicago: The National Reading Conference.

INDEX

CORWIN
PRESS

The Corwin Press logo—a raven striding across an open book—represents the happy union of courage and learning. We are a professional-level publisher of books and journals for K-12 educators, and we are committed to creating and providing resources that embody these qualities. Corwin's motto is "Success for All Learners."